American Babies

---·❖·---

AMERICAN BABIES
Their Life and Times in the 20th Century

Elizabeth A. Reedy

Growing Up: History of Children and Youth
Priscilla Ferguson Clement, Series Editor

PRAEGER

**Westport, Connecticut
London**

Library of Congress Cataloging-in-Publication Data

Reedy, Elizabeth Ann
    American babies : their life and times in the 20th century / Elizabeth A. Reedy.
      p. cm. — (Growing up : history of children and youth)
    Includes bibliographical references.
    ISBN 978–0–275–99088–6 (alk. paper)
     1. Infants—United States—Social conditions—20th century.   I. Title.
  HQ774.R44   2007
  305.2320973'0904—dc22   2007028639

British Library Cataloguing in Publication Data is available.

Library of Congress Catalog Card Number: 2007028639
ISBN: 978–0–275–99088–6
ISSN: 1938–6095

First published in 2007

Praeger Publishers, 88 Post Road West, Westport, CT 06881
An imprint of Greenwood Publishing Group, Inc.
www.praeger.com

Printed in the United States of America

The paper used in this book complies with the
Permanent Paper Standard issued by the National
Information Standards Organization (Z39.48–1984).

10 9 8 7 6 5 4 3 2 1

For Catherine and any babies she may bear

Contents

Series Foreword

Over the years, when I have identified myself as a historian of children, I have often been asked, "Do children really have a history?" Thanks to the outpouring of exciting and substantive work by a variety of excellent historians in recent years, I can answer the question with a resounding yes. Especially since the 1970s, the history of children and youth has been expanding rapidly.

Children have been studied in a variety of contexts including schools (both public and religious), institutions (such as orphanages and juvenile reformatories), and voluntary organizations (such as the Boy Scouts). The toys children play with, the objects they live with, and the ways youngsters spend their money have all been the subjects of recent works. So have the ways young people have influenced the larger culture through their dress, their music, their dances, the movies and TV they watch, and the political action they take—especially during the civil rights movement. Historians have also written about children living in certain time periods, such as the Great Depression, and children growing up in different parts of the country, such as on the western frontier. Many aspects of the lives of boys and girls such as their encounters with the law, with the medical establishment or with family loss, abuse, poverty, disability, work, war, discrimination, and class have also been studied.

The purpose of this series, *Growing Up: The History of Children and Youth*, is to introduce this growing field in history to a larger audience. Authors of books in the series both synthesize much exciting work in the history of young people and present additional original research in the field. All books in the series emphasize the history of children of both genders, diverse ethnic backgrounds, and various social classes. Each book also covers a substantial period of time, and, as much as possible, their authors showcase the experiences of children themselves rather than exclusively adult perspectives on the young.

The present volume by Elizabeth Ann Reedy is a fascinating and instructive book on the history of American babies in the twentieth century. Previously, infants have been studied in various contexts: as middle- and upper-class objects of adoration in the late nineteenth and twentieth centuries, as the youngest and frequently most physically at risk among racial minorities since the seventeenth century, as the objects of various welfare programs in the nineteenth and twentieth centuries, and as the patients of pediatricians, the new medical specialists of the late nineteenth century, whose work has saved the lives and transformed the childhoods of countless infants. Reedy brings all this and more together in her fascinating study of the life of babies from 1901 to 2000. And while she obviously can't tell the history of babies from their point of view, she does an admirable job of ferreting out and vividly describing specific examples of individual babies and their experiences in infancy.

Reedy begins by examining how babies from different social classes experienced life in the first year of the twentieth century. There was not one "babyhood" but many. Next she looks at advice literature on babies, which has proliferated in the twentieth century from the occasional book or magazine article to a flood of books, magazines, and newspaper articles and Internet sites all devoted to helping moms and dads raise babies right. Subsequent chapters demonstrate the enormous progress that has been made in dealing with childhood illnesses and the success of new types of surgery that correct congenital defects of babies. The special care and new treatments that have saved the lives of countless premature babies are also detailed. Reedy shows how expensive it has become to have a baby and how government welfare programs, including various parts of the Social Security Act, were created to help needy parents. The experience of African-American babies and those of immigrants is examined in a chapter that clearly shows the devastating impact of racism on America's youngest citizens. Finally, Reedy discusses not only what has happened to babies but the desire to have them and hence the recent growth in infertility treatments. She concludes her study of babies in the twentieth century with a provocative look at the twenty-first century and the crucial issues that now face babies.

On a personal note, I would like to conclude by remembering that this book series began as one jointly edited by myself and Jacqueline Reinier, a fine historian of eighteenth- and nineteenth-century children and a dear friend and colleague. Jackie died of cancer before this series came to fruition, but without her support, it never would have begun. Thanks, Jackie!

Priscilla Ferguson Clement
Spring, 2007

Acknowledgments

This book would not have been possible without the help and support of many people. In particular, I would like to thank Priscilla Ferguson Clement for approaching me about the idea for the book and for her unwavering support throughout the entire process. Elizabeth Potenza at Praeger has also been a source of encouragement, and a mild push forward when needed. The librarians at the Free Library of Springfield Township and Abington Library in Montgomery County, Pennsylvania, were always friendly and accommodating.

Before I committed to the book, my doubts as to my ability to write it were assuaged by Patricia D'Antonio and Joan Lynaugh at the University of Pennsylvania. Their belief in my skills and abilities span more than a decade and both are wonderful mentors and even better friends. Elizabeth Dowdell of Oreland, Pennsylvania has been a colleague, cheerleader, and most of all a devoted friend throughout this process. Family members also helped with words of encouragement, especially my parents, Bill and Betty Walsh, my aunt and uncle, Kay and John Harkin, and my brother and sister-in-law, Tom Walsh and Frances Chichetti.

As a pediatric nurse I have cared for hundreds, if not thousands, of babies during my career. Most of them were sick, many were premature. I do not recall many names, but I have learned a great deal from each of them. Their ability to bounce back from problems that many adults could not handle is amazing and thrilling to witness. Some of the babies I cared for are grown now and may have babies of their own. I thank all of them and their parents for helping me to grow as a nurse and as a person.

Finally, my husband Brett and daughter Catherine deserve much of the credit for my ability to complete this book. They both supported me with love, affection, and, occasionally, the push I needed to keep going. Both were also amazingly patient with me throughout the process of writing and never failed to keep me grounded.

Introduction

In every child who is born, under no matter what circumstances, and of no matter what parents, the potentiality of the human race is born again.[1]

—James Agee, with Walker Evans, 1941

Between 1901 and 2000 life in the United States changed dramatically for everyone and everything. Babies born in 1901 were cared for by parents who did not possess, or even know about, disposable diapers, car seats, plastic bottles, premoistened diaper wipes, ready-to-eat baby food in jars, or books, video tapes, and DVDs "guaranteed" to increase a baby's intelligence. Most babies born in 1901 did not live long enough to see a home computer, cell phone, or a flat panel television set. Before we conclude that 1901 was a simpler time with a lot less stress we should remember that babies born that year had, in some cities, a greater than 20 percent chance of dying before their first birthday. Other items that ease the care of a baby today such as automatic washing machines and dryers, antibiotics for infections, immunizations to prevent many childhood diseases, and electric breast pumps, simply did not exist in 1901. Throughout the course of the twentieth century these things and other inventions and innovations helped adults cope with the demands of a baby amid the stresses of everyday life. This book explores the world that American babies experienced in the twentieth century. I examine the social, cultural, and economic issues, along with specific challenges for babies, including medical problems, feeding debates, and family and parent issues. I attempt to present these issues within the context of the times. One thing babies cannot do is talk for themselves. We will never know what a baby thinks of his immediate environment, the people who raise him, or the decisions made by American society that influence his world.

Late in the century Americans started classifying babies by the era in which they were born: Silent Generation, Greatest Generation, Baby Boom, Baby Bust, Gen-X, Gen-Y, Millenials, etc. But the first babies born in 1901 did not know all this. When born they were just like all the babies born before them and those that came after them. They needed to be loved, fed, and kept warm and dry. While growing increasingly aware of the world immediately surrounding them, babies in the first year of life are not concerned with the larger outside world or with the latest technological advances designed to ease their care. The outside world does, however, play a major role in babies' lives. It dictates where they live, how well they live, what they eat, their clothing, playthings, and just about everything else. I cannot begin to cover everything about the life of a baby and how it changed in the twentieth century. I discuss some of the major influences on American babies and the changes seen over the course of the last hundred years.

First, a word on terminology. "Baby" has many meanings in American society. It can be a term of endearment for adults and children alike. It can be an insult, as in "You're such a baby!" It is used to describe any number of things that are small, little, tiny, etc. In this book I define baby as the period in a person's life from birth to the first birthday. The child is referred to as an infant or as a baby, interchangeably. The term "neonate" refers to a baby from birth to fourteen (or twenty-eight) days of age. This time period is referred to as the "neonatal" period. Both "neonate" and "neonatal" have been used more in the second half of the twentieth century due to advances in understanding of physiological processes that occur immediately after birth. These terms also more accurately identify causes of infant morbidity and mortality.[2]

In Chapter 1 infancy in 1901 is explored. At the beginning of the twentieth century people celebrated the New Year and new century as one of hope and unlimited potential for the United States. The nation was growing as waves of immigrants, mainly from Southern and Eastern Europe, joined those who had come before from all over Europe, and indeed the globe. Then, as now, who your parents were meant a great deal as the upper and middle classes led comfortable lives and were able to provide the necessities as well as some extras for their babies, while the working and lower classes struggled to provide food and shelter. The Pan-American Exposition in Buffalo heralded the accomplishments of Americans during the nineteenth century and provided a glimpse of life in the twentieth century. Americans continued to move west and to larger cities throughout the country in search of better opportunities for themselves and their babies and children. Progressive Era reformers focused on the health of infants as they pushed to clean up the air, water, and sewers.

Chapter 2 looks at the changing attitudes Americans displayed toward babies early in the century. Babies were suddenly popular, it seemed, in the public mind as never before. Advice, wanted and unwanted, has always been part of motherhood. In the twentieth century it proliferated at an amazing rate. Newspapers, magazines, books, governmental publications, radio, television, and the Internet have provided a means for twentieth-century parents to obtain information about their babies. Physicians, who began to specialize in the care of infants and children in the late nineteenth century, expanded their role and provided advice as well as illness and injury care. Financially babies have traditionally been the recipient of private philanthropy and in the twentieth century their cause was also taken up by the federal government.

The following chapters present more information about specific issues. The health and illness issues faced by babies are discussed in Chapter 3. Major progress has been made in the prevention of devastating childhood illnesses, and new surgical techniques have allowed babies born with congenital defects to live, and live well. Chapter 4 looks at the issue of prematurity. In 1901 "preemies" were not the concern of physicians. They were often labeled weaklings and their death was expected. There were few things one could do for them, although incubators and other technologies were right around the corner—or at least at the Pan-American Exposition where preemies in the new incubators were a major attraction. By the 1950s preemies were cared for in hospitals, by specially trained physicians and nurses. By the 1980s machines that breathed for babies, maintained their body temperature, and provided the appropriate nutrition at the appropriate time and rate were available for any infant born prematurely.

The economics of infancy are discussed in Chapter 5. As anyone who has ever had a baby can testify, they are expensive. Even before it is born, a baby can cost a great deal. Spending money is a social event as well as a necessary one. Deciding on the essential needs of a baby and the amount of money to spend is often a difficult task. In the twentieth century, even as consumer culture discovered babies and dictated new "must-haves" every year, some parents were unable to provide even a few necessities. The country took notice and a variety of governmental assistance programs including the Sheppard–Towner Act, the Social Security Act with all its amendments, and other local, state, and national programs gave tax dollars to the care of babies.

Chapter 6 looks at the impact of racism on American babies. Black babies continue to have the highest infant mortality rate among all racial or cultural groups in the United States. Late in the century attempts to end this pattern were made but more progress is needed before these babies can ever hope to have the same advantages at the start of their lives as other American babies. Population and immigration issues are discussed in Chapter 7. The twentieth century started and ended with a similar difficulty—a perceived threat from too many immigrants from a presumably undesirable area of the world. Will the babies of these new late twentieth-century immigrants contribute as much to twenty-first-century America as the babies born to early twentieth-century immigrants contributed to that century? It is too early to tell, but with all the advances in infant care in the United States described in this book, they should have a good chance.

Making babies is easy for most people, but not for all. In Chapter 8 I have discussed the issue of infertility and the effect it can have on those unable to get pregnant and deliver a baby. There are many reasons for infertility and in the last few decades of the century physicians discovered the means to help infertile couples conceive and carry a baby to term. As with most other discoveries, however, there are risks and benefits. Balancing them is the challenge for the next century. Conclusions and future expectations are presented in Chapter 9. At the beginning of the twenty-first century most American babies are better off than they were in 1901. Overall they are bigger, healthier, and much more likely to survive the first year. But challenges remain. Perhaps by reviewing the events of the past century we can plan to make even more of a difference in the lives of American babies in the next century.

NOTES

1. James Agee, with Walker Evans, *Let Us Now Praise Famous Men, 1941*, in Stephen Donadio, Joan Smith, Susan Mensner, and Rebecca Davison, eds., *The New York Public Library Book of 20th-Century American Quotations* (New York: The Stonesong Press. Inc., and The New York Public Library, 1992), 82.

2. *Webster's New World Dictionary*, 3rd College ed., s.v. "baby," "infant," and "neonate."

American Babies in 1901

O child! O new-born denizen
Of life's great city! on thy head
The glory of the morn is shed,
Like a celestial benison!
Here at the portal thou dost stand,
And with thy little hand
Thou openest the mysterious gate
Into the future's undiscovered land.
—Henry Wadsworth Longfellow, *To a Child*

On January 1, 1901, at 12:03 A.M. Central time, Mr. and Mrs. Francesco Iagolo of Clark Street in Chicago became the proud parents of a baby boy. This baby had the distinction of being named the first baby of the twentieth century to be born in Chicago.[1] In fact, many babies were born that day in the United States and many more would be born over the course of the next 100 years. Twentieth-century America saw one of the greatest population explosions in history. Baby Boy Iagolo and all those who came after him would, as they grew, change the face of not only the nation but the entire world. They would fight in two world wars, several "police conflicts," and help restore their former enemies to prosperity. They would themselves see great prosperity and the Great Depression. From the perspective of their parents these babies might be planned for or unplanned, wanted or unwanted, made easily or made in a laboratory. These babies could be overwhelming or enthralling, good-natured or exasperating, and much, much more. But before they were any of these things and before they could do anything of consequence, babies needed to survive birth and their first year of life. This chapter will explore what America, in a brand new century, had to offer new babies and what challenges America's babies faced.

The beginning of the twentieth century[2] in America brought promises of revolutionary changes in all aspects of life. The country was coming out of the economic depression of the 1890s and prospects for financial gain were much brighter for many. Politically, America was coming into its own. Over the course of the new century it would be instrumental in world affairs and have little difficulty becoming a major influence in all aspects of life for people around the globe. The large cities and towns of the Northeast and Midwestern states grew in size and population, while farming predominated in the South and West. Overall population growth continued, fortified by large numbers of immigrants, but the rate of growth was slowing. Family life was changing too—the ideal family consisted of a working father who provided all the necessary income and a mother who stayed home and cared for the children and the house. In this ideal family fathers did not interfere with the mother and mothers did not seek employment outside the home for wages. However, the reality for many families was quite different as both parents and the older children needed to work to make ends meet both in cities and on farms.[3] Automobiles had already been introduced, but it took an American, Henry Ford, to make them affordable and commonplace. Movies, telephones, air travel, medicines that cured disease, modern surgical techniques, computers, and much, much more, all were created by or significantly influenced by Americans of the twentieth century.

Baby Iagolo was born at a time and in a place where the excitement was palpable and the potential for individual and societal gain was enormous. But his chances for success depended on many things including the family he was born into and their ability to care for him during the first year of his life, his social class, his race, and even his luck. All other American babies were affected by these issues as well as economic and political forces, both national and local.

POPULATION

The population of a country in general and the population of a baby's immediate environment play important roles in the baby's and his family's life. In

1900 the Twelfth Census of the United States showed an increase of almost 21 percent in population from 1890. At the same time the urban population grew by nearly 37 percent.[4] Although the birthrate for native-born white parents began decreasing in the mid-nineteenth century, the new immigrant population kept the nation from experiencing a major slide in population. Some of the increase reflected the great immigration waves of the late nineteenth century as people from Europe came to America to escape poverty, persecution, political uproar, and to seek out the American Dream for themselves. Many young men and women came to start anew and prosper. Often one of their goals was to start a family.

Birthrates and morbidity and mortality statistics for babies in the early years of the twentieth century are, in general, estimates at best. Birth records were beset by many problems. Before 1915 there were no uniform methods of organizing birth records and methods for counting births were haphazard. Many babies were simply not counted. In 1915 the Census Bureau instituted a uniform birth registration system but for only the 31 percent of the population who lived in eight Eastern and two Midwestern states and the District of Columbia. This system was gradually expanded to cover all states by 1933.[5] In addition to those births never reported, some births were discounted, especially among prematurely born infants. In these instances babies born alive but who died within a few hours or even days of birth may have been classified as stillborn, thus skewing both birthrates and mortality statistics. The number of deaths during infancy is difficult to estimate owing to the wide variations in medical diagnoses. Many illnesses, injuries, and deaths were never reported. It should also be remembered that the ability of physicians to diagnose and treat babies was extremely limited compared to today and the infrastructure needed to accurately count births, deaths, and other vital statistics did not exist as it does now.

INFANT MORBIDITY AND MORTALITY IN 1901

Statistics do tell tales however, and nowhere is this more apparent than in the field of infant morbidity and mortality. As a nation the United States has always looked to statistics to compare the well-being of its citizens to those of other nations and cultures. We do know some things about the common illnesses and injuries during the first years of the century, and these statistics paint a scary picture. Although the infant mortality rate (IMR) in New York

City was abysmal, it was actually decreasing. In 1885 the IMR (number of deaths per one thousand live births within the first year of life) was 247.8. By 1900 it was 183.1.[6] Across the country the IMR ranged from 87.2 in Portland, Oregon, to 322.7 in Charleston, North Carolina.[7] More significantly the causes of infant mortality were coming under increasing scrutiny at both national and local levels. During the latter part of the nineteenth century many scientific discoveries, including the germ theory and principles of sanitation, led to a better understanding of the causes of infectious disease. This added knowledge in turn led to the concept of prevention.

By 1901 reformers of the Progressive Era had made much progress in the area of sanitation. The cleanup of sewage systems and of rivers and streams continued and some believed this in itself would result in a dramatic decrease in infant mortality. Cities in general were faulted and parents were encouraged to take their babies to the suburbs or rural areas for fresh air as often as possible. But fresh air and clean water were not the only solutions. Larger changes were needed. Edwin Graham, M.D., a professor of diseases of children at Jefferson Medical College in 1908 called for the control of nuisances, pasteurization of milk during summer months, prenatal care for the poor, better sanitation, paid maternity leave, the teaching of hygiene and motherhood skills, breast-feeding for all babies as far as possible, safe milk supplies and visiting nurses to ensure proper feeding practices, laws to protect children cared for by people other than their parents, and good food.[8]

Disease took far too many of 1901's babies before they learned to walk, talk, or eat by themselves. Dehydration caused by acute diarrhea, pneumonia and other respiratory diseases, prematurity, and congenital birth defects were the principle causes of death among infants. Parents were devastated by the loss of any of their children no matter what their age. Baby Iagolo's parents probably received a great deal of advice on how to prevent infant death from relatives, friends, and a growing number of infant and child care experts. Most of the advice was well intentioned but accurate information was not widely available. Even for those conditions for which a cause was known, specific treatment options were limited; supportive care was the most many families had to offer.

Class

In 1901 class often defined your place in society, and once defined there was little or no chance for change. IMRs were high for the entire population, but then as now were higher for babies born into poor and disadvantaged families.

More likely to die during or at birth, babies from impoverished families were also more likely to be born prematurely, die from congenital diseases, and develop often avoidable diseases and conditions, some leading to death and others leading to permanent disabilities. Babies born into lower class families experienced poor nutrition that hinders growth, leaves infants susceptible to disease, and influences the ability to learn. Impoverished parents were often in poor health which influenced their ability to raise the baby, and parental death left many babies without one or both parents. Poor or disadvantaged parents were more likely to be employed in jobs that exposed them to dangerous and even life threatening situations. In his landmark novel *The Jungle*, Upton Sinclair describes some of these issues within the context of the early twentieth-century meat packing industry.[9] During the early years of the century many industries had mediocre to poor working conditions; many of the child labor laws, health and safety regulations, and increased knowledge of risks in general came along later. Parents' ability to care for their babies and children is directly affected by their own class and standing in society.

Race

Race has been an issue in the United States from colonial times. In 1901 the country was only thirty-six years past the great divisions of the Civil War. Slavery was abolished and Reconstruction was over, but racial prejudices survived. Throughout the country, but especially in the South, racial divisions affected all aspects of American society. Babies born to African-American families had, and still have, a higher chance of dying during infancy than those born to Caucasian families. Little or no prenatal care contributes to the higher death rate of black babies, but poor parental education is a major influence as well. In 1901 many African-American parents had little opportunity for formal education and what was available was in most instances inferior to that available to white parents. Some African-American families left the South where their forebears had been enslaved for the job opportunities of the northern and Midwestern cities. For virtually all African-Americans, limited job opportunities and unfair housing policies added to the poor outlook for babies. Race and class issues will be discussed further in Chapter 6.

Family

In 1901 the notion of family was also undergoing major change. The extended families frequently found in rural areas were becoming rarer. As young men and women moved or immigrated to the cities they left their parents and other relatives behind. For the working classes and the poor the housing stock available in the cities was limited and in many cases not even large enough for a typical family of mother, father, and several children. In tenement housing many people crowded together, related or not. Thus babies born into these circumstances grew up with a number of influences, not all of which could be controlled by their own parents. When their mothers went to work, many babies were left to the care of older siblings or to unemployed family members and friends.

Well-to-do families continued their practice of employing baby nurses, governesses, maids, and others to help care for babies and children. Middle-class families also employed servants to help manage the house and care for babies and children. They had larger houses than the working classes and the poor, and were able to provide separate rooms for the children to sleep in and cribs and smaller furniture specifically made for babies.

The Birth of a Baby in 1901

Until the twentieth century the vast majority of American babies were born at home. At the first signs of labor the mother retreated to her bed and remained there until after the birth. Grandmothers and aunts came to help with the labor and delivery and to assist with the running of the household while the mother was incapacitated. If there were not enough family members, neighbors helped the mother. The father's main job was to stay out of the way. When the birth was imminent, he sent for the midwife, either by sending a note with a messenger, or by going out to escort her himself. Once the baby was born and the mother was recovering the midwife left. Relatives and friends stayed until the mother was able to return to her daily activities, or until they needed to leave to care for their own families. The mother repaid her debt to these women by assisting them during their own confinements.

EVOLUTION OF HOSPITALS

For most of recorded history the care of the sick has occurred at home. Childbirth, not considered an illness, also occurred at home. While hospitals, or institutions for the mentally or physically destitute, have been around for centuries, the hospital-centered medical system that we know today in the United States has its roots in the late eighteenth and nineteenth centuries. The first hospital for the sick was founded by Benjamin Franklin and Dr. Thomas Bond in 1752 in Philadelphia. Pennsylvania Hospital is still in existence, operating at the same location, and now part of the University of Pennsylvania Health System. Initially Pennsylvania Hospital admitted very few pregnant women. Legitimate children should, according to the morals of the day, be born at home and the hospital's directors did not want to encourage immorality. A few babies were born there however and in 1803 a lying-in, or maternity, department officially opened. It closed in 1854 mainly due to high morbidity and mortality caused by puerperal, or childbed, fever. Pennsylvania Hospital did not reopen the maternity department until 1929.[10]

By the late nineteenth and early twentieth centuries the sight of a physician at a home birth became more common, especially among those financially able to hire one. New understandings of the mechanics of birth and the introduction of technical aids helped the physicians gain entry into the birthing room. Physicians also began using the principles of asepsis to help decrease the risk of infection before, during, and immediately after birth, thus saving mothers' lives. But physicians were still guests in the birthing room and often faced an uphill battle trying to win the woman, her family, and friends over to new ideas. Women still made most of the decisions regarding the use of technical aids, such as forceps, at the turn of the twentieth century, but as technology became increasingly complicated they were eventually convinced to turn these decisions over to the physician.[11]

Thus by 1901 medical practice was evolving and obstetricians and pediatricians were becoming more numerous. Obstetrics was a relatively new field of specialized practice for physicians. As they improved their knowledge and skills in the care of the expectant woman they began to push aside the traditional midwife. Midwives, who were generally women with little or no formal training, had attended women at birth for centuries. But with increasing numbers of physicians and the attendant increase in the number of hospitals the home birth was soon to become a thing of the past.

The hospital birth was not embraced immediately by all. For the wealthier families, giving birth in a hospital had negative social ramifications. Hospitalization for any reason signified the inability to provide for oneself or family. Hospitals had long been the last resort for the extremely poor and destitute. Any man unable to provide for medical attention for family members in his own home was considered a failure. Childbirth was no exception.

For much of the nineteenth century those births occurring in hospitals were to women whose moral character was questionable. In other words, they were unmarried, or were prostitutes. They may have been turned out by their families to make their own way, and having no one available to help found a grudging acceptance in the hospitals and lying-in charities. For some, submitting to charity care also meant giving up their babies for adoption.[12] Others became wet nurses for more well-to-do families.

"Lying-in" and charity hospitals had opened in many cities in the nineteenth century. They were initially run by midwives but obstetricians took over many as the century progressed. The fledgling field of obstetrics supported the lying-in hospitals as ideal laboratories for the advancement of their field. As with any medical teaching hospital today, the patients received the latest in medical care. For many medical students these institutions gave them their first and often only experience with childbirth. Men (and a few women) wanting to specialize in the field were able to see many women in labor and giving birth within a short period of time. They could compare notes, conduct studies of different methodologies for treatment, practice their techniques, and observe all the nuances of childbirth. These experiences were invaluable for the physicians once they began their own practices and teaching careers. The women who relied on these institutions received a bed in a warm room, help caring for themselves and their babies after birth, and the knowledge that their babies were born with a better chance at life than if they had been born in a squalid room without anyone even to witness the birth.

Still, births in the nineteenth and early twentieth centuries were not without risks for mothers and babies. Infection among postpartum women was a major cause of maternal death. Despite the advent of the germ theory and studies done on the benefits of hand washing in preventing infection, puerperal fever was a frequent visitor to the hospitalized maternity patient. Puerperal fever, now known to be caused by staphylococcus, has always been a problem for mothers. It was spread, in most cases, by the birth attendant. Midwives and physicians who did not wash their hands between patients carried the bacteria from one to another. Home birth attendants did not frequently go from one home to another within a short time period thus puerperal fever was not a serious problem in home births. Of course it did occur in some situations, especially in cities where two or three women might be in labor at the same time and the attendant finished at one home, then went downstairs to another apartment. Family members could also spread the disease. But hospitals were a perfect breeding ground. In the lying-in hospitals mothers were housed in large wards, with forty and even more patients in one room. Physicians, midwives, and medical students went from one patient to another examining and inspecting the mothers. Thus an infection in one mother could quickly spread to many others. In this time before the discovery of antibiotics the only recourse was to isolate infected patients. In practice this was difficult due to a lack of isolation rooms, and the interval between symptom development and diagnosis. Often the only way to rid a ward of infection was to close it for several days to weeks. Obviously these infections and maternal morbidity and mortality affected the babies. Maternal milk supplies were limited, or in the case of maternal death, cut off completely. Infection passed on to the baby could be fatal as well.[13]

The advent of anesthesia during labor and childbirth solidified the role of the physician in the birthing room. Ether was first introduced in the United States at the Massachusetts General Hospital in 1846. It remained a novelty for much of the rest of the century until the advent of asepsis.[14] Chloroform came along shortly after ether. During the middle years of the nineteenth century using drugs in childbirth was considered unnatural and even immoral. In 1853 Queen Victoria used chloroform during labor with her eighth child and afterwards praised the experience highly.[15] Thereafter ether gained popularity in the United States with chloroform the agent of choice in England.

During the early twentieth century anesthesia and pain control during surgeries of all types gained wider acceptance among medical practitioners and the general public. Surgeons stopped operating in people's homes and moved their practices to the cleaner and eventually sterile atmosphere of the hospital operating room. Anesthesiologists, physicians trained in the principles and practice of anesthesia, became accepted and as their knowledge and expertise increased hospital-based surgery became standard. For mothers-to-be these innovations, along with an increasing respect for physicians and hospitals in general, dictated that most future childbirths would be in the hospital.

INFANT CARE

A baby's care after birth depended on many things. Born in a tenement in New York City, her residence would have been a small apartment, possibly shared not only with her family, but with boarders as well. Living space was at a premium and privacy rare. Her parents might have been immigrants, new to America, with limited English language skills. Their possessions would have been few and money for luxuries, including medical care, would have been nonexistent. Baby care was the responsibility of her mother, and possibly any siblings old enough to manage. She would have been wrapped in blankets or cloth to keep her warm and given to her mother for feeding. Depending on her family's circumstances she may have slept in a crib or bassinette, been placed in a dresser drawer that was lined with newspaper or cotton blankets, or taken into her mother's bed. Like most babies she spent her first days and weeks mainly sleeping or eating. Her world expanded as she grew and became mobile. Then, as now, safety was a major concern. However there were no safety locks or gates or childproof caps. A baby's safety depended solely on her family watching out for her.

Accidents were common in all families, especially for a family living in an urban tenement. Falls down unprotected stairs, burns from faulty stoves and heaters, accidents in the streets, and any number of minor or major injuries awaited the unsuspecting baby of 1901. Opportunities for fresh air were also limited in the overcrowded tenements lined up shoulder to shoulder among factories operating long before environmental protection laws. Water and sewage, while certainly considered a problem that required action, nevertheless remained a major concern in many areas. The changes of the Progressive Era continued and cleaner water would soon be seen.

Even after a healthy birth and uneventful neonatal period, a baby's chances of dying before his first birthday were high. In New York City, Philadelphia, Boston, Chicago, St. Louis, Atlanta, and other major cities, towns, and rural areas, babies died frequently. One of the major causes of these deaths was dehydration and diarrhea due to acute gastroenteritis. Bacteria caused the disease; the disease caused the diarrhea that led directly to dehydration. Without enough fluid major organs ceased to function and death followed relatively quickly. It was an ugly death and in the early 1900s most people had no idea what caused it or how to prevent it. The disease was widely known as "summer complaint" as it was worse and more lethal during the summer months. Since younger babies were much more susceptible, those born during the spring months of 1901 were at an especially high risk. The mother would have needed to be extra vigilant with a baby born during those months. In Chapter 3 this issue as well as other diseases and conditions of infants will be discussed in more detail.

A baby born to native-born, middle- or upper-class parents living in New York City in 1901 might have lived in luxurious accommodations on the other side of the city. During the summers the family would often leave the squalor of the city behind for a country house in the mountains. The family would probably have had a physician present for the baby's birth and trained nurses hired to care for baby and mother after birth. If health problems developed a pediatrician might have been called. Not immune to "summer complaint" the well-off baby would nonetheless have had less chance of catching the disease due mainly to her less frequent contact with other babies. However her chances of dying from the disease, once it was established in her body, were still high.

General baby care for infants of the middle and upper classes was often supplemented by the employment of baby nurses or governesses. These women were responsible for changing diapers, bathing and dressing the baby, playing with her, taking strolls in the park, and presenting her to the parents when required. The extent of this supplemental care varied considerably among families from those that used the baby nurses for all baby-related care to those who used them for short periods of time when the mother was unavoidably absent from the home. It would be easy to think of these arrangements as detrimental to the baby's mental health, however many of the baby nurses remained in a family's employ for many years and the babies grew to think of them as part of an extended family. Some of the social obligations placed on the mothers in the middle and upper classes took them away from their children frequently; having a devoted and trusted woman to provide consistent care and nurturing was a significant help to the family. These servants would soon become rare as new opportunities for women opened up in the twentieth century.[16]

Feeding the Baby

Breast-feeding a baby was once the only method of providing nourishment to a young infant. In 1901 a mother could breast-feed, bottle-feed, or hire a wet nurse to feed the baby. Breast-feeding, long considered the best and most highly recommended method of infant feeding, was falling off in the late nineteenth century. Prominent physicians, while not abandoning their ingrained beliefs about the benefits of breast milk, warned that many mothers, especially those considered "nervous" or "sickly" might actually harm their infants by continuing to breast-feed. By 1901 many mothers, especially in the middle and upper classes chose to bottle-feed their babies. In order to bottle-feed babies, artificial formulas were concocted. Physicians prescribed formulas; usually cow's milk with some additives, and mothers mixed them at home. The cow's milk available to many mothers, however, was contaminated and frequently led to a number of different problems including dehydration and malnutrition.[17]

Wet-nursing was a traditional form of providing breast milk to babies whose mother was unable, due to illness or death, or unwilling to breast-feed. Wet nurses were women who had recently borne a baby and usually because of poverty, needed to support themselves by breast-feeding other women's babies. The wet nurse either took the baby to her own home and kept it until it was weaned, or moved into the family's home where she was generally placed in the category of a servant. Those who moved into the family home did not often keep their own baby with them. This was the dark side of wet-nursing. In order to have an adequate milk supply a woman must have recently given birth. Her own baby was usually not wanted in her employment situation as he or she would interfere with the milk supply for the employer's baby. Therefore her baby was left with relatives and fed by a friend or relative who also happened to be nursing, or given substandard concoctions such as watered down milk or corn syrup preparations. Such arrangements contributed to significantly higher morbidity and mortality among the babies of wet nurses.[18]

CONCLUSIONS

Baby Iagolo and all the other babies born on January 1, 1901, in the United States became citizens of a country on the cusp of greatness. Their parents were rich, poor, and anywhere in between. They lived on farms, in new suburbs, and in increasing numbers in big cities where their health often suffered due to crowded and dirty conditions. But the adults in their lives, parents, relatives, politicians, and the general public, were, to an extent never before seen, interested in their survival. In the flowery prose of the time the *Chicago Record* wrote that Baby Boy Iagolo was born "while horns were blowing, bells ringing and whistles shrieking a clamorous salute to the incoming century .... [The] babe opened its eyes in the second story of a smoke-besmirched and dust-begrimed building and Chicago made its first gift to the manhood of a new era .... [The parents] are proud of the little one, and are looking with eyes glowing with delight upon their gift to the century."[19] This gift of new life, represented by every newly born baby, signified the hope that the twentieth century would, for the first time, bring health and prosperity to all babies as well as their families. In the following chapters I will explore the many issues facing Baby Iagolo and all the others who followed after him.

NOTES

1. "Century's First Baby," *Chicago Record*, January 2, 1901, 1.
2. I use 1901 as the starting point for the twentieth century as it is the first year of the century. Unlike the excitement surrounding the advent of the year 2000, 1901 was seen

by most people living in that time as the correct and actual start of a new century and was celebrated as such. *The New York Times*, January 1, 1901, headlines read: "Twentieth Century's Triumphant Entry," and " . . . Yesterday was the Nineteenth, Today, the Twentieth . . . ." *The Philadelphia Inquirer* headline of January 1, 1901, spanned the entire width and two large lines of the paper "Hail, Twentieth Century! Farewell to the Old and a Happy New Year to one and All." The paper also printed two pictures above the fold—the first showed a picture of the clock on City Hall Tower at 11:59 P.M. with "the last minute of old century" printed underneath and the second showed another picture of the clock at midnight with "Birth of the New Century."

3. David I. Macleod, *The Age of the Child—Children in America, 1890–1920* (New York: Twayne Publishers, 1998), 1–3, 8–10.

4. William R. Merriam and William C. Hunt, "Census Reports," in *Twelfth Census of the United States, Taken in the Year 1901*, Vol. 1 (Washington, DC: U.S. Census Office, 1901), xxxi–xxxviii. "Urban" was considered any city or incorporated entity with a population of 4,000 or more.

5. Richard A. Meckel, *Save the Babies—American Public Health Reform and the Prevention of Infant Mortality, 1850–1929* (Ann Arbor: The University of Michigan Press, 1990), 111, 269; Halbert L. Dunn, Robert D. Grove, Iwao M. Moriyama, Sam Shapiro, Hugh Carter, Carl C. Dauer, Hazel V. Aune, Frank S. Morrison, and Howard West "Analysis and Summary Tables with Supplementary Tables for Alaska, Hawaii, Puerto Rico and Virgin Islands," in *Vital Statistics of the United States, 1950*, Vol. 1 (Washington, DC: U.S. Government Printing Office, 1954), 2–19. The original ten states were Connecticut, Maine, Massachusetts, Michigan, Minnesota, New Hampshire, New York, Pennsylvania, Rhode Island, and Vermont, along with Washington, DC. Rhode Island was removed from the registration area in 1919 and put back in 1923.

6. Meckel, *Save the Babies*, 90.

7. Ibid., 106.

8. Edwin E. Graham, "Infant Mortality," *Journal of the American Medical Association* 51(13) (1908): 1045–1050.

9. Upton Sinclair, *The Jungle* (New York: Penguin, 1990).

10. "Obstetrics. A Brief History of Obstetrical Care at Pennsylvania Hospital," *Historical Timeline*, (n.d.), www.uphs.upenn.edu/paharc/timeline/1801/tline10.htm; Charles E. Rosenberg, *The Care of Strangers—The Rise of America's Hospital System* (Baltimore, MD: The Johns Hopkins University Press, 1987), 19.

11. For an in-depth analysis of the changing nature of childbirth in America see Judith Walzer Leavitt, *Brought to Bed: Childbearing in America, 1750–1950* (New York: Oxford University Press, 1986); and Leavitt, "The Growth of Medical Authority: Technology and Morals in Turn-of-the-Century Obstetrics," in Judith Walzer Leavitt, ed., *Women and Health in America*, 2nd ed. (Madison: The University of Wisconsin Press, 1999).

12. Rosenberg, *The Care of Strangers*, 304.

13. Sherwin B. Nuland, *The Doctors' Plague. Germs, Childbed Fever, and the Strange Story of Ignác Semmelweis* (New York: W.W. Norton & Company, 2003). Ignác Semmelweis, a Hungarian obstetrician practicing in Vienna, demonstrated the benefits of hand washing in controlling puerperal fever in the 1840s. His results were generally ignored by his contemporaries, and in any case he did not publish his findings for a wider audience.

14. Rosenberg, *The Care of Strangers*, 92, 114, 144–145.

15. Murdina MacFarquhar Desmond, *Medicine and Society—European Background and American Practice (1750–1975)* (Austin, TX: Eakin Press, 1998), 48–50.

16. Steven Mintz and Susan Kellogg, *Domestic Revolutions—A Social History of American Family* Life (New York: The Free Press, 1988), 123–124; Geraldine Youcha, *Minding the Children—Child Care in America from Colonial Times to the Present* (New York: Scribner, 1995), 243–250.

17. Meckel, *Save the Babies*, 55–59, 62–91.

18. Janet Golden, *A Social History of Wet Nursing in America: From Breast to Bottle.* (New York: Cambridge University Press, 1996).

19. "Century's First Baby," 1.

The General Public and Babies:
Attitudes, Advice, and Altruism

In spite of the six thousand manuals on child raising in the bookstores, child raising is still a dark continent and no one really knows
anything. You just need a lot of love and luck—and, of course,
courage.

— Bill Cosby, Fatherhood, 1986

In the spring of 1999 I was pregnant with my first and only child. I believed
I knew a lot about babies as I had been a pediatric nurse for more than
fifteen years. I also had seven nieces and nephews and many friends with
their own babies. I expected advice from my mother and sisters, and even
a few close friends. But advice from strangers in the supermarket or in the
mall? Even in the bookstore, while selecting from among the thousands of
tomes on pregnancy, childbirth, and baby care, I received unsolicited advice
on which book worked best. Everyone, it seemed, had an opinion—about
breast-feeding versus bottle-feeding, the use of disposable versus cloth diapers,
developmental toys versus pure playing, babysitters, day care versus stay-at-
home moms, sleeping habits—the list was endless. I purchased several baby
care books and along with the pamphlet handed out by the pediatrician after
our daughter's birth tried to make sense of it all. This task proved impossible.
One expert advised picking up a crying baby at once while another expert with
similar impressive credentials advised letting the baby cry for a while. The

contradictions in advice were everywhere. Eventually my husband suggested that we get Dr. Spock's *Baby and Child Care*[1] book and forget about the rest. After all, Spock worked for his mother! I put the books away, we bought Dr. Spock's book and referred to it sparingly, preferring at last to rely on our own instincts. We asked for advice only when we felt it was needed. This decision still did not stop the advice. We were, like many other new parents, the recipients of a century's worth of generally well-meaning baby care advice.

The twentieth century witnessed major changes in the way the American public perceived babies. Early in the century babies, born at home and the sole responsibility of women, were generally ignored by the outside world. Initially unable to contribute to the family or to society at large, they were often seen as a drain on limited resources. But change came. Declining birthrates, hospital births, wars, and financial disaster, served to bring babies to the attention of the general public, and changed babies from financial burdens to symbols of prosperity and hope.[2]

Along with this change in attitude came advice, lots of it. Traditional sources of advice included grandmothers, mothers-in-law, and other relatives as well as trusted friends. In the twentieth century, however, it suddenly seemed everyone was an expert when it came to raising the American baby. Not only family and friends, but also strangers, government officials, and medical professionals all had opinions on babies and voiced them to prospective parents repeatedly. Mothers especially felt inferior in the face of this "help" and spent many hours sifting through it all. Several physicians including L. Emmett Holt in the early years of the century, Benjamin Spock at mid-century, and T. Berry Brazelton during the 1960s to 1990s were authors of the most popular baby advice books. Spock would become the most widely read child rearing expert in the United States. His book *Baby and Child Care* is said to be the world's second best-selling book after the Bible. By the century's end parental advice books filled entire sections in bookstores.[3]

Babies cost a lot of money and in the early twentieth century the needs of the poor and indigent were finally noticed. Progressive Era reformers began "Americanization" classes for infants of immigrants. Government-sponsored programs in the 1920s and 1930s laid the groundwork for federal and state support of infant care. President Franklin Roosevelt's New Deal and his Social Security program in the 1930s and President Lyndon Johnson's Great Society programs in the 1960s expanded the scope of government intervention into the lives of babies. Later in the century many of these programs came under scrutiny because of the money spent on them and while some were cut, others survived and thrived. Private philanthropy has always been a part of American life and babies have generally been seen as "worthy" of monetary and material giving. This chapter will explore the attitudes and advice that, for better and worse, helped change the lives of American babies forever.

CHANGING ATTITUDES

The attitudes of Americans toward babies early in the twentieth century reflected attitudes people had held for centuries. Most couples expected to reproduce and offspring were a natural part of life. Farmers expected to have children who could, as they grew, help out and eventually take over the family farm. Until the twentieth century women often began having babies while in their teen years, as the average life expectancy was less than fifty years.[4] Infant mortality rates (IMR) were high also. Thus a woman with children could expect at least one, and often more of her children to die before reaching adulthood; the majority of such deaths occurred in infancy due to disease. Accidents were less common among babies than among older children but still were a concern. Parents could often do nothing to prevent these deaths. Looking back from our vantage point in the early twenty-first century we might ask: Did parents not demand to know why their babies died? Why did the general public not rise up in anger against whatever was causing the deaths? Why did people continue to have babies if so many of them succumbed during the first year of life? Despite the continued high IMR in the United States today as compared to other highly developed countries, if infant mortality reached the levels of 1901 today it would certainly cause a major public outcry, demands for explanations and fixes, and searches for persons to blame, no doubt followed by a congressional inquiry and a movie of the week.[5]

Some might conclude that the parents of the late nineteenth and early twentieth centuries did not care about their babies as much as we do today but that conclusion is wrong. Information about how to prevent infant death was simply lacking. Babies died for many reasons. Some died from congenital diseases that today would be considered easily fixable. Congenital heart disease is a major example. The surgical ability to correct life-threatening heart defects was simply not available until well into the twentieth century. Prematurity is another example. Until the 1960s a baby born before it was able to breathe on its own died. Ventilators for breathing and medicines necessary for survival would not become a realistic expectation until the second half of the century.

Antibiotics to treat infectious diseases were not readily available to the general public until after World War II. The general nutrition of the public at large also played a part. Poor nutrition can hinder the body's ability to recover from illness or infections, thus directly and indirectly affecting mortality rates. The connection between diet and disease was not well known among scientists until the mid-1910s and decreases in disease rates attributable to dietary changes not seen until the mid-1920s. Traumatic accidents are common at all times but the inability to cure or treat many of them significantly influenced early twentieth century morbidity and mortality.[6]

Despite the apparent lack of outrage parents did grieve the death of their babies. They accepted such deaths and went on with their lives because that is how they saw their own parents handle the death of siblings, and how the rest of their neighbors, friends, and family members coped. There was simply not enough knowledge to reduce infant deaths significantly. Viviana Zelizer provided an insightful analysis of the value of babies and children in the United States in her 1985 book *Pricing the Priceless Child: The Changing Social Value of Children.* She documented the social, cultural, and economic changes seen in late nineteenth and early twentieth century America that influenced the way parents, families, and the general public viewed and valued babies and children. In the early years of the nation a new baby meant the arrival of not only another mouth to feed, but the potential for economically necessary labor beginning at young ages—children as young as four years routinely helped on the family farm, or in urban areas by assisting the mother with piece work, or other household work. By age seven or eight children worked in factories and coal mines as well as more "traditional" childhood occupations such as newspaper delivery. According to Zelizer, by the last quarter of the nineteenth century children's economic value had reached an all time high. The withdrawal of children from the economic world began among the upper class, spread to the middle class by the mid- to late nineteenth century, and by the 1920s reached the lower classes. The sentimental value of children increased and, in Zelizer's terminology, the "sacralization" of child life began.[7]

The advent of the germ theory in the 1870s which identified microscopic organisms as the cause of disease and the idea of asepsis led to many reforms in the United States during the late nineteenth and early twentieth centuries. The Progressive Era reformers of that time encouraged Americans to focus their efforts on cleaning up the cities' air, water, and sewage that they saw as harbingers of filth, disease, and death. Reformers focused on the welfare of babies and children in their activities. Publicizing the staggering infant death rates helped convince communities and government to act. Within a few years, the death of any baby became a cause for outrage, not only within the family but for the entire nation.[8]

The health of babies had become a major concern by 1901. Reformers called for active government involvement in the cause and by 1908 New York City opened the first child health bureau in the nation. Baby milk stations, staffed by public health nurses and physicians, provided clean milk for new mothers in an expanded effort to decrease the spread of gastrointestinal tract infections that caused so much suffering and death among the city's infants. When statistics demonstrated uneven responses to these early efforts, reformers turned their attention to the mothers. The milk stations became places for education and advice for mothers in the "proper" care of infants and children. Clean milk was fine, but if the mothers did not keep it safe at home by providing a proper environment for the milk the babies who ingested it would remain at risk. Domestic hygiene, a renewed emphasis on breast-feeding, and infant hygiene were stressed and mothers were expected to follow the recommendations of the public health professionals.[9]

At the beginning of the twentieth century advice expanded as the public at large became more educated. Physicians began specializing in the care of children toward the end of the nineteenth century. They made science the basis of their authority in all matters concerning babies. Volunteers set up settlement houses in impoverished areas of large cities and frequently focused on the plight of infants. There was much less advice available to rural mothers but the regular mail service brought newspapers and magazines replete with the advice urban mothers received locally. In 1912 local and regional efforts became a national priority with the establishment of the United States Children's Bureau. Under the direction of Julia Lathrop the bureau initially focused almost exclusively on infant mortality. The Children's Bureau even sponsored local exhibitions that attempted to educate mothers about baby and child care. In March 1916 National Baby Week was held for the first time and included many more of the instructional programs held at the smaller exhibitions, free reading materials to take home, parades of mothers carrying their infants, and "best mother contests."[10]

By the mid-1910s progressive reform efforts were in full swing. Middle-class reformers encouraged members of their social class and the poor to educate themselves about the care of babies and to do everything possible to ensure the health and well-being of the next generation of Americans. Cleanliness was stressed and mothers taken to task for allowing their homes and children to be dirty. As physicians came to believe that breast-feeding was better for babies, their emphasis on infant feeding changed from the provision of clean milk to the encouragement of breast-feeding for all infants. They still did, however, prescribe complex formulas for mixing milk with other ingredients for babies who were not breast-fed. The urban settlement house workers assisted the poor adjust to life in a big city. Poor immigrant populations flooding the cities from southern and eastern Europe were thought by many to be especially in need of education in the ways of American baby and child care. Middle-class reformers established "Americanization" programs aimed at bringing these supposedly "ignorant, backward, and superstitious" people up to the standards of mainstream (i.e., middle class, white) American families.[11]

ADVICE FOR EVERYONE (ESPECIALLY MOTHERS)

In 1909 L. Emmett Holt, M.D., published *The Care and Feeding of Children* which was the first widely available parental advice book. It had been originally published in 1894 as a manual for nursery maids working in a hospital. The author realized that nursery maids privately employed by the upper-class families and mothers of the middle and lower classes were also buying and using the manual. He therefore revised the book and put out a new edition specifically for home use. Holt covered the physical care of infants and children, feeding babies, the diet of older children and miscellaneous advice on diseases, emergencies, playtime, and baby temperament. Holt wrote the book in a question and answer format and included much that could be considered common sense. He emphasized the importance of breast milk and supported this fact by citing decreased mortality rates among breast-fed infants. He concluded "there is no perfect substitute for good breast feeding." Holt was a realist, however, and while he devoted nine pages of his book to breast-feeding, including when, why, and how to wean the baby by one year of age, he devoted sixty pages to the ins and outs of artificial feeding.[12]

The last section of *The Care and Feeding of Children* directs mothers to start training the child's bowels at less than two months of age by placing him over a small chamber twice a day. Holt claimed this could lead to full training by three months.[13] This form of toilet training, seemingly unrealistic to many, has been in vogue at various times in history, and had a growing following during the 1990s and 2000s.[14] Holt also recommended that the baby not be rocked or played with to avoid nervousness, irritability, and indigestion among other ailments. He objected to kissing the baby on the grounds that it could cause infection transmission and other serious but unidentified problems. While kissing can transmit infection from a sick person, Holt does not make this point. All kissing is taboo. Some of his information reflects more modern thinking and also reflects debates that have raged on and off throughout the twentieth century. For instance he discusses "bad habits" of young children including sucking, nail-biting, dirt-eating, bed-wetting, and masturbation, and believes these should be broken as soon as possible. But he does suggest that in breaking the habits, rewards work better than punishment. He also discusses the issue of bed sharing and is firmly against it, warning about the danger of smothering and the "injurious" effect of breast-feeding during the night for mother and baby. He does not specify why this would be injurious, but the issue of bed sharing is one that still has polarizing effects on parents, pediatricians, and others.[15]

Holt provided a concise volume of information for the early twentieth century mother or nursemaid. He appears to assume that the advice given will be taken at face value and used accordingly. His answers to the questions posed in the text are short and written in easily understood language. While he describes some of the common childhood diseases, their symptoms, and basic treatment, he states clearly that sick babies should be treated by a physician.[16]

The U.S. Children's Bureau provided many services to families and children throughout the 1910s and 1920s. A major project was the publication and distribution, free of charge, of an advice manual. *Infant Care* was initially published in 1914 and served not only to help Americanize the immigrant and urban populations but also to bring expert advice to mothers in small towns and rural areas where health care was limited at best. Mothers learned to clothe, feed, and care for their babies according to the beliefs of the Children's Bureau professionals. *Infant Care* included the symptoms of common diseases, suggestions for bedding and proper activities for babies. The pamphlets were mailed by request or handed out by Congressmen. Mothers' letters to the Children's Bureau came by the thousands and covered a wide range of concerns. Bureau workers answered each letter received, basing their information on that espoused by authorities such as L. Emmett Holt, M.D., the preeminent pediatrician of the day and the author of *The Care and Feeding of Children*, described above. The letters also served to help the Bureau tailor planning for future endeavors, including legislation.[17]

The Children's Bureau *Infant Care* was a straightforward publication that provided clear, succinct information for mothers. The 1923 edition of the pamphlet included recommendations for birth registration that reflect the urgency reformers felt for statistical evidence. On page two the pamphlet states, in capital letters, "See that the birth of your baby is registered." The initial pages focused on the best home for the baby. Parents were advised to select a home that was "sunny, well ventilated, and dry." Apartments were thought to be unsuitable as they did not provide enough space for a growing child. "Tenements with dark rooms are not fit homes for children. Suburban homes or those in the outskirts of cities or close to public parks give to city children of the average family the best chance for proper growth and development." These descriptions of middle-class norms reflect the background of the middle-class reformers at the Children's Bureau. The ability of the working class and poor to achieve these goals is not discussed.[18]

Infant Care goes on to include sections about clothing the baby, care of diapers, bathing (including cool, salt, starch, soda, and bran baths), care of special organs, habits, sleep, and exercise. It differentiated care of the city baby and of the country baby. City mothers were told they had a more difficult time raising their babies due to overcrowding, lack of fresh air and sunshine, and the heightened urban potential for disease. The benefits of the new health centers and professional medical attention were stressed. Country mothers were advised to take advantage of the advice of public health nurses at county fairs or in traveling clinics. More than half of the pamphlet was dedicated to feeding the infant. This included breast- and artificial formula feeding, the introduction of solid foods, and even recipes for appropriate infant foods, courtesy of the Office of Home Economics of the U.S. Department of Agriculture.[19]

Private businesses also jumped into the advice business during these years. The Metropolitan Life Insurance Company, chartered in 1868, was insuring the lives of millions of Americans by the 1910s. In 1909 its vice president, Haley Fiske, had announced that "insurance, not merely as a business proposition, but as a social program" would be the company's guiding philosophy.[20] In conjunction with Lillian Wald, the founder of the Henry Street Settlement House in New York City, MetLife (as it is now known) instituted visiting nurse services in New York City to provide health care to its policyholders and their families. By 1911 the company expanded these services nationwide and by 1916 nearly 10 million policyholders were eligible.[21] The company produced, printed, and distributed information to help their clients care for themselves and their children. These activities while altruistic also made good business sense. Saving lives meant fewer payments and increased profits. *The Child* was one of MetLife's influential publications. This small pamphlet was published in 1916 and reflects much of the information found in Holt's *The Care and Feeding of Children*. It covers care of the home, advising mothers that "dirt means danger" and that "clean homes, pure water, pure air, clean milk and clean streets are a protection to the children." The information on the care of the baby up to one year of age is straightforward and easy to read. It emphasizes cleanliness, sleeping at regular times, fresh air every day, and breast-feeding. The pamphlet states in capital letters "every mother who can nurse her own baby should do so." It goes on to say "this is her most important duty" and that if a mother cannot breast-feed the doctor should be consulted at once. Instructions for bottle-feeding are included with the caveat that this be done under the supervision of a doctor. *The Child* also suggests bowel training for the infant as young as three months and counsels the mothers against pacifier use. It provides a brief introduction to the treatment of babies with diarrhea, colic, colds, convulsions, and rickets but stresses "that sickness be noticed as soon as possible and the doctor sent for."[22]

Magazines and newspapers also entered the baby care arena. Some hired writers specifically to address the needs of the new mother. L. Emmett Holt contributed columns titled "Happy Baby" for *The Delineator* magazine.[23] Other magazines, including *Cosmopolitan* and *The Atlantic Monthly* published articles beginning in the 1900s and 1910s. *Parents' Magazine*, founded in 1926 as *Children: the Magazine for Parents*, was quite popular by the 1930s when it reached national and even international audiences.[24] In addition to *The Delineator*, other women's interest magazines were enjoying increased circulations and found baby advice columns and stories popular among their readers.[25]

Newspapers realized the popularity of infants and young children and did not neglect to provide advice. *The New York Times* published many articles between 1901 and 1945 that alerted readers to the potential problems babies faced if not cared for properly. They praised official efforts to educate mothers and provide counseling for those in need. In 1910 several articles illustrated the efforts of officials to promote better health for babies. On June 26 Mrs. H. Ingram, the superintendent of Relief for the New York Association for Improving the Condition of the Poor wrote an article with suggestions for caring for babies during the hot summer months.[26] A week later the magazine section printed an article describing the efforts of a visiting nurse in the tenements to keep a set of "drooping" twins alive in the heat of the summer.[27] On July 27, the newspaper reported on "serious mortality" since the beginning of the month and the health commissioner's firm conviction that the infants' deaths were preventable and the responsibility "rests with the mothers themselves."[28]

By the 1920s *The New York Times* was reporting on the decrease in the IMRs as well as publishing advice articles.[29] In the 1930s and 1940s one reporter, Catherine Mackenzie, published many articles covering the latest in baby care advice.[30] After the onset of World War II the newspaper adapted advice for the needs of wartime mothers and babies.[31]

These articles were typical of the kind of advice mothers (and fathers) could expect from "authoritative" sources and many of them relied greatly on professionals for their information. For parents living in rural environments without access to relatives or even neighbors these written sources of support gave not only advice but peace of mind.

The race of babies was not addressed as a separate issue during the first half of the century. It was well known that African-American babies had significantly higher mortality rates than white, native-born infants. However the differences were generally ascribed to "innate and acquired characteristics and customs." That blacks had the highest rates of infant mortality was considered "a result of their being the most racially and culturally backward and most neglectful of their children." The racism inherent in American society effectively excluded African-American babies from the attention of early Progressive Era reformers. For example, New York City welfare workers did not enter black neighborhoods until 1916 and it would take federal legislation to bring infant welfare for blacks into the southern states in the 1920s.[32] I will discuss much further the inequities of racism and its effects on babies in Chapter 6.

ALTRUISM

Progressive reformers knew that to keep the public's attention on the welfare of babies they needed to get the attention of the politicians. Money was needed and while private groups did put up generous amounts of money, only tax dollars would adequately fund programs deemed necessary for baby saving. The first major federal attention to the issue of infant welfare came during the initial White House Conference on Children held in 1909. Called by Progressive Republican President Theodore Roosevelt, conference attendees supported the idea of a separate governmental department to oversee the welfare of infants and children. After much debate the Congress passed a bill and the U.S. Children's Bureau was established. President William Howard Taft signed the bill into law on April 9, 1912. The Children's Bureau immediately began a national campaign to reduce infant mortality and to implement birth registration (birth certificates) in order to accurately record the number of babies born each year. Throughout the 1910s the Children's Bureau expanded its work and began to push for further federal legislation. The result was the passage of the Sheppard–Towner Maternity and Infancy Act in 1921. This act provided funding for the Children's Bureau to encourage states to promote programs aimed at decreasing disease and death among all children. Activities supported included child health and prenatal clinics, educational materials for home use, and visiting nurse services. The focus was on education—nurses, physicians, and others working in the field as part of the Sheppard–Towner programs were not permitted to diagnose or treat physical illness or injury in babies or children. Referrals to private physicians were made when problems were identified. Parental response to the various programs was positive.[33]

Sheppard–Towner was controversial as was the Children's Bureau. Many groups, including the Roman Catholic Church opposed the bureau on the grounds that it interfered with family life and parental control over their offspring. Critics of the 1920s, including the influential American Medical Association, called the Sheppard–Towner Act "socialized medicine" and worked vigorously to repeal it. The AMA and other conservatives were successful and the Act was not renewed in 1929. The Children's Bureau was successful in many ways. The IMR dropped from 75.6 per 1,000 live births in 1921 to 67.9 in 1929. By 1929 the vast majority of infant births were recorded.[34] The importance of this achievement cannot be underestimated. Almost all future legislation regarding the welfare of babies would be based on these statistics.

The middle years of the century were dominated by the Great Depression of the 1930s and World War II. Babies were affected along with all Americans. Financial and material shortages and cutbacks during the Depression caused nutritional problems as babies and mothers often went without food. For some families the loss of a job and any savings they might have had led to homelessness. Babies in these families suffered from exposure as well as malnutrition. A baby's inability to adequately regulate her body heat made these problems especially acute for the smallest babies. The birthrate in the United States continued to decline, aided no doubt by parents' decisions to put off having more children until their financial problems resolved.[35] The Social Security Act of 1935 revived some of the infant and child care programs that had been developed under Sheppard–Towner. Aid to Families with Dependent Children (AFDC), a part of the Social Security Act, helped destitute parents provide food, clothing, and shelter to their children. These programs and their impact will be discussed in more detail in Chapter 5.

With the start of World War II in Europe in 1939 and the U.S. entrance into the war in 1941 the American economy rebounded tremendously. Factories switched to war production and hired many men and women to build the tanks, ships, guns, jeeps, and other equipment needed by the armed services. Women, including mothers of babies and small children, entered the workplace to take the place of men headed overseas to fight. The public attitude to babies changed somewhat during the war with increased acceptance of day care programs for the children of some mothers employed in the war effort. While federally funded day care centers were established they served only about 10 percent of the children needing care and, with few exceptions, only children over two years of age. The Child Welfare League of America and the Children's Bureau vigorously opposed day care for infants. Despite this, infants were cared for in a few private agencies, but most mothers of babies continued to rely on relatives, older children, or friends. The federally supported and many private day care programs closed at the war's end.[36]

The public's positive attitude toward babies continued throughout the 1930s and 1940s. Baby parades and contests took on a patriotic cast during the war. Photos of babies were used to urge citizens to purchase war bonds.[37] Infants also graced the covers of magazines. The *Saturday Evening Post's* January 3, 1942, cover showed a chubby baby astride a world globe; it was sitting on top of the map of the United States holding a rifle and with an Army overseas cap on its head. A sign pasted across the middle of the globe said "No Trespassing."[38] These depictions of babies as patriotic citizens encouraged older children and adults to step up and do their part to ensure victory. The pictures also served to remind people that the suffering required of all citizens in wartime was to secure the future for all American babies.

AFTER THE WAR—BABIES IN THE "MODERN AGE"

At one second after midnight on January 1, 1946, a baby girl was born at St. Agnes Hospital in Philadelphia, Pennsylvania. The next day the *Philadelphia Inquirer* reported her birth as the first of the New Year. That baby, Kathleen Casey, was the first of more than 76 million babies born between 1946 and 1964.[39] Later dubbed the "Baby Boom," the years immediately after World War II produced the largest generation of Americans ever. This surge in the number of births, actually begun during the war, reflected a belief in a better future as the country came out of the Depression and war years. It was also a significant factor in the postwar economy as the babies and their families needed places to live, play, and eventually go to school. New suburban neighborhoods sprung up seemingly overnight along with schools, hospitals, roads, and businesses. The consumer culture blossomed in this atmosphere. An automobile became a necessity for many middle-class families. It seemed that babies grew up in cars—they were brought home from the hospital in them, driven to pediatrician offices in them, and were taken shopping in them with their strollers stored in the back.[40]

Babies were symbols of the American Dream in the 1950s. New products were brought out to make the care of them easier. Disposable diapers were conceived in the 1930s and 1940s but started the climb to dominance in the diaper market in the 1950s. Plastic baby bottles followed a similar path.[41] A renewed emphasis on infant and child health captured the imagination as polio, the debilitating and too often fatal paralyzing disease of summer was controlled by new vaccines. Other dreaded diseases including measles, mumps, and rubella would be targeted in the 1960s. Of course babies could always anticipate other "shots" including the DPT (diphtheria, pertussis, and tetanus)[42] and various booster shots. Parents were strongly encouraged to take advantage of these opportunities and in many areas the vaccines became required by law for entry into school. While most parents welcomed the availability of immunization against disease others began to question the government's ever-increasing role in their individual family's lives.[43]

By the mid-1960s the baby boom was over. The Vietnam War was at its peak and the babies of the late 1940s and 1950s would change the nation in ways never before seen. Rebelling against the staid lives of their parents, they helped spearhead cultural, civil rights, and sexual revolutions. When President Lyndon Johnson declared the "War on Poverty" he proposed programs that included the enactment of Medicare and Medicaid which helped the poor finance medical care, a mother and infant nutrition program called WIC, Women, Infants and Children, and the distribution of food stamps so the impoverished could purchase nutritious food.[44] With the exception of Medicare's focus on the elderly, these programs directly affected the lives of infants. Medicaid provided money for health care and WIC and food stamps helped ensure adequate nutrition.

Even entering the world changed dramatically in the late 1960s and 1970s. While nearly 100 percent of American babies were born in hospitals in 1950, with many of their mothers sound asleep at the time of birth, by the 1980s women were once again choosing when, where, and how to have their babies.

Although most continued to give birth in hospitals, "natural" birth, or birth without the use of any pain medication or anesthesia, became more important to many women. Birthing centers opened in some areas and were staffed by certified nurse-midwives with obstetrician and hospital backup for emergencies. These centers provided a more home-like environment for those with an uncomplicated and low-risk pregnancy.[45] Marshall Klaus and John Kennell's 1976 book, *Maternal-Infant Bonding*, convinced a generation of mothers that being awake and alert during and immediately after birth so that they could hold, cuddle, and nurse their babies in those first few minutes was vital to both the mothers' and babies' long-term mental and physical health.[46] Although later studies have discredited this notion,[47] by the 1990s immediate interaction between the newborn infant and its mother and often its father was a part of most American births.

Attitudes toward babies continued to evolve throughout the 1980s and 1990s. Positive views of infants were the norm; however the differences between and among babies were still emphasized. Babies born to married couples in a stable relationship and home environment were celebrated. Those born to single women, teenagers, and lower class families without the means to support them were considered suspect. Resentment toward those members of society requiring public assistance grew and babies did not escape the outrage of many people. Single women who chose to bear babies or adopt babies without a husband were commended by some and criticized by others for contributing to the demise of the traditional American family. Births to teen mothers were alarming because they were less likely than mothers twenty or older to finish high school, go to college, or obtain a well-paying job. Births to teenagers peaked in 1991 and then steadily dropped throughout the 1990s.[48]

Infertile couples could take advantage of new technology to have "test tube babies" as they were initially termed. By the 1990s in-vitro fertilization (IVF) was commonplace and while successful less than half the time it was used, offered couples who could afford it a second chance at parenthood. One of the results of IVF was an increase in the number or twins, triplets, and higher order multiple births. Sets of quadruplets, quintuplets, sextuplets, and even septuplets were born and became instant celebrities. While most of the publicity was positive, questions about the propriety of attempting to carry three or more babies to term were asked. Since the chances of miscarriage and significantly premature birth are quite high in these cases people questioned if the price the babies paid in physical and mental disabilities was equal to the price parents paid to become parents.[49]

"Trust yourself. You know more than you think you do."[50] With those words Benjamin Spock ushered in *Baby and Child Care*, the most widely read advice book of the twentieth century. First published in 1946, at the start of the postwar Baby Boom, it provided a straightforward, almost folksy approach to the care of babies and children. His success spawned many imitators. Sales of parental advice books grew throughout the second half of the twentieth century and show no signs of abating. Advice is everywhere—the bookstore, magazines, the Internet, television, radio, friends, relatives, strangers, etc. Books on the topic range from *Parenting for Dummies* to the *Children's Hospital of Philadelphia Book of Pregnancy and Child Care* and other prestigious medical institution publications.[51] Parents, especially mothers, are told they are smart, dumb, and everywhere in between. Mothers are told to rely on themselves, on their girlfriends, and on medical professionals, read books and watch videos, keep the baby with them at all times, take scheduled breaks from the baby, involve the baby's father, have babies by themselves, go back to work and stay at home, take him out for fresh air and keep him inside to avoid germs, and on and on. Specialty books on breast-feeding, bottle-feeding, introduction of solid food, growth and development, reading to baby, classical music for baby, teething, clothing, supplies, and many others line the shelves of libraries and bookstores.

A book that provided an alternative to Spock was written by T. Berry Brazelton, M.D., and originally published in 1967. In *Infants and Mothers: Differences in Development* Brazelton sought to assure mothers that while their babies were unique, they were not abnormal. Brazelton's influence was immense and he continued to publish widely on all aspects of infant care throughout the 1990s.[52]

In the 1990s the Internet became the newest entrant in the baby advice field. Major manufacturers of baby equipment as well as the neighbor down the street set up Web sites to help parents care for their babies. Chat rooms brought mothers from all around the country together online to discuss, question, and support each other. The Internet meant that the speed of information available to mothers had compressed from weeks and months in the early 1900s to near instantaneous by 2000. In the 1910s a mother with a baby care question that was unanswerable in her immediate surroundings could write to the Children's Bureau and wait for a reply. Depending on her location and the post office this entire process might take several weeks. In 2000 she could access the Internet from her home computer at 2:00 A.M. if necessary and find an answer within minutes. Hospitals and pediatricians also embraced the

Internet and Web sites written by and directed by them were set up across the country. Unfortunately not all information found on the Internet is reliable. Many sites contain potentially misleading or even false content. Determining the truth is often impossible for parents, especially during the stressful first weeks of a baby's life.

Public and private philanthropy continued to be a major source of assistance for parents of new babies in the second half of the century. Medicaid has been controversial and amended several times. In 1996 the Personal Responsibility and Work Opportunity Reconciliation Act signed by President Bill Clinton replaced AFDC. To receive aid, needy mothers had to meet work or school requirements and respect lifetime limits on assistance.[53] The growth and influence of private charitable organizations devoted to the problems of babies was felt across the country in the 1980s and 1990s. One of the larger and most successful charities is the March of Dimes, an organization founded in 1938 to help cure polio. It raised money through a nationwide campaign made all the more poignant because of President Franklin Roosevelt's bout with the disease as a young man. The general public was encouraged to send in their dimes to the White House to help conquer this terrible affliction. Success came in the mid-1950s with the introduction of vaccines that virtually eliminated polio in the United States by 1980. The March of Dimes switched their focus in 1958 to the prevention of premature birth, birth defects, and low birth weight.[54] Other groups have come together to combat a myriad of diseases and conditions. Religious groups routinely include the needs of babies in their charitable works. Americans also prove their ability to come together to help babies when disasters such as earthquakes and hurricanes strike. Baby formula, diapers, and other necessities are frequently provided by private citizens and by corporations for the needy in these circumstances.[55]

CONCLUSION

The general public embraced babies during the twentieth century as never before. Babies benefited immensely. Progressive Era reforms that focused on babies as indicators of the status of the nation brought many changes. Once ignored by all but their mothers and fathers, babies became adored members of the family, loved by all who saw them. Death in infancy was no longer expected or accepted and the IMR dropped significantly. By 2000 the United States had the lowest IMR in its history, although it still lagged behind other developed countries. The changed attitudes toward babies prompted local, state, and federal laws designed to maintain and improve infant lives. Public and private programs, beginning with the settlement houses in the early part of the century, provided assistance with everything from milk to money to medical care.

But as babies became more important to the society at large they seemed more of a mystery to their parents. Not that the parents were without help. Advice came from everywhere and seemed to feed on natural parental anxiety about the care of a new baby. Americans do not necessarily want someone to tell them how to raise babies, but they do want positive affirmation that what they are doing is at the very least not harmful and possibly extraordinary. Especially after World War II Americans relied more on professional "authorities" for advice and affirmation and less on their friends, families, and natural instincts. As science and medicine advanced enormously, advice from scientific and medical experts on everything, including infant care, became widely trusted. The increased mobility of Americans also contributed to their greater reliance on expert advice on babies. Earlier in the century grandparents lived with or close to their children and grandchildren. Other relatives and close friends were nearby. When families live far away from these traditional sources of support and advice they often look for help in other places. In that regard the advice manuals and Internet sites fill a void and convey a sense of security. Although Spock and Brazelton satisfied many parents during the 1940s to early 1970s, the parents of the last quarter of the century were accustomed to greater choices in all aspects of life. Book publishers responded with an array of offerings. Magazines geared toward parents and the rise of the Internet in the 1990s provided even more. Too much advice, however, can overwhelm parents and even disrupt their ability to make appropriate decisions for their babies. While parents continue to seek perfection for their baby they might be wise to read the second paragraph of Dr. Spock's advice book where he states "don't take too seriously all that the neighbors say. Don't be overawed by what the experts say .... take it easy [and] trust your own instincts."[56]

NOTES

1. Benjamin Spock and Steven J. Parker, *Dr. Spock's Baby and Child Care*, 7th ed. (New York: Pocket Books, 1998).

2. Viviana A. Zelizer, *Pricing the Priceless Child: The Changing Social Value of Children* (Princeton, NJ: Princeton University Press, 1985).

3. A very unscientific survey done on January 17, 2006, revealed 3,005 titles when Amazon.com was searched for "new parents." A Google search on January 19, 2006, revealed more than 1.8 million results for "attitudes about babies." Spock's book is called the second best-selling book in the world after the Bible in many places, by many people. I have not located a definitive source for that claim. One author cites sales of 1 million copies a year by the mid-1960s. Ann Hulbert, *Raising America—Experts, Parents, and a Century of Advice about Children* (New York: Alfred A. Knopf, 2003), 12, 243.

4. National Center for Health Statistics, *Health, United States, 2006 with Chartbook on Trends in the Health of Americans* (November 2006), 127, http://www.cdc.gov/nchs/data/hus/hus06.pdf#027 and www.cdc.gov/nchs/about/major/dvs/mortdata.htm.

5. Donna L. Hoyert, Mary Anne Freedman, Donna M. Stobino, and Bernard Guyer, "Annual Summary of Vital Statistics: 2000," *Pediatrics* 108(6) (2001): 1241–1255. In 1998 the infant mortality rate (IMR) in the United States was 7.2 deaths per 1,000 live births. This ranked twenty-third in a list of developed countries. Hong Kong had the lowest IMR at 3.2, closely followed by Switzerland, Sweden, and Japan. Canada ranked fifteenth.

6. Jeffrey P. Baker, *The Machine in the Nursery* (Baltimore, MD: Johns Hopkins University Press, 1996); Thomas E. Cone, Jr., *History of the Care and Feeding of the Premature Infant* (Boston, MA: Little, Brown and Company, 1985); Julius H. Hess and Evelyn C. Lundeen, *The Premature Infant: Medical and Nursing Care*, 2nd ed. (Philadelphia, PA: J.B. Lippincott Company, 1949); Robert M. Freedom, James Lock, and J. Timothy Bricker, "Pediatric Cardiology and Cardiovascular Surgery: 1950–2000," *Circulation* 60 (2000): IV-58–IV-68; Environmental Protection Agency. United States Department of Agriculture. Center for Food Safety and Applied Nutrition, Food and Drug Administration. Div. of Nutrition Research Coordination, National Institutes of Health. National Center for Health Statistics; National Center for Environmental Health; National Center for Infectious Diseases; National Center for Chronic Disease Prevention and Health Promotion, Centers for Disease Control and Prevention. "Achievements in Public Health, 1900–1999: Safer and Healthier Foods," *Morbidity and Mortality Weekly Report* 48(40) (1999): 905–913; Steve Collins, Nicky Dent, Paul Binns, Paluku Bahwere, Kate Sadler, and Alistair Hallam, "Management of Severe Acute Malnutrition in Children," *Lancet* 368 (2006): 1992—2000.

7. Zelizer, *Pricing the Priceless Child*, 3–21.

8. Michael B. Katz, *In the Shadow of the Poorhouse—A Social History of Welfare in America* (New York: Basic Books, 1986), 137–142; and Richard A. Meckel, *Save the Babies: American Public Health Reform and the Prevention of Infant Mortality, 1850–1929* (Ann Arbor: University of Michigan Press, 1990), 71–91.

9. Meckel, *Save the Babies*, 77–81, 93–102, 120–123; and Katz, *In the Shadow of the Poorhouse*, 37–42.

10. Meckel, *Save the Babies*, 46–49, 111, 130, 141–143, 146–148. For an in-depth look at the popular baby contests of the day see Annette K. Vance Dorey, *Better Baby Contests: The Scientific Quest for Perfect Childhood Health in the Early Twentieth Century* (Jefferson, NC: McFarland & Company, 1999).

11. Meckel, *Save the Babies*, 130–132, Steven Mintz, *Huck's Raft—A History of American Childhood* (Cambridge, MA: Belknap Press of Harvard University Press, 2004), 205–206; and Thomas E. Cone, *History of American Pediatrics* (Boston, MA: Little, Brown and Company, 1979), 186–187, 249.

12. L. Emmett Holt, *The Care and Feeding of Children*, 9th ed. (New York: D. Appleton and Company, 1912), 7–8, 41–114.

13. Holt, *The Care and Feeding of Children*, 154–155.

14. Molly Ladd-Taylor, *Raising a Baby the Government Way–Mothers' Letters to the Children's Bureau, 1915–1932* (New Brunswick, NJ: Rutgers University Press, 1986), 39; Min Sun and Simone Rugolotto, "Assisted Infant Toilet Training in a Western Family Setting," *Journal of Developmental and Behavioral Pediatrics* 25(2) (2004): 99–101; Anna Kuchment, "Parenting: Ditching Diapers," *Newsweek*, September 26, 2005, p. 9; and Tina Kelley, "A Fast Track to Toilet Training for Those at the Crawling Stage," *The New York Times*, October 9, 2005, p. 1. http://www.nytimes.com/2005/10/09/nyregion/09diapers. *The New York Times* article was reprinted in newspapers across the country. There are many Web sites devoted solely to infant toilet training as well as parenting sites, "woman's" magazine sites and infant and child health sites that discuss the issue.

15. Holt, *The Care and Feeding of Children*, 155, 168, 183–185; Task Force on Sudden Infant Death Syndrome, "The Changing Concept of Sudden Infant Death Syndrome: Diagnostic Coding Shifts, Controversies Regarding the Sleeping Environment, and New Variables to Consider in Reducing Risk," *Pediatrics* 116(5) (2005): 1245–1255; Marian Willinger, Chia-Wen Ko, Howard J. Hoffman, Ronald C. Kessler, and Michael J. Corwin, "Trends in Infant Bed Sharing in the United States, 1993–2000; The National Infant Sleep Position Study," *Archives of Pediatric and Adolescent Medicine* 157 (2003) 43–49; International Lactation Consultant Association, "ILCA Responds to Policy Statement by AAP Task Force on SIDS," *World Alliance for Breastfeeding Action*, (n.d.), http://www.waba.org.my/ilca_sids_response; and Attachment Parenting International, "Attachment Parenting International Position Paper Regarding the New Recommendations by the American Academy of Pediatrics," *Attachment Parenting International*, October 12, 2005, http://www.attachmentparenting.org/aappp.

16. Holt, *The Care and Feeding of Children*, 8.

17. Ladd-Taylor, *Raising a Baby the Government Way*, 1–6, 32–46.

18. Mrs. Max West, *Infant Care*, No. 8. (Washington, DC: Government Printing Office, 1923), 2, 11–17.

19. West, *Infant Care*, 17–36, 40–41, 47–76.

20. Metropolitan Life Insurance Company, "Helping and Healing People," (n.d.), http://www.metlife.com/Applications/Corporate/WPS/CDA/PageGenerator.

21. Karen Buhler Wilkerson, "The Call to the Nurse: Our History from 1893 to 1943," *Visiting Nurse Service of New York*, http://www.vnsny.org/mainsite/about/a_history_more.

22. Belle Lindner Israels, *The Child* (New York: Metropolitan Life Insurance Company, 1916): 6, 16, 27.

23. Hulbert, *Raising America*, 70. The *Delineator* was a popular women's fashion magazine published by the Butterick Publishing Company from 1873 to 1937.

24. Hulbert, *Raising America*, 70–71, 105.

25. See for example, Lola Wangner, "My First Baby," *Lady's Home Journal* (October 1904): 5–6; Evelyn Linda Cooledge, "The Young Mother's Calendar," *Lady's Home Journal* (December 1904): 30; Caroline Wormely Latimer, "How Can I Keep My Baby from Crying?" *Lady's Home Journal*, (January 1912): 35, 48; and T. Wood Clarke, "The Baby in the Small City," *Lady's Home Journal* (July 1914): 61.

26. H. Ingram, "Some Simple Helps," *The New York Times, Sunday Magazine*, June 26, 1910, p. 6.

27. "Saving the Lives of Babies in Congested Districts; What a Visiting Nurse from the Health Board Does to Keep Alive Drooping Children of the Tenements," *The New York Times*, July 3, 1910, p. SM11.

28. "Health Department Appeals to Mothers; Tells How to Care for Their Babies during the Period of Hot Weather," *The New York Times*, July 27, 1910, p. 8.

29. For example: "What State's Doing for Better Babies," *The New York Times*, November 3, 1926, p. 38; "Infant deaths in Summer: Baby Centres and Visiting Nurses Do Much to Reduce Them," *The New York Times*, July 18, 1920, p. 18; and "Tries to Improve Long Island Babies: State Health Department Starts Campaign to Spread Gospel of Breast Feeding," *The New York Times*, 17 April 1923, p. 27.

30. Catherine Mackenzie, "Children and Parents," *The New York Times*, November 19, 1939, p. D7; Catherine Mackenzie, "Child and Parent," July 28, 1940, p. 85; Catherine Mackenzie, "Handling a Sick Child," February 23, 1941, p. SM20; Catherine Mackenzie, "The Second Baby vs. the First," March 2, 1941, p. SM22; Catherine Mackenzie, "Mental Tests for the Baby," March 30, 1941, p. SM23; Catherine Mackenzie, "Bringing Up the Baby," January 2, 1944, p. SM19; and Catherine Mackenzie, "Good and Bad Discipline," July 30, 1944, p. SM26.

31. "Medical Group Will Advise Young Wives of Service Men How to Care for Babies," *The New York Times*, March 17, 1945, p. 18; and Catherine Mackenzie, "Bringing Up the Baby," *The New York Times*, January 2, 1944, p. SM19.

32. Meckel, *Save the Babies*, 131—132, 142

33. Ibid., 200–219.

34. Kriste Lindenmeyer, *'A Right to Childhood'—The U.S. Children's Bureau and Child Welfare, 1912–46* (Urbana: University of Illinois Press, 1997), 100–104; and Meckel, *Save the Babies*, 214–219.

35. Centers for Disease Control and Prevention (CDC), "Table 1-1. Live Births, Birth Rates, and Fertility Rates, by Race of Child: United States, 1909–1980," in *Vital Statistics of the United States, 1997, Volume I—Natality* (Hyattsville, MD: National Center for Health Statistics, 1997), http:// www.cdc.gov/nchs/data/statab/t991x01.pdf. In 1935 the birthrate was 18.7/1000. This was the lowest mark the birthrate reached before rebounding to 19.4 in 1940. It would not dip below 1935 levels until 1966 when the baby boom was over.

36. William M. Tuttle, Jr., *"Daddy's Gone to War"—The Second World War in the Lives of America's Children* (New York: Oxford University Press, 1993), 71, 75–77, 80–82; and Geraldine Youcha, *Minding the Children: Child Care in America from Colonial Times to the Present* (New York: Scribner, 1995), 307–319.

37. One poster has a picture of an infant in a highchair holding a U.S. savings bond in his hand. The caption of the poster is "For Baby's Future BUY WAR BONDS." Series World War II posters, Record Group 44, Data Control Group LCS, U.S. Archives, Washington, DC.

38. J.C. Leyendecker, "No Trespassing," *Saturday Evening Post*, January 3, 1942, Cover.

39. Landon Y. Jones, "Swinging 60s? The First Baby Boomer Looks Back—and Forward-On the Eve of a Milestone," *Smithsonian Magazine*, January 6, 2006, http:// smithsonianmag.com/issues/2006/january/presence.

40. Mintz, *Huck's Raft*, 256, 275–279.

41. "Cloth without Looms," *Time*, May 25, 1942, www.time.com/time/printout/ 0,8816,766607,00.html; "No Boiling, No Burps," *Time*, March 17, 1947, www.time.

com/time/magazine/article/0,9171,793435,00.html; "Summer 1957," *Time*, July 29, 1957, www.time.com/time/printout/0,8816,825154,00.html; "How to Make a Buck," *Time*, July 29, 1957, www.time.com/time/magazine/article/0,9171,825227,00.html; and "The Great Diaper Battle," *Time*, January 24, 1969, www.time.com/time/magazine/article/0,9171,900601,00.html.

42. An antitoxin for the treatment of diphtheria was first available in the 1890s; tetanus and pertussis vaccines were combined with it during the 1940s.

43. Mintz, *Huck's Raft*, 278–279; and CDC, and National Immunization Program, "Achievements in Public Health, 1900–1999. Impact of Vaccines Universally Recommended for Children—United States, 1990–1998," *Morbidity and Mortality Weekly Report* 48(12) (1999): 243–248.

44. Mintz, *Huck's Raft*, 311–314; and Katz, *In the Shadow of the Poorhouse*, 264–266.

45. Howard Blanchette, "Comparison of Obstetric Outcome of a Primary-Care Access Clinic Staffed by Certified Nurse-Midwives and a Private Practice Group of Obstetricians in the Same Community," *American Journal of Obstetrics and Gynecology* 172(6) (1995): 1864–1871; and Marian F. MacDorman and Gopal K. Singh, "Midwifery Care, Social and Medical Risk Factors, and Birth Outcomes in the USA," *Journal of Epidemiology and Community Health* 52 (1998): 310–317.

46. Marshall H. Klaus and John H. Kennell, *Maternal-Infant Bonding* (St. Louis, MO: Mosby, 1976).

47. Susan Goldberg, "Parent-Infant Bonding: Another Look," *Child Development* 54(6) (1983): 1355–1382.

48. "Teen Birth Rate Continues Decline, Fewer Childhood Deaths, More Children Immunized Children More Likely to Live in Poverty, Be Involved in Violent Crime," Federal Interagency Forum on Child and Family Statistics (July 20, 2005), http://www.nichd.nih.gov/news/releases/americas_children05.cfm; and Stephanie J. Ventura, T.J. Matthews, and Sally C. Curtin, "Declines in Teenage Birth Rates, 1991–98: Update of National and State Trends," *National Vital Statistics Reports* 47(26) (1999): 1–9. Between 1991 and 2003 the teen birthrate dropped more than 40 percent.

49. Claudia Kalb, "Families: The Octuplet Question," *Newsweek*, January 11, 1999, p. 33; Linda Kulman, "Cigars All Around," *U.S. News & World Report*, December 1, 1997, p. 14; Michael D. Lemonick and Jeffrey Kluger, "It's a Miracle," *Time*, December 1, 1997, pp. 34–39; John McCormick and Barbara Datrowizt, "The Magnificent Seven," *Newsweek*, December 1, 1997, pp. 58–62; Wendy Wasserstein, "Annals of Motherhood—Complications," *New Yorker*, February 21 and 28, 2000, p. 87; "Question Time," *People Weekly*, January 11, 1999, p. 72; Susan Schindehette, "Coming Up Roses," *People Weekly*, December 8, 1997, pp. 54—60; and "Once Used by Government, Dionne Quints Recoup a Loss," *Philadelphia Inquirer*, March 7, 1998, pp. A1 and A8.

50. Spock and Parker, *Dr. Spock's Baby and Child Care*, 1.

51. Sandra Hardin Gookin, *Parenting for Dummies*, Dan Gookin (Ed.) (Foster City, CA: IDG Books Worldwide, Inc, 1995); and Patrick S. Pasquariello, Jr., senior ed., *The Children's Hospital of Philadelphia Book of Pregnancy and Child Care*. (New York: John Wiley, 1999).

52. T. Berry Brazelton, *Infants and Mothers: Differences in Development* (New York: Delacourt Press, 1967).

53. Meckel, *Save the Babies*, 264, 274–291; Joanne L. Goodwin, "'Employable Mothers' and 'Suitable Work'—A Reevaluation of Welfare and Wage Earning for Women in the Twentieth-Century United States," *Journal of Social History*

29 (1995): 253–274; and Personal Responsibility and Work Opportunity Reconciliation Act of 1996, H.R. 3734 (August 22, 1996), http://thomas.loc.gov/cgi-bin/query/F?c104:1:./temp/~c104HIrfhm:e19928.

54. March of Dimes Foundation, "Uniting to Beat Polio," *March of Dimes, About Us* (n.d.), http://www.marchofdimes.com/aboutus/789_821.asp.

55. Hurricane Andrew in August 1992 devastated South Florida. It hit Louisiana hard as well. Private and public donations began almost immediately. See for example, "Foundation Is Giving $10 Million to Help South Florida to Rebuild," *The New York Times*, September 19, 1992, p. 8; "After the Storm: As Army Gears Up, Floridians Rely on Private Relief," *The New York Times*, August 30, 1992, p. 1; and Roberto Suro, "After the Storm: Overwhelmed by Kindness, Louisiana Begins Rebuilding," *The New York Times*, September 3, 1992, p. 18.

56. Spock and Parker, *Dr. Spock's Baby and Child Care*, 1.

Health, Illness, and the
American Baby

" ... we have demonstrated that the door of hope is open to the littlest of our citizens, and that under the worst conditions it is possible to solve at least a part of the infant mortality problem."
— S. Josephine Baker, M.D., 1912[1]

Medical advances during the twentieth century enhanced and elongated life for all Americans. The discovery of medicines such as insulin and antibiotics changed life expectancies for diabetics and for anyone with any type of bacterial infection. Surgical techniques, radiological procedures, and other diagnostic tools allowed physicians to identify and treat health problems as never before. During the immediate post–World War II years it seemed that there was nothing that could not be treated and cured by American medicine. Perhaps nowhere was this optimism more pronounced than for babies. In the course of 100 years babies went from being forgotten or ignored by medical personnel to being arguably the most important patient population in the nation. By the 1990s treatments extended even into prenatal life with the advent of fetal surgery. In this chapter I will explore some of the major advances made in the care of babies including the identification of babies as a distinct category of patients requiring treatments precisely catered to their needs, the impact of antibiotics on infectious disease, and the dramatic decline in common childhood illnesses because of immunizations. I will also discuss some of the newer problems facing babies in the later years of the century including emerging infections and allergies.

In America by 2000 parents of a newborn infant, unless the baby had a serious birth defect, congenital disease, or prematurity, expected their young-ster not only to live, but thrive. The infant mortality rate (IMR) in 2000 stood at 6.8 deaths per 1,000 live births.[2] Earlier, in the first two decades of the century, surviving infancy was not so easy. For every thousand babies born in 1915 ninety-five would die before their first birthday. Congenital diseases and defects were the cause of many deaths. Prematurity accounted for approxi-mately 6 percent of all births and many of these babies died shortly after birth.[3] In otherwise healthy infants, gastrointestinal infection and respiratory infec-tion were the predominant causes of illness and death. Accidents, abuse, and neglect also took a toll. The course and outcome of all illnesses and injuries are naturally affected by the environment in which they take place. Living conditions, access to professional medical care, race and cultural biases, ge-ographical considerations, and parents' own knowledge all played a part in a baby's chances for a healthy life.

MEDICAL CARE AVAILABLE TO INFANTS IN 1901

There was little medical care specific to the care of infants available to the general public at the beginning of the twentieth century. At this time as for most of history, babies were the responsibility of their mothers. Mothers provided nutrition, bathed a feverish baby, concocted alternative feedings for a colicky or vomiting baby, and understood the pros and cons of traditional healing methods. When patent medicines were available mothers decided what would be appropriate and when to administer them. A mother's intelligence as well as a lot of luck determined a baby's chances of surviving what we now think of as minor illnesses. If a mother died, whether in childbirth or after, the baby was lucky if her father or another female relative took over care and feeding. In some situations fathers sent their babies and young children to relatives, friends, or neighbors to be raised. When the father remarried he might retrieve his children.

As the nineteenth century progressed physicians became increasingly edu-cated and increasingly numerous. Their influence was expanding to include the areas of public health and nutrition and many began to consider the care of the middle and lower classes worthy of their attention. Except for a few physicians this attitude did not extend to the care of sick babies.

There were many reasons for this lack of interest in babies. First, as previously discussed, the number of babies dying within the first few hours and days of birth remained high. Doctors attributed these deaths to congenital disease, defect, or prematurity and labeled babies "weak" or "congenitally debilitated."[4] Physicians had limited ability to diagnose, treat, and cure babies suffering these fates. Second, as we know now, a baby's anatomy and physiology are very different from that of an adult. Richard Meckel, in his 1990 book *Save the Babies: American Public Health Reform and the Prevention of Infant Mortality, 1850–1929* stated: " . . . earlier pediatric writers, while recognizing that children were not miniature adults, had assumed that the diseases of infancy and childhood were unique, rather than the infants and children themselves."[5] Thus treatments for similar conditions but tailored to the anatomy and physiology of an adult usually did not work for babies. For instance babies' upper airways are anatomically different—they are relatively smaller and narrower than adults'. This causes babies to be more susceptible to respiratory infection that can swell and clog the airways, causing difficulty in breathing. This can occur rapidly, often within hours, and in the days before antibiotics it frequently led to death. The third reason why there was little interest in treating babies in the nineteenth century was that parents, physicians, and others expected some babies to die, as they had done for centuries. If a baby did not die of some illness or condition present at birth, a gastrointestinal or respiratory illness could kill them before their first birthday. Fourth, physicians generally did not begin to specialize in the care of certain populations until the nineteenth century and pediatricians were one of the later groups to come together.[6] Pediatrics as a specialty was first recognized by the American Medical Association in 1880 and the American Pediatric Society was founded in 1888. The American Academy of Pediatrics did not organize until 1930.[7] While respected hospitals in the major East Coast cities in 1901 had pediatricians available on staff, the majority of American babies never saw a pediatrician at all. General practitioners, of course, were available and could diagnose and treat some conditions, but since medical education was not standardized across the country they might have had little or no training in the specific care of babies.[8]

TYPICAL DISEASES/CONDITIONS CAUSING ILLNESS, AND DEATH IN 1901

At the beginning of the twentieth century there were many illnesses that could potentially harm or even kill a baby. Some of them are all but forgotten now due to advances in medicine and technology. Others are only now receding into collective memory. A few continue to afflict babies, although in most cases the ability to diagnose and treat the illnesses has improved dramatically. There are also new diseases such as HIV/AIDS that only came to light late in the century. In 1901, however, there were two major classifications of diseases causing death and illness among babies. Diseases of the gastrointestinal tract and of the respiratory tract caused the most illnesses and deaths among previously healthy infants.[9] We know today that bacteria and viruses cause many of these infectious diseases. In the early years of the twentieth century the germ theory of disease was new and not widely supported. It would be easy to fault physicians and scientists of the time for not knowing how to prevent disease and to treat its' consequences but it would be unfair and wrong. The twentieth century has witnessed drastic changes in the amount of knowledge available to the general public as well as professionals involved in medical care. The development of medical specialties such as pediatrics and subspecialties such as neonatology and pediatric surgery was necessary to the dissemination of the information that seemingly doubled every few weeks. While the physicians and scientists of 1901 had significantly more information available to them than did their predecessors fifty years before, they would have had a hard time conceiving of the changes to come over the next 100 years.

Gastrointestinal Tract Problems

Gastrointestinal problems are multifaceted. They are caused by several different viruses and bacteria, none of which were easily identified in the early years of the century. The most common gastrointestinal problem for babies, then and now, is diarrhea, vomiting, and dehydration, most often caused by a virus. In the 1800s and early 1900s it was often referred to as "summer complaint" since many cases originated in the summer season. It generally started with diarrhea and vomiting. If the baby could not keep down enough liquids he became dehydrated. For the majority of babies the illness lasted for several days, and, while it made them miserable, it went away. A mother's biggest challenge was getting the baby to take breast milk, artificial formula, or water. For although not proven nor widely known until the 1910s, the actual cause of death in most infants suffering from summer complaint was dehydration.

In its most violent manifestation summer complaint involved explosive, watery, malodorous, and recurrent stools along with severe vomiting. A baby with a bad case of summer complaint demonstrated signs of acute and severe dehydration very quickly. Urine output decreased and kidney function was rapidly affected. With little physical reserves and no effective treatment death was common.

Summer complaint, sometimes known in the eighteenth and early nineteenth centuries as cholera infantum, was at one time thought to be caused by excessive summer heat and impure air in the cities. In colonial times it was seen in April and May in the cities of the Deep South, while in Philadelphia it appeared by late June or early July and ran until mid-September. Many physicians were convinced that sending city babies to the countryside would help decrease the problem by exposing them to fresh air. By the 1820s it was apparent that bottle-fed babies were more likely to be afflicted with the disease.

By the late 1890s a few physicians suggested the use of fluid replacement via hypodermoclysis which involved injecting a salt solution into the soft tissues of the baby's trunk or thighs. In a few cases this worked to alleviate the dehydration but in many cases it was not enough. Physicians also prescribed calomel, castor oil, bismuth, and opium to rid the body of the foul material and to soothe the bowel. None were very effective and many physicians continued to espouse the removal of sick infants to suburban and rural areas. In Boston a barge was rented and mothers with sick infants were taken for a one-day cruise around the harbor to expose the babies to the salt air and fresh breezes. The Boston Floating Hospital continued this practice until 1931 when a permanent, land-based hospital was opened.[10]

Thus in 1901 while physicians and most parents were aware of the seasonal nature of infant diarrhea and the increased prevalence among artificially fed babies, effective treatments were still in the future. Irritating foods, combined with excessive heat and foul air were thought to attack the baby's delicate intestinal tract causing the diarrhea. Physicians tried to help by prescribing bland diets. Some suggested using elaborate formulas that changed the biochemical composition of cow's milk to better suit the baby's digestive system. Breast milk then was in all practicality the only preventative measure that could be prescribed for the majority of babies. Breast-feeding advice however was erratic—although recommended it was also considered difficult for mothers to get it right.[11]

In the major cities concerned citizens set up milk stations initially to provide clean milk to mothers at reduced rates. Public health officials provided mothers with education about infant feeding and infant care. They learned the proper methods of mixing milk formulas at home and the best ways to keep the milk safe. The stations also served to "Americanize" the immigrant mothers flooding the cities. Efforts to banish "old wives tales" from child care initially focused on the mothers, but soon found a receptive audience among the older daughters of the mothers. These girls, and some were as young as eight or nine years of age, provided baby and child care in many households. When the mother needed to work the young girls fulfilled their mothers' traditional role. By focusing on this group of eager learners, the public health workers assured themselves that at least the next generation would benefit.[12]

Outbreaks of summer complaint declined by 1920. Success was attributed to public health initiatives aimed at individuals and the community. The discovery of viral and bacterial causes has led to better preventative measures including hand washing and safer food-handling procedures at home and in the marketplace. Public health workers taught parents how to prevent disease and dehydration and how to cope with them successfully when they did occur. The advent of the well baby exam sparked by the Children's Bureau and the Sheppard–Towner Act brought babies to the attention of health care providers on a more regular basis where problems were often noticed before they became life-threatening.[13] Throughout the rest of the century outbreaks of diarrheal diseases decreased dramatically. Indoor plumbing and improved water supplies as a result of better built and maintained sewage treatment plants helped keep infants and children from playing in and drinking contaminated water.

Infants still suffer from intestinal disturbances, including diarrhea and vomiting. The development of oral rehydration solutions and the advances made in intravenous fluid replacement have both decreased substantially the morbidity and mortality related to dehydration.[14] Rarely do babies die from diarrhea and dehydration today. Some studies suggest that prematurity, low birth weight, and exclusive breast-feeding are risk factors, as is being born to a first-time mother. Premature and low birth weight babies are at higher risk because of associated conditions that make it harder for the baby to recover from the dehydration. Babies who are exclusively breast-fed and those born to a first-time mother are at risk when the parents are not adequately educated to understand the symptoms and treatment associated with positive outcomes. Identification of those at risk and the provision of appropriate education may reduce the risk for these babies.[15]

Respiratory Tract Problems

Babies who survive the first year of life without any respiratory tract illnesses are rare even today. For most it is a mild and time-limited issue, highlighted by a runny nose, mild to moderate coughing, fatigue, and a low-grade fever. Most babies recover quickly with no long-term complications. But for some babies respiratory illnesses are life-threatening. In 1901 infant morbidity and mortality related to respiratory illness was significant.

As previously stated, the anatomy of an infant's respiratory tract differs from that of older children and adults. The upper and lower airways are proportionately smaller and narrower. This is not a problem unless there is irritation or infection causing the tissues of the airways to swell and/or fill with mucous. While this happens to everyone experiencing respiratory symptoms, in babies the airways become compromised quicker, sometimes within an hour or two. In addition, babies less than six months old are often unable to handle the secretions from their upper airways easily. Without the ability to effectively clear their own airways, babies cannot take in enough oxygen which leads to oxygen deficits in every organ of their bodies.[16]

In 1901 the typical baby with a respiratory tract illness suffered from a viral or bacterial infection transmitted from a family member or other person exhibiting signs of illness. The severity of the illness depended on several things including the baby's age and any other diseases or conditions that might have weakened the baby's immune system. Very young infants, unable to turn their heads or cough effectively were at extremely high risk.

The range of respiratory illnesses diagnosed among infants in 1901 included pneumonia, bronchitis, and bronchopneumonia and influenza. While these illnesses took fewer lives than the gastrointestinal disorders they did account for the third-highest number of deaths. Prematurity-related problems remained the cause of the most infant deaths.[17] Many physicians believed, with some reason, that poor nutrition contributed to these illnesses as well. A baby fed a poor diet was more likely to be underweight, have a weakened immune system, and so was less able to fight off infection of any kind. Treatment of these illnesses focused on improved nutrition, fresh air, and patent medicines.[18] Croup, a common disease even today, could be treated by sitting the child in a room filled with steam, or by going outside in cold weather. Both these techniques are initial treatments still today, but when they are ineffective, corticosteroids, oxygen, mist tents, and bronchodilators can be used to help the baby breathe easier.[19] In 1901 these additional treatments were simply unknown.

The ability to diagnose and treat babies with respiratory illnesses improved steadily throughout the century. The introduction of oxygen as a common treatment helped many. Antibiotics cured pneumonias and other respiratory tract infections. Immunizations prevented many respiratory problems. Diphtheria and epiglottitis can cause severe illnesses of the throat and often resulted in death due to acute respiratory failure. Diphtheria antitoxin was introduced in 1894 and helped decrease deaths considerably.[20] An immunization to prevent *Haemophilus influenzae* type b was not introduced until the mid-1980s. It too dramatically decreased the number of illnesses and deaths.[21] Increased knowledge about the causes of diseases and about preventative measures has also helped. Hand washing was another simple yet impressive weapon in the fight against morbidity and mortality. As with gastrointestinal diseases, hand washing before and after changing a baby's diaper or wiping his nose can decrease dramatically the number of infectious organisms transmitted to other babies, children, and adults.

Other Diseases and Conditions

Respiratory and gastrointestinal diseases were rampant at the turn of the twentieth century but were not the only causes of sickness and death among American babies. Cancer, while rare, did occur and the outlook was grim. Most babies developing any type of cancer eventually died from the disease. Kidney and urinary tract defects and infections also caused suffering and death in some cases. Without antibiotic treatment, these infections can cause scarring of the urinary tract and eventual kidney damage from progression of the infection. Accidental injury and death, while more common among older children, was also an issue for infants. By six months of age most babies are able to turn themselves over, and rapidly progress to sitting alone, standing, crawling, and sometimes walking by their first birthday. This newfound mobility is a major milestone in life, but it does put the baby at risk for falls, ingestions of poisons, burns from pulling hot liquids onto themselves, and other problems related to their developmentally appropriate curiosity. As the century progressed the proliferation of automobile use placed infants and children in danger while passengers or playing in the street. It was not until the 1970s and 1980s that legislators passed comprehensive child safety laws which required manufacturers of everything from medicine bottles to cars, water heaters, clothing, strollers, toys, and a myriad of other products to adhere to stringent guidelines. These laws have saved countless lives but still require the acknowledgement of risk by the baby's parents and their adherence to the regulations.

IMMUNIZATIONS

It could be argued that immunizations have accounted for at least as much of the decline in infant mortality as any other single advance of the twentieth century. In 1901 a baby could die from, among other things, whooping cough (pertussis), measles, mumps, rubella, polio, tetanus, chicken pox, *Haemophilus influenzae* type B, and several other types of influenza. All these diseases occurred frequently around the country. Many were sporadic, occurring seasonally or on an annual basis. Polio, for example, often occurred in the spring. Some diseases were always present but spiked in certain areas at certain times for no discernable reason. One community might experience a measles outbreak while another ten miles away had a difficult year with influenza. These diseases affected all children and some adults; however infants with their immature immune systems were more likely to have severe cases, experience complications, and to die from the effects of any of these diseases.[22]

The decrease in morbidity and mortality among American infants as a result of the proliferation of immunizations during the twentieth century was extraordinary. It is difficult today to imagine that less than one hundred years ago some parents watched while one or more of their children died due to diseases that are now routinely prevented. The aim of researchers was to develop the means to prevent disease in children, including infants. Smallpox was fading at the time as vaccinations were developed in the eighteenth century and became routine in the nineteenth century. But other diseases killed seemingly at random. Diphtheria killed all the children in many families during increasingly frequent outbreaks of the disease. There was no cure or even treatment for the severe pain. Physicians were implored by parents to do something. In 1894 the diphtheria antitoxin for the first time promised relief if administered within the first three days of the disease's onset. Parents were ecstatic. Unfortunately the antitoxin's effects were temporary. In 1924 active immunization affording permanent protection was introduced. The development of other vaccines as the twentieth century progressed followed a pattern of reaction to epidemic illness. Scientists and physicians collaborated in the laboratory to manufacture the vaccines and politicians and private benefactors helped provide the money necessary for the work. The media played a part in publicizing the search for a cure, especially for polio. Parents waited anxiously for help, and when it came, many willingly brought their children to be immunized. Babies were not always the first to get immunizations as there was concern that they would be inadvertently hurt and it was believed safer to administer the vaccine to older children. Even so babies benefited because an older sibling's immunity frequently meant that the baby would not be exposed to the disease. The U.S. military played a large role in the development of immunizations. Of course, this did not directly affect babies as the main focus was vaccinating the soldiers and sailors needed in the various branches of the military. However, again babies benefited indirectly as their chances of exposure to disease diminished as more persons were vaccinated. Immunizations may have been rare and unusual in the early years of the century, but by 1970 those who did not take advantage of their availability were considered outsiders.

The development, production, and distribution of immunizations throughout the twentieth century have served virtually to eliminate some of these diseases and have dramatically limited the scope and severity of others. Possibly the most dramatic example is the development of the polio vaccine in the 1950s. Polio was a menace to all Americans. It paralyzed babies, children, and adults. In its most virulent form it killed quickly. Parents learned to dread the coming of spring and another potentially severe polio season. They kept their babies and children inside, away from others to avoid exposure. Polio struck harder in some years than in others. In 1916 it claimed many victims in one of the worst outbreaks in the United States. Franklin Delano Roosevelt, who developed the disease in 1921, was arguably the most famous polio survivor and a catalyst in the search for a cure. During his presidency the March of Dimes organization began to raise money for scientific research aimed at the development of a vaccine. Success came in April 1955 when Dr. Jonas Salk announced the results of his research and clinical trials. Families across the nation lined up to have all their children immunized. Seemingly overnight the scourge of polio was severely limited, and by the late 1970s physicians and scientists could confidentially state that wild polio, or polio not caused by exposure to the live virus in vaccines, would no longer paralyze and kill American children. Since 1979 there have been no cases of wild polio diagnosed in the United States. A few cases transmitted by the secretion of live polio virus in the stools of recently immunized babies have struck immuno-compromised adults. Since the late 1990s all polio immunizations have been of the killed, or inactivated, type and pose no risk of transmission. Since 1994 polio has been eliminated from North and South America.[23] The World Health Organization (WHO) hopes to certify the world free of polio by 2010.[24]

Medical researchers developed the rubella vaccine in 1969 after an epidemic of rubella (often referred to as "German measles") in the United States between 1962 and 1965 caused the deaths of more than 13,000 infants before or shortly after birth.[25] It also caused congenital rubella syndrome (CRS) among approximately 20,000 babies born to mothers who contracted the disease during pregnancy, especially during the first trimester. CRS is a group of birth defects usually including heart defects, blindness, and deafness. Medical personnel administered the vaccine to children, and between 1969 and 1976 the number of rubella cases declined by 78 percent and congenital rubella syndrome showed a similar dramatic drop. During the late 1970s and early 1980s rubella outbreaks among adolescents and young adults prompted the development of additional vaccines aimed at this population. Despite an upsurge in the number of rubella cases during the late 1980s and early 1990s, continued emphasis on vaccination led to the elimination of endemic rubella in the United States by 2000. The disease itself has not been eliminated but due to vaccinations the likelihood of disease transmission among native-born Americans has been reduced substantially.[26]

The polio vaccine, along with others designed to prevent diphtheria, tetanus, pertussis (whooping cough), measles, mumps, and rubella became a standard part of well baby care. Today infants receive, at the recommendation of the Centers for Disease Control, thirteen to fifteen immunizations by their first birthdays and twenty-four by age two.[27] Federal and state legislation requires that all children receive the CDC recommended immunizations prior to starting school. Many day care centers and nursery schools require the recommended immunizations for admission as well. Legislation and public pressure have led welfare agencies and insurance companies to cover the financial costs of these immunizations.[28]

Nonetheless, outbreaks of preventable disease have occurred. For example there was a significant outbreak of measles during the years between 1989 and 1992.[29] In 1991 officials reported 500 cases of measles between January and March in Philadelphia. Six children from families belonging to churches where medical care was shunned and faith healing relied upon died after contracting the disease. None had received any immunizations. The courts ordered other children of the congregations vaccinated over the objections of the families and the churches. Officials cited the health of the children and of the community as reasons for the order. Clearly, the decisions parents make regarding vaccination of their babies has potentially lethal implications during childhood and adulthood.[30]

Immunizations have created controversy as they can cause reactions ranging from mild to severe in nature. The vast majority of reactions are quite minor and include pain and soreness at the injection site, slight fever, irritability, and sleepiness. In some babies these symptoms are more exaggerated and can be frightening for the parents but nonetheless are not dangerous. During the 1980s and 1990s immunizations came under attack from various people who blamed them for a wide variety of conditions including asthma, autism, attention deficit hyperactivity disorder, seizures, and other neurodevelopmental disabilities in children. The combination vaccines of diphtheria, tetanus, and pertussis (DTP) and measles, mumps, and rubella (MMR) have been singled out as two of the most problematic. Clinical research, however, has not supported a link between these immunizations and any of the conditions attributed to them.[31]

It might be said that immunizations are a victim of their own success. Most parents and even many grandparents today have not seen any infants or children with immunization preventable diseases and have no recollection of their horrors. My own recollections do not include the diseases themselves but I do remember my parents' reactions to real and potential problems. My brother and sisters and I contracted rubella during the 1964 epidemic. I do not remember being sick, however, my mother, who also contracted the disease, was pregnant at the time and the baby died. My parents rarely talk about the loss but are obviously still affected. When the rubella vaccine became available my siblings and I all received the shot despite having acquired natural immunity as a result of the disease itself. The other situation I recall happened one day when my sister and I were in grade school during the mid-1960s. One morning she woke up complaining that her legs hurt. I remember that my mother became very alarmed and urged her to lie down while she called the doctor. Sensing the very real possibility of a day off from school, I also started complaining about leg pain. We both were able to stay home from school but since we had been immunized with the polio vaccine and had no other symptoms the pediatrician convinced my mother we did not have polio. I did not realize the terror we inflicted on our mother until years later.

With the exception of polio and smallpox (the last U.S. case was in 1949 and the World Health Assembly certified the world as free of naturally occurring smallpox in 1980), the other diseases of infancy and childhood that are preventable by immunization have not gone away.[32] During the 1990s pertussis outbreaks have occurred among older children, adolescents, and adults. While for most this means a persistent harsh cough lasting up to several months, for unvaccinated babies exposure to someone with pertussis can mean a serious illness, hospitalization, and in some cases, death. The first pertussis vaccination occurs at two months of age; thus newborns are at particularly high risk. New vaccines against pertussis for older children and adolescents are now being tested. Since the immunity developed after the early childhood vaccinations wears off after several years, a booster shot will likely be recommended for them.

SURGERY

The use of surgery to cure and alleviate suffering has a long history. Most people have heard tales of barbers operating on people and physicians using handsaws to amputate extremities injured in war or accidents. The advent of the use of anesthesia in a more controlled manner during the nineteenth century propelled surgical techniques forward as surgeons could probe farther into the human body. The twentieth century witnessed the continuation and refinement of these changes. Anesthesia was placed firmly within the walls of the hospital and special training was instituted for physicians and nurses wishing to administer the drugs. Aseptic technique, sterilization of surgical instruments, and the use of gowns and gloves by the surgeons, nurses, and others involved in the operation decreased fatalities due to infection. Surgery would prove lifesaving for many babies. It offered hope for infants with previously untreatable congenital conditions such as spina bifida or with cancerous tumors of the abdomen or extremities.

Pediatric surgery is a medical subspecialty today that requires extra years of training for those involved. Earlier in the century general surgeons frequently operated on babies and children. Their expertise was gained through experience and possibly mentoring from another surgeon. Several major issues differentiate it from adult surgery. First is the size of infants and children. Surgical instruments need to be smaller than those used for adults. Babies' internal organs and structures are naturally smaller than those of adults but may also be in slightly different places and at different angles within the body. The relative size of an organ within the body of a child or adult may also differ.[33]

Second, babies need surgery for different reasons than adults. Babies may be born with a condition requiring surgery. In the past many of these congenital problems caused death at an early age. One example is spina bifida, a set of defects in the spinal column. In its most severe form, known as myelomeningocele, nerves, membranes that normally surround the spinal column and the cord itself, protrude through an opening anywhere along the spinal column. This mass must be maintained intact until surgery can be performed within the first few hours of life. Without a permanent covering, infection will occur causing meningitis and possibly death. Even with surgery many babies born with myelomeningocele will experience varying degrees of paralysis, loss of bowel and bladder control, and other lifelong disabilities. Improvements in medical and surgical techniques allowed the survival of many more of these babies than in the past and also decreased the severity of complications. During the 1990s surgeons began to develop techniques to correct this condition during fetal life. Surgery involves opening the mother's uterus, removing the fetus, correcting the defect, and returning the fetus to the uterus. The mother is monitored carefully for the rest of the pregnancy as she is at high risk of premature labor and delivery. Research studies are currently evaluating the effectiveness of this surgery compared to early closure after birth. The prevention of spina bifida is also a major focus of pediatricians and many studies have pointed to the important preventive role of folic acid in a mother's diet before and during the first trimester of pregnancy. All women of childbearing age are now counseled to maintain appropriate levels of folic acid through diet and the use of supplements. These dietary changes have resulted in a 24 percent decline in the rate of spina bifida during the 1990s.[34]

Other surgical conditions are not congenital but are unique to infancy. For instance in some babies, mainly boys, a condition called pyloric stenosis can develop within the first two months of life. The pylorus muscle that connects the stomach to the small intestine fails to grow with the growing infant and prevents passage of milk through the stomach. A baby with pyloric stenosis can become dehydrated quickly. The only cure is surgical resection of the muscle. Symptoms include projectile vomiting, dehydration, and weight loss despite a voracious appetite. The baby is hungry as nothing he eats is getting past his stomach. The condition starts slowly and quickly escalates requiring prompt diagnosis and treatment. The diagnosis can be difficult and some mothers are told they are just being nervous and silly before a definitive cause for the symptoms is established. However, once identified pyloric stenosis now requires minimally invasive surgery with discharge to the home within twenty-four to forty-eight hours. Mortality from the condition decreased from 100 percent before 1904 to less than 2 percent today. The first operations to correct pyloric stenosis occurred during the first decade of the twentieth century and proved successful 40–50 percent of the time. In 1911 Conrad Ramstedt, a German surgeon, revised the surgery and within the next decade the mortality rate decreased to 10 percent and by 1931 it had come down to 2 percent. The Ramstedt procedure remains the standard treatment today.[35]

A third important difference among babies needing surgery is communication. Surgeons often depend on patients' ability to describe their symptoms which is obviously impossible with babies. Parents can describe what they see, but pediatric surgeons and nurses must rely much more on observation and physical examination than their counterparts in adult surgery. The advanced imaging techniques including x-rays, ultrasounds, magnetic resonance imaging (MRI), and computerized tomography (CT) scans have helped immensely in this area.

Surgery has saved the lives of many infants with cancer, gastrointestinal tract anomalies, and airway blockages. It has also made life better for infants with non-life-threatening but disabling or disfiguring conditions such as cleft lip and palate, other facial anomalies, and numerous other problems. Surgery has also influenced the lives of babies suffering burn injuries by restoring function and improving cosmetic appearance. By 2000 infants were able to have surgery and after recovery lead normal lives. Of course surgery can not save all infants but for those it can the outcome is extraordinary.

ANTIBIOTICS

Many of the great innovations in world history occurred accidentally. The discovery of penicillin is perhaps the greatest of them all. In 1928 British scientist Alexander Fleming returned from vacation to discover that a fungus, *Penicillium notatum*, was secreting a substance that killed samples of bacteria inadvertently left on his workbench. More than a decade later penicillin would save the lives of countless soldiers injured during World War II and revolutionize the practice of medicine everywhere.[36] For babies this meant that previously fatal infectious illnesses could be treated and even cured. Ear infections would no longer lead in some infants to meningitis and potentially serious complications or death. Group B streptococcus, a major source of infection in the newborn, could be treated with improved outcomes. And parents learned not to fear infections in their babies.

Penicillin was initially considered a "miracle drug" as it seemingly worked to cure infections of all sorts. It is effective against a wide range of bacteria. It was not the first drug developed to treat infections. During the 1930s sulfonamides became available to treat certain infections[37] but were not effective against the range of infections penicillin would cover. Some bacterial infections proved unaffected by penicillin. Other classes of antibiotics have been developed since the advent of penicillin to attack these bacteria. A sizeable number of people are allergic to penicillin and some have died after contact with the drug. In the last few decades the emergence of penicillin-resistant bacteria has required the development of new antibiotics specifically tailored to circumvent this problem.[38]

Antibiotics, despite the problems inherent with any drugs that are overused or used for inappropriate problems, have saved the lives of countless babies. They have prevented surgical complications and hearing loss. They have prevented brain damage and permanent mental disabilities. Babies will always get infections. Most will be mild and some will not even need antibiotics. Recent clinical research has demonstrated that some ear infections in older children will go away without the use of antibiotics. This has significance in that the less often antibiotics are used, the fewer side effects from them are seen, and the less chance there is for antibiotic-resistant organisms to flourish.[39] Penicillin may not have been the miracle drug some thought it would be, but it, and newer antibiotics, have led to better lives for several generations of American babies.

CANCER

The treatment of cancer in infants and children made tremendous strides during the twentieth century. For infants and children cancer was a death sentence during the first half of the century. Few survived six months after diagnosis and almost none survived two years. Since then the ability to diagnose accurately and treat cancers of childhood has vastly improved. Survival is expected for most children diagnosed with cancer in childhood. Unfortunately for infants the news is not as good. Infants suffer 10 percent of all cancers diagnosed in children less than fifteen years of age. While neuroblastoma, a tumor of the nerve tissue along the spine, in the chest or in the adrenal glands is the most common cancer of infancy with an 80 percent survival rate as of 1996, the other cancers found in babies are more likely to be fatal. Leukemia in infants has a particularly poor prognosis compared to older children. By the late 1990s the cure rate for children with leukemia diagnosed after their first birthday averaged 70 to 85 percent. Some children could anticipate up to 95 percent cure rates based on the specific type of leukemia. But for infants leukemia associated with genetic defects has a cure rate of less than 50 percent. For those diagnosed before the age of six months, the outlook can be worse. Current research is focused on innovative therapies designed specifically for infants.[40]

ACHIEVEMENTS AND SETBACKS

The major advance of the first third of the twentieth century was the decline in overall infant mortality. Diarrheal diseases fell off sharply in the 1920s as communities cleaned up their water supply and sewer systems. Better understanding of the role of dehydration in causing infant death also improved the prognoses of sick babies. Increased access to medical practitioners allowed parents to seek professional opinions sooner when their baby became ill. The medical specialty of pediatrics was expanding and nurses also began to specialize. Hospitals specifically and only for children expanded nationally along with separate pediatric wards in general hospitals.[41]

The work of the U.S. Children's Bureau is vital to this story. The Bureau operated from 1912 until 1969. During its most influential years, 1912–1946, the Bureau focused its considerable energies on infant and child health. The Sheppard–Towner Act of the 1920s was one significant outcome of Children's Bureau activities and, although short-lived, provided well baby and child care to many. The Social Security Act of 1935 also provided aid to babies and children. These legislative efforts will be discussed further in Chapter 5. By the 1930s the health and well-being of babies was a national priority. Education, preventative measures, and well baby care were emphasized.[42]

Between 1930 and 1949 there was a rapid decline in infant mortality and then a much slower decline from 1950 to 1965. During the earlier years antibiotic and fluid replacement therapies reduced the infant death rate substantially. By the 1950s and 1960s many of the infant deaths were those of high-risk babies. This included those with low birth weight and those born prematurely. The ability to respond to these issues had not advanced yet to a level where the mortality rate was significantly affected.[43]

The passage of the Medicaid laws and the introduction of other federal programs in the mid-1960s aimed at improving the health care of all children helped accelerate the decline in the mortality rate. During the 1970s the care of babies, especially those born prematurely or with serious life-threatening conditions was regionalized in many parts of the country. By moving babies to hospitals with the experienced staff and facilities to treat them, many lives were saved. In the early 1990s infant mortality again declined sharply. For prematurely born infants new medicines and new technologies allowed the survival of increasingly smaller babies.

One cause of death among infants that confounded parents, physicians, and scientists for centuries is Sudden Infant Death Syndrome (SIDS). Previously termed Crib Death, it occurred when an apparently healthy baby was put to sleep at naptime or at bedtime and was subsequently found dead in his/her crib. When no other cause of death could be found the diagnosis of SIDS was made and parents left to wonder what possibly could have happened. This tragedy defied simple solutions although better prenatal care and overall improved infant health accounted for some minor decreases in the rate of SIDS over the course of the twentieth century. During the early 1990s researchers discovered that babies who slept on their backs had significantly lower rates of SIDS than those who slept in the traditional stomach down position. It is believed that sleeping on the back allows the baby to breathe easier and to avoid rebreathing expired air with decreased oxygen levels. While these situations themselves are not believed to cause SIDS, they may trigger the condition in babies at high risk for SIDS. The U.S. Public Health Service, the American Academy of Pediatrics, and several SIDS awareness groups set up a national campaign, called "Back to Sleep," to encourage parents to put all babies to sleep on their backs instead of on their stomachs. The National Infant Sleep Position Study reported a 38 percent decline in the rate of SIDS by 1998.

In 1995 statistics compiled by the National Center for Health Statistics estimated that 75 percent of the decline in the overall postneonatal (between one month and one year of age) mortality rate between 1992 and 1995 was directly related to the change in sleep position. Not all parents, however, have changed their practices. By the end of the 1990s the number of babies put to sleep on their backs began to plateau. Researchers were turning their attention to ascertaining cultural and other reasons for people to distrust or simply ignore the recommendations and to developing new ways of getting the message across.[44]

PROBLEMS IN THE LATE TWENTIETH CENTURY

The advances in the health care of babies over the first eighty years of the twentieth century and the overall improved health of the nation's babies led many to believe that most of the illnesses of infancy could be identified and treated without difficulty. Infectious disease was controllable through immunizations and antibiotics. Surgical problems were easier to correct and newer imaging techniques were making it safer to operate on specific areas of the infant's body. The majority of babies were better fed than they had been in 1901 and breast-feeding, discouraged in the 1940s and 1950s by the medical profession and society, was making a comeback throughout the 1970s. Americans could take pride in these accomplishments, but were unable to "rest on their laurels."

By the 1980s the general public expected that American babies would be born healthy, experience a few minor but treatable respiratory or gastrointestinal problems during infancy and enter the toddler stage of life happy and ready for the challenges of the twenty-first century. The IMR had decreased steadily throughout the twentieth century to 7.2/1000 live births by 1997. This represents a decrease of more than 90 percent since 1915. Despite these dramatic numbers the United States lagged behind many other nations and ranked twenty-fifth in infant mortality among the world's developed nations in 1997. These numbers also mask the discrepancies among people of different races and ethnicities. Black babies are twice as likely to die during infancy than white babies. These and other issues related to race and discrimination will be discussed in Chapter 6.[45]

HIV/AIDS

The emergence of HIV/AIDS in the United States and around the world during the early 1980s had a devastating effect on babies. Although it was once thought by the general public to be solely a disease of gay men, it was soon apparent that no one was immune. Babies became infected with the virus in one of two ways. Doctors found blood transfusions transmitted the disease, and during the early 1980s babies as well as older children and adults were infected in this manner. Surgery and hemophilia were the two major reasons for blood transfusions.[46] By the early 1990s strict guidelines for blood donations and blood transfusions decreased this risk significantly and by the late 1990s the chances of contracting HIV/AIDS from a blood transfusion were 1 in 1.9 million.[47] The other way for babies to get HIV/AIDS was through maternal transmission occurring during the birth process. The number of babies affected peaked in 1992 with 902 cases reported. By 1999 the total had dropped to 156.[48] The treatment available for babies with HIV/AIDS has improved greatly. Women of childbearing age are advised to be tested for HIV/AIDS before becoming pregnant and once they are pregnant. Maternal transmission has been decreased through the administration of antiretroviral drugs to the mother during the pregnancy and to the baby after birth. Treatment of all people with HIV/AIDS has also improved and many are living much longer lives than previously anticipated. It is hoped that this will lead to a decrease in the number of children orphaned when their parents die from the disease.[49]

Obesity

On the Fourth of July, 1903, the *Journal of the American Medical Association* published a short narrative ridiculing the popular notion that fat babies are healthy babies. Fat babies nearly always won first prize at baby shows and artificial infant formulas were advertised using pictures of obese infants. Most mothers felt that a fat baby would fight off infection and other diseases easier than a thinner baby. However, the writer points out, most physicians of the day believed that obese infants were "especially prone to succumb to certain diseases [and are] predisposed to nervous complications in any serious disease."[50] Despite these medical insights of 100 years ago the image of a fat baby still resonates with the American public today. Many mothers still believe that a heavy baby is a healthy baby and the weight is indicative of their ability to parent effectively.[51] The potential health risks are easily ignored when fat is equated with the ideals of health, wellness, and prosperity.

Americans are in the midst of an obesity crisis as more than 60 percent of adults and more than 15 percent of children aged six to nineteen are now considered overweight. The effect on overall health can be staggering. Heart disease, hypertension, lung disease, orthopedic injury, diabetes, depression, certain cancers, and other major problems can be caused directly and indirectly by obesity.[52] Adult-onset diabetes (Type II) is often triggered by excess weight and for the first time is being seen in children as young as ten years of age.[53] While these problems do not directly affect babies, many experts believe that the tendency to gain excess weight begins in infancy. A study by the National Health and Nutrition Examination Survey found that slightly more than 11 percent of children from birth through twenty-three months of age were also overweight. The figures for racial and ethnic minority children are even worse. More than 18 percent of non-Hispanic black children in this age category are overweight. The numbers reflect an increasing trend in overweight and obese children over the last thirty years.[54]

The importance of these statistics lies in their relevance to health later in life for infants affected by overweight or obesity. During the 1990s researchers began to look at babies and the risk of obesity. There is some data that point to the benefits of breast-feeding in decreasing the risk of becoming overweight or obese. Babies who are fed only breast milk for at least six months appear to have a diminished risk of obesity later in childhood. Breast milk is known to be the best form of nutrition for infants with many documented health benefits. The potential to prevent health problems related to obesity should be one more reason to advocate its use for at least one year.[55]

CONCLUSIONS

American babies in the twentieth century benefited from some of the most dramatic advances in medical care ever known. The overall IMR drop of more than 90 percent can be attributed to improvements in all aspects of life. Although it is tempting to point to one surgical technique or one drug or class of drugs as the most important development in the health of babies during the twentieth century it would be more accurate to acknowledge the changes in attitudes about babies. Babies became more important to families and their well-being important to the country as a whole. Advances in sanitation and knowledge about infection control that came about in the late nineteenth century helped to keep babies healthy and to emphasize the importance of preventive care. The expansion of medical and scientific knowledge has also had tremendous influence. Pediatrics as a medical specialty came about only at the end of the nineteenth century and was not available to the majority of babies at the time. Since then the practice of pediatrics has grown immensely and parents nationwide look to pediatricians for guidance as they care for their babies. Immunizations took preventive care to a new level and antibiotics have certainly saved the lives of countless babies. The improvement in surgical techniques for babies has also resulted in better lives for many.

For parents, knowledge and communication have also greatly improved and influence a baby's health in myriad ways. The telephone itself has probably saved lives as parents could call a doctor instead of sending a message with someone on foot or on horseback. Automobiles made health care facilities and professionals much more accessible. During the 1990s the Internet has put health care information literally at one's fingertips. This resource has proved both good and bad. Legitimate medical authorities have posted advice and other information on the Internet based on sound research and experience. However the Internet's open nature has also allowed medical information of dubious validity to be presented in a manner that suggests legitimacy. Some of the information is simply wrong and some may be harmful. It is often difficult for the average person to sort out the conflicting information. A personal connection between health care professionals and parents of infants remains essential at the end of the twentieth century.

While the vast majority of American babies are healthier than ever, there are some who continue to lag behind. Babies of racial and ethnic minority groups have higher mortality rates than white babies and tend to have less access to health care, in part because of poverty that persists despite state and national welfare programs. These issues and others will be addressed in Chapters 5 through 7. During the twentieth century the care of premature infants and the ability to correct congenital cardiac defects have been truly transformed. Once ignored, babies with either or both of these conditions are now treated with all the technological skill and expertise available in medicine. I will discuss these issues in Chapter 4.

NOTES

1. S. Josephine Baker, "The Reduction of Infant Mortality in New York City," *American Journal of Diseases of Children* 5 (1913): 151–161.

2. Arialdi M. Minino, Elizabeth Arias, Kenneth D. Kohanek, Sherry L. Murphy, and Betty L. Smith, "Deaths: Final Data for 2000," *National Vital Statistics Reports* 50(15) (2002): 1–120.

3. Richard A. Meckel, *Save the Babies: American Public Health Reform and the Prevention of Infant Mortality, 1850–1929* (Ann Arbor: University of Michigan Press, 1990), 238. It is difficult to determine the rate of premature birth in the United States before 1950 because birth certificates simply did not ask for gestational age in a meaningful manner until then. Estimates of premature birth range from 3 percent to 15 percent although most experts believe that 6–7 percent is most accurate. Leona Baumgartner, "Nation-wide Plan for Reduction of Premature Mortality," *Journal of the American Medical Association* 146 (July 7, 1951): 893–896; Jeffrey P. Baker, "The Incubator Controversy: Pediatricians and the Origins of Premature Infant Technology in the United States, 1890–1910," *Pediatrics* 87(5) (1991): 654–662; and Theodore E. Cone, *History of American Pediatrics* (Boston, MA: Little, Brown and Company, 1979), 63.

4. Jeffrey P. Baker, *The Machine in the Nursery* (Baltimore, MD: Johns Hopkins University Press, 1996), 38–42, 137, 155, 157.

5. Meckel, *Save the Babies,* 46–47.

6. Meckel, *Save the Babies,* 45–46; and Charles E. Rosenberg, *The Care of Strangers: The Rise of America's Hospital System.* (Baltimore, MD: Johns Hopkins University Press, 1987), 169–175.

7. Cone, *History of American Pediatrics*, 102–104, 203–204; Stanford T. Shulman, "The History of Pediatric Infectious Diseases," *Pediatric Research* 55(1) (2004): 163–176; and Meckel, *Save the Babies*, 46.

8. Andrew H. Beck, "The Flexner Report and the Standardization of American Medical Education" (Reprinted), *Journal of the American Medical Association* 291(17) (2004): 2139–2140.

9. Cone, *History of American Pediatrics*, 159.

10. Cone, *History of American Pediatrics*, 23, 44–45, 74, 79–80, 112–114, 152. The Floating Hospital is now part of the Tufts-New England Medical Center and includes pediatric and neonatal intensive care units as well as many other inpatient and outpatient services, http://www.tufts-nemc.org/home/aboutus/childrens.htm.

11. David I. Macleod, *The Age of the Child: Children in America, 1890–1920* (New York: Twayne Publishers, 1998), 34–38.

12. S. Josephine Baker, "The Reduction of Infant Mortality in New York City," 151–161.

13. Meckel, *Save the Babies*, 124—158, 220–236.

14. Mathuram Santosham, Edward Maurice Keenan, Jim Tulloch, Denis Broun, and Roger Glass, "Oral Rehydration Therapy for Diarrhea: An Example of Reverse Transfer of Technology," *Pediatrics* 100(5) (1997): 10–12; and M.S. Murphy, "Guidelines for Managing Acute Gastroenteritis Based on a Systematic Review of Published Research," *Archives of Disease in Childhood* 79 (1998): 279–284.

15. Umesh D. Parashar, Paul E. Kilgore, Robert C. Holman, Matthew J. Clarke, Joseph S. Bresee, and Boger I. Glass, "Diarrheal Mortality in US Infants," *Archives of Pediatric and Adolescent Medicine* 152 (1998): 47–51; and Gabriel J. Escobar, Veronica M. Gonzales, Mary Anne Armstrong, Bruce F. Folck, Blong Xiong, and Thomas B. Newman, "Rehospitalization for Neonatal Dehydration," *Archives of Pediatric and Adolescent Medicine* 156 (2002): 155–161.

16. Marilyn J. Hockenberry, *Wong's Nursing Care of Infants and Children*, 7th ed. (St. Louis, MO: Mosby, 2003), 496; and Moya L. Andrews, *Voice Treatment for Children & Adolescents* (Clifton Park, NY: Thomson Delmar Learning, 2001), 12–13.

17. Macleod, *The Age of the Child*, 40–41.

18. Edward Bok, *The Americanization of Edward Bok* (New York: Charles Scribner's Sons, 1921), 340–351; and S.H. Adams, "The Great American Fraud," *Colliers Magazine*, October 7, 1905, p. 14. Patent medicines, some containing alcohol, opiates, and other unregulated drugs were commonly used in the late nineteenth and early twentieth centuries. Adams published a series of eleven articles about patent medicines in *Colliers Magazine* in 1905 and 1906 that helped educate the public about the dangers associated with such concoctions. Along with the publication of *The Jungle* by Upton Sinclair in 1906, Adams' articles were a catalyst in the formation of the Food and Drug Administration. Upton Sinclair, *The Jungle* (Cutchogue, NY: Buccaneer Books, 1906).

19. Joseph W. Luria, Javier A. Gonzalez-del-Rey, Gregg A. DiGiulio, Constance M. McAneney, Jennifer J. Olson, and Richard M. Ruddy, "Effectiveness of Oral or Nebulized Dexamethasone for Children with Mild Croup," *Archives of Pediatric and Adolescent Medicine* 155 (2001): 1340–1345; and Julie C. Brown, "The Management of Croup," *British Medical Bulletin* 61 (2002): 189–202.

20. Macleod, *The Age of the Child*, 41.

21. Centers for Disease Control and Prevention (CDC), "Hib Immunization," *American Academy of Pediatrics*, 2006, http://www.cispimmunize.org/ill/ill_main.html.

22. J.A. Dudgeon, "Immunization in Times Ancient and Modern," *Journal of the Royal Society of Medicine* 73 (1980): 581–586; Cone, *History of American Pediatrics*, 22, 32–40, 84–85, 108–111, 171–173, 213–214; and Andrew W. Artenstein, "History of U.S. Military Contributions to the Study of Vaccines against Infectious Diseases," *Military Medicine* 170(4) (April Supplement, 2005): 3–11.

23. Jeffrey Kluger, *Splendid Solution. Jonas Salk and the Conquest of Polio* (New York: G.P. Putnam's Sons, 2004); and John F. Modlin, "Poliomyelitis in the United States, the Final Chapter?" *American Journal of Medicine* 292(14) (2004): 1749–1751.

24. UNICEF, "UNICEF in Action: Eradicating Polio," *Immunizations Plus* (2006), http://www.unicef.org/immunization/index_polio.html; and World Health Organization, "Global Polio Eradication Initiative," *Global Polio Eradication Initiative* (2006), http://www.polioeradication.org/.

25. CDC and National Immunization Program, "Rubella—In Short (German Measles)" (2001), http://www.cdc.gov/nip/diseases/rubella/vac-chart.htm. Rubella is "a respiratory disease caused by a virus ... spread by coughing and sneezing." Its generally mild symptoms include "rash and fever for two to three days."

26. CDC, "Achievements in Public Health: Elimination of Rubella and Congenital Rubella Syndrome—United States, 1969–2004," *Morbidity and Mortality Weekly Report* 54(11) (2005): 279–282.

27. CDC, "Recommended Childhood and Immunization Schedule for Persons Aged 0–18 Years—United States, 2007," *Morbidity and Mortality Weekly Report* 55(51) (January 5, 2007): Q1–Q4, provides current recommendations.

28. Kathryn M. Edwards, "State Mandates and Childhood Immunization," *Journal of the American Medical Association* 284(24) (2000): 3171–3173; Walter A. Orenstein and Alan R. Hinman, "The Immunization System in the United States—The Role of School Immunization Laws," *Vaccine* 17(3) (1999): S19–S24; K. B. Robbins, D. Brandling-Bennett, and A.R. Hinman, "Low Measles Incidence: Association with Enforcement of School Immunization Laws," *American Journal of Public Health* 71(3) (1981): 270–274.

29. CDC, "FAQs (frequently asked questions) about Measles," *National Immunization Program* (2001), http://www.cdc.gov/nip/diseases/measles/faqs.htm. "Measles is an infectious viral disease that occurs most often in the late winter and spring. It begins with a fever that lasts for a couple of days, followed by a cough, runny nose, and conjunctivitis (pink eye). A rash starts on the face and upper neck, spreads down the back and trunk, then extends to the arms and hands, as well as the legs and feet. After about five days, the rash fades the same order it appeared." Measles are sometimes referred to as "regular measles" or "eight-day measles" to differentiate it from rubella—German measles.

30. Jane E. Brody, "Personal Health; for the Vaccine-Wary, a Lesson in History," *The New York Times*, October 3, 2000; Karen DeWitt, "Putting Faith over the Law as Pupils Die," *The New York Times*, February 23, 1991; Tamar Lewin, "Epidemic in Philadelphia Raises Issue of Religion vs. State's Interest," *The New York Times*, February 25, 1991; Michael deCourcy Hinds, "Judge Orders Measles Shots in Philadelphia," *The New York Times*, March 6, 1991; Michael deCourcy Hinds, "Philadelphia Again Told to Immunize Youths," *The New York Times*, March 8, 1991; "Sixth Child Dies in Philadelphia; 5 Others Are Given Measles Shots," *The New York Times*, March 9, 1991; and "Vital Signs: Prevention; U.S. Edges toward Measles Eradication," *The New York Times*, September 7, 1999. See also Robert L. Davis, Piotr Kramarz, Kari Bohlke, Patti Benson, Robert S. Thompson, Hohn Mullooly, Steve Black, Henry Shinefield, Edwin, Lewis, Joel Ward,

S. Michael Marcy, Eileen Eriksen, Frank Destefano, and Robert Chen for the Vaccine Safety Datalink Team, "Measles-Mumps-Rubella and Other Measles-Containing Vaccines Do Not Increase the Risk for Inflammatory Bowel Disease," *Archives of Pediatric and Adolescent Medicine* 155 (2001): 354–359; and Kumanan Wilson, Ed Mills, Cory Ross, Jessie McGowan, and Alex Jadad,, "Association of Autistic Spectrum Disorder and the Measles, Mumps, and Rubella Vaccine," *Archives of Pediatric and Adolescent Medicine* 157 (2003): 628–634.

31. William E. Barlow, Robert L. Davis, John W. Glasser, Phillip H. Rhodes, Robert S. Thompson, John P. Mullooly, Steven B. Black, Henry R. Shinefield, Joel I. Ward, S. Michael Marcy, Frank DeStefano, Virginia Immanuel, John A. Pearson, Constance M. Vadheim, Viviana Rebolledo, Dimitri Christakis, Patti J. Benson, Ned Lewis, and Robert T. Chen for the Centers for Disease Control and Prevention Vaccine Safety Datalink Working Group, "The Risk of Seizures after Receipt of Whole-Cell Pertussis or Measles, Mumps, and Rubella Vaccine," *New England Journal of Medicine* 345(9) (2001): 656–661; M.R. Griffin, W.A. Ray, E.A. Mortimer, G.M. Fenichel, and W. Schaffner, "Risk of Seizures and Encephalopathy after Immunization with the Diphtheria-Tetanus-Pertussis Vaccine," *Journal of the American Medical Association* 263(12) (1990): 1641–1645; Gregory A. Poland, and Robert M. Jacobson, "Vaccine Safety: Injecting a Dose of Common Sense," *Mayo Clinic Proceedings* 75 (2000): 135–139; John Henderson, Kate North, Mancell Griffiths, Ian Harvey, Jean Golding, and the Avon Longitudinal Study of Pregnancy and Childhood Team, "Pertussis Vaccination and Wheezing Illnesses in Young Children: Prospective Cohort Study," *British Medical Journal* 318 (1999): 1173–1176; and Robert M. Wolfe, Lisa K. Sharp, and Martin S. Lipsky, "Content and Design Attributes of Antivaccination Web Sites," *Journal of the American Medical Association* 287(24) (2002): 3245–3248. Studies that document the lack of any ties between autism and the MMR vaccine include Wilson et al., "Association of Autistic Spectrum Disorder and the Measles, Mumps, and Rubella Vaccine" and Kreesten Meldgaard Madsen, Anders Hviid, Mogens Vestergaard, Diana Schendel, Jan Wohlfahrt, Poul Thorsen, Jørn Olsen, and Mads Melbye, "A Population-Based Study of Measles, Mumps, and Rubella Vaccination and Autism," *New England Journal of Medicine* 347(19) (2002): 1477–1482.

32. CDC, "Vaccinia (Smallpox) Vaccine: Recommendations of the Advisory Committee on Immunization Practices (ACIP)," *Morbidity and Mortality Weekly Report* 50(rr10) (June 22, 2001): 1–25.

33. Hockenberry, *Wong's Nursing Care of Infants and Children*, 494–497, 1258, 1303–1308, 1344–1345, 1417, 1466, 1642.

34. March of Dimes, "Spina Bifida," Pregnancy and Newborn Health Education Center (April 2006), http://www.marchofdimes.com/pnhec/4439_1224.asp; P. Mersereau, K. Kilker, H. Carter, E. Fassett, J. Willams, A. Flores, C. Prue, L. WIllams, C. Mai, J. Mulinare, "Spina Bifida and Anencephaly Before and After Folic Acid Mandate—United States, 1995–1996 and 1999–2000," *Morbidity and Mortality Weekly Report* 53(17) (May 7, 2004): 362–365; and Joseph P. Bruner, Noel Tulipan, Ray L. Paschall, Frank H. Boehm, William F. Walsh, Sandra R. Silva, Marta Hernanz-Schulman, Lisa H. Lowe, and George W. Reed, "Fetal Surgery for Myelomeningocele and the Incidence of Shunt-Dependent Hydrocephalus," *Journal of the American Medical Association* 282(19) (1999): 1819–1825.

35. Marta Hernanz-Schulman, "Infantile Hypertrophic Pyloric Stenosis," *Radiology* 227(2) (2003): 319–331.

36. Richard Sykes, "Penicillin: From Discovery to Product," *Bulletin of the World Health Organization* 79(8) (2001): 778–779; F.W. Diggins, "The True History of the Discovery of Penicillin, with Refutation of the Misinformation in the Literature," *British Journal of Biomedical Science* 56(2) (1999): 83–93; and William L. Laurence, " 'Giant' Germicide Yielded by Mold," *The New York Times,* May 6, 1941.

37. Cone, *History of American Pediatrics,* 202.

38. Barbara E. Murray, "Can Antibiotic Resistance Be Controlled?" *New England Journal of Medicine* 330(17) (1994): 1229–1230; Diana A. Palmer and Howard Bauchner, "Parents' and Physicians' Views on Antibiotics," *Pediatrics* 99(6) (1997): e6–e10; and Edward A. Belongia, Bradley J. Sullivan, Po-Huang Chyou, Elisabeth Madagame, Kurt D. Reed, and Benjamin Schwartz, "A Community Intervention Trial to Promote Judicious Antibiotic Use and Reduce Penicillin-Resistant Streptococcus pneumoniae Carriage in Children," *Pediatrics* 108(3) (2001): 575–583.

39. Murray, "Can Antibiotic Resistance Be Controlled?"; Palmer and Bauchner, "Parents' and Physicians' Views on Antibiotics"; Belongia et al., "A Community Intervention Trial to Promote Judicious Antibiotic Use and Reduce Penicillin-Resistant Streptococcus pneumoniae Carriage in Children"; and Subcommittee on Management of Acute Otitis Media, "Diagnosis and Management of Acute Otitis Media," *Pediatrics* 113(5) (2004): 1451–1465.

40. Gregory H. Reaman, "Treatment Outcome and Prognostic Factors for Infants with Acute Lymphoblastic Leukemia Treated on Two Consecutive Trials of the Children's Cancer Group," *Journal of Clinical Oncology* 17(2) (1999): 445–455; Fernando Marco, "High Survival Rate in Infant Acute Leukemia Treated with Early High-Dose Chemotherapy and Stem-Cell Support," *Journal of Clinical Oncology* 18(18) (2000): 3256–3261; and Carolyn A. Felix, Beverly J. Lange, and Judith M. Chessells, "Pediatric Acute Lymphoblastic Leukemia: Challenges and Controversies in 2000," *Hematology 2000* 1 (2000): 285–302.

41. Cone, *History of American Pediatrics,* 201–202; and Rosemary Stevens, *In Sickness and In Wealth: American Hospitals in the Twentieth Century* (New York: Basic Books, 1989), 102, 172.

42. CDC "Achievements in Public Health, 1900–1999: Healthier Mothers and Babies," *Morbidity and Mortality Weekly Report* 48(38) (1999): 849–858.

43. Ibid.

44. Ibid; Marian Willinger, Howard J. Hoffman, Kuo-Tsung, Jin-Rong Hou, Ronald C. Kessler, Sally L. Ward, Thomas G. Keens, and Michael J. Corwin, "Factors Associated with the Transition to Nonprone Sleep Positions of Infants in the United States," *Journal of the American Medical Association* 280(4) (1998): 329–335; and Marian Willinger, Chia-Wen Ko, Howard J. Hoffman, Ronald C. Kessler, and Michael J. Corwin, "Factors Associated with Caregivers' Choice of Infant Sleep Position, 1994–1998," *Journal of the American Medical Association* 283(16) (2000): 2135–2142.

45. CDC, "Achievements in Public Health, 1900–1999: Healthier Mothers and Babies," 849–858.

46. D.A. Scheinberg, G.Y. Minamoto, K. Dietz, J.W.M. Gold, T. Gee, D. Armstrong, J. Gabrilove, B. Clarkson, N. Chein, L. Reich, D.L. Morse, M. Batt, H.J. Miller, B. Stevko, L.A. Chambers, L. Kunches, and G.F. Grady, "Human Immunodeficiency Virus Infection in Transfusion Recipients and Their Family Members," *Morbidity and Mortality Weekly Report* 36(10) (March 20, 1987): 137–140.

47. Simone A. Glynn, Steven H. Kleinman, George B. Schreiber, Michael P. Busch, David J. Wright, James W. Smith, Catharie C. Nass, and Alan E. Williams for the Retrovirus Epidemiology Donor Study (REDS), "Trends in Incidence and Prevalence of Major Transfusion-Transmissible Viral Infections in US Blood Donors, 1991 to 1996," *Journal of the American Medical Association* 284(2) (2000): 229–235; and Janet M. Torpy, Tiffany J. Glass, and Richard M., "Blood Transfusion," *Journal of the American Medical Association* 292(13) (2004): 1646.

48. Division of HIV/AIDS Prevention, National Center for HIV, STD, and TB Prevention, CDC, "HIV and AIDS—United States, 1981–2000," *Morbidity and Mortality Weekly Report* 50(21) (June 1, 2001): 430–434. See also "Erratum: Vol. 50, No. 21," *Morbidity and Mortality Weekly Report* 50(47) (November 30, 2001): 1066; and Hockenberry, *Wong's Nursing Care of Infants and Children*, 1572–1576.

49. Edward M. O'Connor, Rhoda, S. Sperling, Richard Gelber, Pavel Kiselev, Gwendolyn Scott, Mary Jo O'Sullivan, Russell VanDyke, Mohammed Bey, William Shearer, Robert L. Jacobson, Eleanor Jimenez, Edward O'Neill, Brigitte Bazin, Jean-Francois Delfraissy, Mary Culnane, Robert Coombs, Mary Elkins, Jack Moye, Pamela Stratton, and James Balsley, for The Pediatric AIDS Clinical Trials Group Protocol 076 Study Group, "Reduction of Maternal-Infant Transmission of Human Immunodeficiency Virus Type 1 with Zidovudine Treatment," *New England Journal of Medicine* 331(18) (1994): 1173–1180; Mary Jane Totheram-Borus, Patricia Lester, Pin-Wen Wang, and Qing Shen, "Custody Plans among Parents Living with Human Immunodeficiency Virus Infection," *Archives of Pediatric and Adolescent Medicine* 158 (2004): 327–332; and American Academy of Pediatrics, Committee on Pediatric AIDS, "Planning for Children Whose Parents Are Dying of HIV/AIDS," *Pediatrics* 103(2) (1999): 509–511.

50. "Fat Babies and Health," *Journal of the American Medical Association* 41 (1903): 37 (Reprinted), *Journal of the American Medical Association* 289(14) (2003): 1866.

51. Amy E. Baughcum, Kathleen A. Burklow, Cindy M. Deeks, Scott W. Powers, and Robert C. Whitaker, "Maternal Feeding Practices and Childhood Obesity," *Archives of Pediatric and Adolescent Medicine* 152 (1998): 1010–1014.

52. David L. Katz, Meghan O'Connell, Ming-Chin Yeh, Haq Nawaz, Valentine Jnike, Laurie M. Anderson, Stella Cory, and William Dietz, "Public Health Strategies for Preventing and Controlling Overweight and Obesity in School and Worksite Settings," *Morbidity and Mortality Weekly Report* 54(rr10) (October 7, 2005): 1–12.

53. American Diabetes Association, "Type 2 Diabetes in Children and Adolescents," *Diabetes Care* 23(3) (2000): 381–389.

54. Cynthia L. Odgen, Katherine M. Flegal, Margaret D. Carroll, and Clifford L. Johnson, "Prevalence and Trends in Overweight among US Children and Adolescents, 1999–2000," *Journal of the American Medical Association* 288(14) (2002): 1728–1732.

55. Baughcum et al., "Maternal Feeding Practices and Childhood Obesity"; Rudiger von Kries, Berthold Koletzko, Thorsten Sauerwald, Erika von Mutius, Dietmar Barnert, Veit Grunert, and Hubertus von Voss, "Breast Feeding and Obesity: Cross Sectional Study," *British Medical Journal* 319 (1999): 147–150; Matthew W. Gillman, Sheryl L. Rifas-Shiman, Carlos A. Camargo, Jr., Catherine S. Berkey, A. Lindsay Frazier, Helaine R. H. Rockett, Alison E. Field, and Graham A. Colditz, "Risk of Overweight among Adolescents Who Were Breastfed as Infants," *Journal of the American Medical Association* 285(19) (2001): 2461–2467; Mary L. Hediger, Mary D. Overpeck, Robert J. Kuczmarski, and W. June Ruan, "Association between Infant Breastfeeding and Overweight in

Young Children," *Journal of the American Medical Association* 285(19) (2001): 2453–2460; William H. Dietz, "Breastfeeding May Help Prevent Childhood Overweight," *Journal of the American Medical Association* 285(19) (2001): 2506–2507; and T. Kue Young, Patricia J. Martens, Shayne P. Taback, Elizabeth A.C. Sellars, Heather J. Dean, Mary Cheang, and Bertha Flett, "Type 2 Diabetes Mellitus in Children," *Archives of Pediatric and Adolescent Medicine* 156 (2002): 651–655.

From Weaklings to Fighters

"...If ever he have child, abortive be it, Prodigious, and untimely brought to light."
—William Shakespeare in *Richard III*, Act I, Scene II

INTRODUCTION

Parents of prematurely born infants are often, and quite understandably, anxious about their newborn's chances for survival. While not wanting to be unrealistic, physicians and nurses are interested in keeping parents' hope alive and will often point out other babies who were born prematurely and survived. Many Neonatal Intensive Care Units display pictures of babies they have treated over the years. Parents often send in updated pictures as the babies go to school, and reach other developmental milestones. One parent commented on the Preemie-L Web site, "I know a source that gave me great relief and helped me 'keep it together' was seeing photos of the babies who had graduated the NICU ... I would scan the board for all babies close to twenty-nine weeks and gain such relief looking at the 'before' and 'after' pictures."[1] New parents have also been told of famous men who were apparently born prematurely including Isaac Newton, Napoleon Bonaparte, and Winston Churchill. In the 1990s online communities formed to connect parents of preemies and provide support from those who have already been through such a traumatic time.[2]

By the close of the twentieth century prematurely born infants had a greater chance of survival than at any other point in history. Babies born as early as twenty-two weeks gestation, or more than four months early, are routinely saved. That is not to say that all babies born early survive. Many still die despite the extensive knowledge and the increasingly sophisticated technology available to help keep them alive. Many others survive with short- or long-term disabilities. But the changes during the twentieth century in not only the ability to care for these babies, but the desire to do so, have been extraordinary.

Although immediate and highly technological care for babies born too soon is now accepted as standard treatment, it is a relatively recent development in the care of infants. Prior to the 1970s most babies born more than three months premature died because of the lack of ability to breathe on their own for more than a short time. There were no reliable mechanical ventilators for these infants.

By the end of the twentieth century premature infants were commonly found in large and small hospitals throughout the United States. Their care was solidly ensconced within the walls of hospital-based Neonatal Intensive Care Units (NICU's) where specially trained physicians, nurses and an army of other health care personnel anticipated and met their every need. While the limits of viability of prematurely born infants continue to be debated, those born at twenty-four weeks gestation and after have increasingly optimistic prognoses.

Babies born with congenital cardiac defects also had very grim prognoses in 1901. If they survived the neonatal period their lives often became a constant struggle and were inevitably shortened. In 2000 congenital heart defects were surgically corrected as soon as possible after birth. Some unfortunate babies are born both prematurely and with cardiac defects. These too have a good chance of survival.

In this chapter I will explore the expansion of premature infant care in the United States during the twentieth century and the dramatic changes in the treatment of babies born with congenital heart defects. These two areas are both emotionally charged. Premature infants have captured the imagination of Americans as the tiniest of them are often portrayed in the media as superstar survivors. The heart has always been seen as the center of our existence. Terms such as "the heart of the matter," "heart broken," and "he has a good heart" testify to its power. By 2000 surgeons were able to fix most defective infant hearts either completely or enough to allow life.

PREMATURE INFANTS

In 1901 a baby born prematurely (before thirty-eight to forty weeks gestation) faced a difficult time. Except for a few scattered pockets of medical interest, "preemies" had generally dismal prospects for survival. Simply put, the interest, knowledge, expertise, and technology necessary to help these infants were not available. Preemies who survived more than a day or two were often labeled "weaklings" or "congenitally debilitated." Their survival depended on many factors, chief of which was their degree of prematurity. In other words, their chances of survival depended on how early they were born and their weight at birth.

There have always been babies born too soon. Over the centuries, parents of these babies employed various techniques to keep them alive. In Africa some preemies were wrapped in castor oil plant leaves and placed in a large pot heated by the sun.[3] English, Scottish, and eventually American parents wrapped their premature babies in cotton or wool and placed them by a constantly attended fire in order to preserve body temperature.[4] Despite these parental attempts, the Western mainstream medical profession generally ignored the plight of premature infants until the latter years of the nineteenth century.

French physicians introduced the closed infant incubator in the 1880s in response to governmental mandates to decrease the overall dismal French infant mortality rate (IMR).[5] Parisian obstetrician Dr. Pierre Budin published the first major textbook on the care of preemies. In 1901 his book, *The Nursling: The Feeding and Hygiene of Premature and Full-Term Infants*, appeared in France and by 1907 American readers could buy it. It became the standard for physicians, nurses, and others interested in premature babies.[6] A few American hospitals opened short-lived premature infant stations during the 1900s. Funding issues and a lack of interest caused them to close.

Thus by the early twentieth century premature infants remained in general the province of mothers and female attendants. Resuscitation of nonbreathing newborns depended largely on the experience of birth attendants. Questions of viability and the ethical dilemmas inherent in the resuscitation of "weak" or "congenitally debilitated" infants remained. Should these infants, so obviously abnormal, be saved? And if so, what could be done for them and who should do it?

During the years between approximately 1910 and 1922 the plight of premature infants was overshadowed by America's abysmal general IMR. Premature babies were not the focus of reformers. But once deaths of otherwise healthy babies decreased, prematurity became a more visible problem. In other words, when fewer infants were dying, of those deaths that did occur, more were due to prematurity than had previously been the case.

Infant incubators were part of the problem as well. Faulty designs often proved more harmful than helpful as infants were either under- or overheated, both potentially fatal errors. Physicians relying on anecdotal rather than statistical evidence dismissed the incubator as ineffective and even dangerous.[7] Some hospitals provided care for preemies using other measures of providing warmth, including traditional methods such as warm bricks in cradles and rooms heated to ninety degrees or more.[8]

By the early 1920s premature infant care was at a crossroads. Based mainly in the home in 1920, over the next two decades it moved permanently into the hospital. A variety of social, cultural, and technological factors combined to foster this transition and make hospital-based, medically directed premature care the standard in the United States. As knowledge about the physiologic details of prematurity and the popularity of premature infants in general grew, the demand for premature care expanded.

Increasing knowledge of the causes and results of premature birth and a desire to alleviate its associated morbidity and mortality marked the early years of "modern" premature care. In the United States this desire culminated in the identification of prematurity as a new disease or condition worthy of treatment by medical professionals. It also meant the separation of premature infants from other newborns and from their parents. Identifying and isolating premature infants allowed physicians to focus on and specifically treat problems different from those of other infants. These methods, initially unchallenged, were presented to the public as the only possible hope to save these previously doomed babies.

AMERICAN HOSPITALS AND PREMATURE INFANTS

The basic goals of premature care are based on traditional, commonsense care. They include maintaining warmth, providing adequate nutrition, and preventing infection. Pierre Budin trumpeted these goals in his classic 1907 text and they were the basis for all hospital premature care. They are still used today.

In 1922, two events occurred to help place premature care permanently within the realm of physician-directed and hospital-based premature nurseries.

One was the establishment of a premature infant station at the Michael Reese Hospital in Chicago under the direction of Dr. Julius Hess. At Michael Reese medical personnel separated premature infants from the "normal" newborn and pediatric populations. The hospital hired nurses solely to care for and to develop specific procedures to aid the premature babies.[9]

The premature station at Michael Reese received a great deal of financial support from the Infants' Aid Society of Chicago, a local women's philanthropic group organized in 1914. An endowment of $85,000 secured the station's future. The Society also provided clothing and other baby care items to the indigent. The support of the Infants' Aid Society influenced the direction of premature care and demonstrated the importance of philanthropic support from the private sector.[10]

The other significant event of 1922 was the publication of the first major *American* textbook devoted to the care of premature infants. Julius Hess' *Premature and Congenitally Diseased Infants* provided the most detailed account of hospital-based premature infant care in 1922.[11] The premature station at Michael Reese soon became the acknowledged leader in premature care. It hosted physicians and nurses from around the country eager to learn and implement the latest in premature care. Thus, through his writings and willingness to teach, Hess's ideas and practices quickly became standard treatment for all premature infants.

During the 1920s, reports on experiences with premature infants multiplied in the professional literature. Most articles were positive, often citing impressive survival rates that discounted infants who expired during the first twenty-four hours in the premature unit.[12] The case of a one and a half pound infant surviving more than two years is reported, but the general consensus remained that a birth weight of approximately two pounds represented the limit of viability in most situations.[13] The usefulness of incubators for heat received continuing attention. One study concluded that the infant's body temperature be used to regulate the incubators' heat. This was a new idea at the time.[14]

Through observation and clinical studies physicians began to understand that premature infants needed individual attention and care. Heated incubator rooms and homemade warming cribs could not maintain constant temperature control for individual babies. The addition of oxygen as a treatment for the respiratory distress prevalent in premature infants sealed the need for an individual approach to climate control. The commercially manufactured, mechanical incubator that physicians almost universally disavowed by the mid-1910s was subsequently accepted in a revised form in the 1930s. In March 1938, Charles Chapple, M.D., of Philadelphia submitted an application for a patent for an incubator.[15] The Chapple incubator, named for its inventor was the predecessor of the Isolette brand of incubator that captured the market by 1950 and, with updates and revisions is still produced and used widely today.

Premature infants experience respiratory difficulties directly related to the degree of prematurity. In other words, the shorter the gestational period, the more likely the infant will experience serious breathing problems. In the 1930s, oxygen slowly gained a reputation for easing the cyanosis and asphyxia associated with prematurity. Several studies published in the professional journals identified expected benefits of its use and suggested, as one article concludes, "a continuous supply of oxygen seems to be of advantage in treating feeble, premature babies."[16] Physicians administered oxygen for cyanosis, respiratory embarrassment, feebleness, asphyxiation, a birth weight under 1200 grams, and "all others whom it was believed might be benefited."[17]

By the early 1940s oxygen was a standard treatment not just for respiratory distress in premature infants, but for prematurity itself. This standard rested on the knowledge of the poor prognosis for premature infants suffering respiratory distress. Babies who could not breathe on their own died. Since there appeared to be no negative consequences of oxygen and respiratory distress happened so frequently, oxygen administration to all premature infants could be justified. Along with the individualized warmth provided by the new incubators, oxygen seemed to promise an end to the most significant causes of morbidity and mortality.

NUTRITION AND FEEDING

What, when, and how to feed premature babies has always been a challenge for caregivers. Breast milk was considered essential to survival and was the feeding of choice throughout the 1920s. Wet nurses breast-fed babies when the mother was unavailable or unable to breast-feed. Some doctors proposed alternatives including chymogen milk (a mixture of boiled cow's milk, rennet, and milk sugar), boiled milk, skimmed milk, and buttermilk.[18] In professional journals different physicians put forth their own ideas and methods on the timing of the first and subsequent feedings. Babies unable to suck were fed by dropper or feeding tube. In addition to milk, babies received plain water or sugar water between feedings to maintain the proper fluid balance, orange juice beginning in the third week to prevent scurvy, and cod liver oil beginning in the fourth week to prevent rickets.[19]

During the 1930s the value of breast milk came under greater scrutiny and physicians experimented with various formulas for artificial feedings. Some used commercially produced infant formula such as SMA and Similac for the first time.[20] Although at least one physician called the sole use of breast milk "a relic" of earlier times, by 1940 most returned to the belief that breast milk was the best nutrition available for premature infants and should be used whenever possible.[21] Opinion continued to sway, however, and much of the debate can be traced to the issue of supply and demand. As hospital care became standard treatment, physician control over the lives of the premature infant increased. With limited access to their infants, mothers of preemies found their milk supply dried up quickly. Commercial infant formulas, rare in the 1930s, were ubiquitous by the postwar years. Publicity in the form of free samples to new mothers helped formula companies increase their market. Thus by the end of the 1940s, while breast milk was not considered bad for the premature infant, many hospitals fed all premature infants mixtures of cow's milk, vitamins, and other additives.

Not until the 1960s did popular opinion again strongly support breast milk for all babies. Since then doctors have encouraged mothers of preemies to breast-feed when at all possible. When distance or their infant's frail health prevents direct breast-feeding, mothers are encouraged to pump breast milk. Medical personnel can then bottle feed it to babies or freeze it for later use. Clinical evidence of breast milk's benefits for all babies abounds.[22]

PUBLIC HEALTH CAMPAIGN

Public health officials caught up with premature infants during the 1930s. The Children's Bureau became a "significant campaigner" for premature care during that decade, advising local efforts and providing funding. The Bureau also supported premature infant research and a follow-up clinic in New York City.[23] Public health departments in cities and states began to devise strategies aimed at bringing the premature infant to the attention of hospitals, physicians, and nurses.

By 1940 the Children's Bureau reported that twenty-eight states, the District of Columbia, and Hawaii had community plans either in place or set to begin to ensure the special care premature infants required. In 1935 Congress passed the Social Security Act as part of President Franklin Roosevelt's New Deal aimed at preventing financial disaster for the elderly and the infirm. Title V, part 1 of the Act included the provision of funds to help set up the community plans for premature births. Medical and nursing education was often part of the plans. Public health nurses and pediatricians traveled to premature centers in Boston and Chicago for in-depth training, and returned to their home states to teach and advise their professional colleagues.[24]

The entry of the United States into World War II in 1941 postponed many public health efforts, including a major plan for New York City. When the war was over cities and states across the country renewed these efforts and the resulting plans encompassed the revision of hospital standards, transportation of premature infants to hospitals, financial assistance, and more educational programs to train physicians and nurses.[25]

During the 1940s premature infants treated in the most up-to-date nurseries could expect to lead normal healthy lives once discharged. At least that is what physicians promised their parents. Although some premature infants demonstrated long-term neurological problems, at the time the risk did not seem too large. Other conditions lasting past the neonatal period doctors traced to prenatal influences or poor home conditions.[26] Treatment alternatives increased as physicians adopted apparently successful ideas and procedures used by others. Many times these worked successfully, but by 1950 it was obvious that something was going wrong in the nation's premature nurseries.

UNEXPECTED CONSEQUENCES—THE DISCOVERY OF RETROLENTAL FIBROPLASIA

In 1942 the *American Journal of Ophthalmology* published an article by Dr. Theodore Terry, a Boston ophthalmologist, about an apparently new condition associated with premature infants.[27] Termed retrolental fibroplasia (RLF) by the following year, this disorder of the retinal vasculature became the leading cause of blindness among children in the United States by 1950. RLF became the first acknowledged complication of the treatment of prematurity. Physicians and scientists worked zealously trying to identify a cause for RLF. They examined the medical and nursing care of the infants for any discrepancies or omissions that might have triggered RLF. They focused on newer treatments including vitamin therapy, blood transfusions, various medicines, and hormonal supplements. Geography, heredity, lack of prenatal care, and early exposure to light were all ruled out as causes. The use of oxygen to treat the anoxia (lack of sufficient oxygen resulting in blue discoloration of the mouth and skin) prevalent among premature infants came into use during the 1930s but researchers did not seriously consider it in the search for a cause of RLF until the early 1950s. Researchers in England and Australia, where oxygen for premature infants was not prescribed until after World War II, noted a similar, later increase in the number of cases of RLF. They questioned the use of oxygen and published their observational data in the professional literature. By the early 1950s American researchers had also begun to question the role of oxygen in the development of RLF and began a large-scale, multihospital study of its effects. The study culminated in 1956 with solid evidence pointing to oxygen as the culprit.[28] Oxygen use was immediately curtailed throughout the world and rates of RLF dropped dramatically. Unfortunately, deaths due to respiratory failure and the lack of oxygen treatment increased by 1960 and the incidence of RLF began to increase again. Known now as Retinopathy of Prematurity (ROP), it continues to affect preemies today.[29] Physicians now believe it has many causes. Standard screening procedures identify infants at risk early and treatment is planned. Clinical studies continue to sort out the best way to prevent the disease and to treat it once developed. The overall aim, preventing blindness, remains the same.

BEATING THE ODDS, 1960–1990

Between 1960 and 1990 the pace of advancement in the care of premature infants accelerated dramatically. Neonatology became a medical subspecialty of pediatrics requiring a year or more of postgraduate training for physicians after they served a pediatric residency. Clinical research studies of treatments became standard in the large academic health centers. Incubator technology continued to evolve. The wooden boxes of the 1930s gave way to clear plexiglass models allowing direct visualization of the infant without disrupting the flow of heated air. For the smallest and sickest preemies open warming tables allowed immediate access in emergencies while maintaining the necessary environmental temperature. Other innovations included improved venous and arterial access, better antibiotics, and expanded use of imaging techniques to quickly and accurately identify gastrointestinal, cardiac, neurological, and other abnormalities or complications. Perhaps the most important innovation involved the development and refinement of the ability to support and maintain the premature baby's respiratory efforts.[30]

Babies born before twenty-eight weeks are, in most cases, unable to breathe on their own for more than a few minutes. Until the advent of mechanical ventilation these babies inevitably died of respiratory failure. Although ventilators had been a staple of adult intensive care units for several years, the technology necessary for the physiologically different neonate did not become available and effective until the 1970s.[31] By the mid-1980s babies born as early as twenty-four weeks gestation could survive their early entry into the world with ventilators, warming beds, and effective medical and nursing care.

There were complications, however. One major problem was that babies born before thirty-two to thirty-four weeks gestation frequently lacked sufficient levels of surfactant to keep their lungs inflated. Early mechanical ventilators saved many lives but often damaged the babies' lungs in the process. Bronchopulmonary dysplasia (BPD) was a frequent result of long-term ventilation and caused scarring of the lungs with resultant decreases in lung function. Babies with the most serious cases of BPD required tracheotomies. Mechanical ventilation continued in some cases for several years and often played a part in growth and developmental delays. Artificial surfactant therapy, developed during the 1980s and widely available by the early 1990s led to a significant decrease in the length of time premature infants required mechanical ventilation and eliminated the need in some. This led to a concomitant decrease in the frequency and severity of BPD.[32]

Another highlight of the era included the introduction of objective measures to assess the newborn premature baby. Until the 1970s preemies were identified mainly by weight. Both the American Academy of Pediatrics in 1935 and the World Health Assembly in 1948 cited birth weights of five and a half pounds or less as the definition of prematurity.[33] By the late 1960s it was obvious this was not enough. The gestational age, or the number of weeks the pregnancy lasted, was more specific but was difficult to determine since calculating it relied on several often-conflicting factors. Mothers determined gestation based on the date of their last menstrual period, a method beset by problems associated with irregular cycles, first trimester bleeding, and embarrassment due to conception prior to marriage. Medical professionals based gestational age on personal experiences, which obviously varied. Although these methods usually resulted in a fairly accurate determination of gestational age, consistent assessments based on a standardized scoring system did not appear until the early 1970s.[34] Today a combination of physical and neurologic findings, the mother's estimation of gestation, and sonographic studies determine the degree of prematurity. In some cases amniocentesis may also help determine fetal maturity.[35]

NEW CHALLENGES, 1990–2000

The last decade of the twentieth century witnessed the continued decrease in mortality associated with premature birth. At the same time, however, there was a rise in the overall number of babies born prematurely to approximately 11 percent of all births in the late 1990s.[36] This increase can be explained in several ways. First, maternity care continued to improve. Women who might have miscarried in an earlier era were able to give birth to a live, albeit premature baby. On the other hand, at-risk mothers such as those living in poverty and adolescents continued to have a lower rate of prenatal care and higher rates of premature births. A third and more publicized reason is the increase in multiple births as a result of infertility treatments. These treatments increase the chances of a multiple birth (twins, triplets, etc.). There is a documented increase in risk for prematurity with multiple births, and the risk increases with the number of babies.[37]

The 1990s was also a time when the limits of viability, always a point for debate among medical professionals, appeared to stall at about the twenty-two to twenty-four week gestation time. For babies born at or before this time parents and professionals must choose to initiate resuscitative procedures or let the baby die. And if begun, what parameters should guide decisions to keep going or to stop? In most cases there is no clear answer.[38]

PREMATURE BABIES IN THE PUBLIC EYE

The advancement of neonatal intensive care in the United States throughout the twentieth century is a story with many heroes. Physicians, nurses, public health officials, and parents have all had a hand in making the United States the world leader in neonatal care. In addition, as with any cause, garnering the attention of the public at large and securing financial support are essential for success. By the late 1990s premature births, particularly those involving more than one baby, attracted widespread media attention, speculation, and unsolicited opinions.[39]

In some respects this intense coverage represents a continuation of public interest which began with the display of premature infants at national fairs and exhibitions in the late 1890s and continued until approximately 1940. Held across the country, these exhibitions featured scientific, technological, and cultural advances and innovations. The fairs also included popular entertainment along the "midways." Amusement rides, games of chance, and "freak shows" were popular. It was within this environment that incubator shows flourished. The small size of the infants, their placement in a machine similar to those used on farms for poultry incubation, and the encouragement of carnival-style barkers stimulated the interest of the fair going public.[40]

The earliest incubator exhibits took place in Europe and were a popular success. Dr. Martin Couney, the self-proclaimed incubator doctor, ran the major shows in Europe and brought them to the United States in the late 1890s.[41] The first American incubator show took place in 1898 in Omaha, Nebraska, at the Trans-Mississippi International Exposition. The incubator exhibit was located in a large building on the midway and visitors filed past the rows of incubators after paying an entrance fee.[42] The next major American fair was hosted by Buffalo, New York, in 1901 at the Pan-American Exposition.[43] In St. Louis, the 1904 Louisiana Purchase Exposition also hosted an exhibition. There, Dr. John Zahorsky, a St. Louis pediatrician, was in charge.[44] Exhibitors generally obtained infants locally from physicians who often believed they would die anyway. St. Louis newspapers ran advertisements that promised free care and attracted parents of preemies. Zahorsky made several studies of the care of the babies in the incubators and recognized the value of educating the public about the care of the babies. His studies were published in 1904, but were poorly received and generally ignored by the medical establishment.[45]

While entertaining, the incubator exhibit's identification as a sideshow and location among midway entertainment spectacles prevented mainstream physicians, struggling to assume a professional identify of their own, from embracing it as substantive progress. Additionally, in 1904, the costs of caring for all premature babies in incubators would have been prohibitive. Hospitals of the era were ill-equipped, poorly staffed, and unable to afford to provide such a service. Most middle- and upper-class women still gave birth at home and the incubator was a cumbersome machine that was simply not a viable domestic alternative.[46] A few local hospitals took advantage of the exhibitions and purchased the used incubators and other equipment to expand their own programs.[47]

Media attention to the shows was sporadic. Dramatic descriptions of the infants and the methods required to care for them appeared in papers and magazines along with criticisms of mothers who neglected to provide the proper atmosphere and care.[48] The New York Society for the Prevention of Cruelty to Children characterized the exhibits as mercenary rather than charitable and questioned promoter Couney's tactics.[49] Other large incubator shows were held in Portland, Oregon, in 1905 and San Francisco, California, in 1915.[50] Dr.

Couney operated summer exhibits at Coney Island in New York City until the early 1940s and in Atlantic City for several years during the 1910s and 1920s.[51]

The Century of Progress Exposition—Chicago, 1933–1934

The 1930s brought the public and premature infants even closer together with the opening of the Century of Progress Exposition in Chicago in 1933. It was an immediate success and was renewed for the 1934 season. The Baby Incubator show, located on the midway, promised "living babies."[52] The public health department referred premature babies and local hospitals transferred them to the fair exhibit. In addition, parents brought babies to the exhibit where they received care free of charge. Fair-goers paid admission fees to support the exhibit.[53] An unofficial fair guidebook listed the incubator babies as one of the outstanding amusement attractions at the fair.[54]

This incubator show was a major success. It attracted much attention from fair-goers and provided professional care for premature babies. Nurses from Michael Reese Hospital staffed the exhibit.[55] It is difficult to determine the benefits, if any, for the premature infants as their day-to-day care was probably similar to that received in the hospital. One exception was the constant parade of people past the incubators, a practice forbidden by most hospitals at that time.[56] The influence of this practice on infection rates and thus morbidity and mortality is unknown.

The Century of Progress incubator show expanded public interest in premature infants immensely. Press coverage focused on the extremely small size of premature newborns, the special equipment required, heroic physicians and nurses, and the fight for life by the infants themselves.[57] These accounts kept the issue of prematurity in the public eye throughout the Great Depression.

Dionne Quintuplets

In May 1934 the birth of the Dionne quintuplets in Quebec, Canada, dramatically increased interest in prematurity, particularly instances involving multiple births. They were born prematurely on May 28, 1934, in Corbeil, Ontario, Canada. Incubators obtained from Chicago and breast milk collected from volunteer donors in Toronto, Montreal, and Chicago warmed and nourished the five girls.[58] The press circulated the story worldwide and the enormous public interest led the Canadian government to take legal guardianship of the girls away from their parents soon after birth. Although cared for in a specially built hospital across the road from their home by full-time nurses and a local physician the infants rarely saw their parents and family. They were exhibited daily to tourists who paid a fee to see them. This arrangement ensured a substantial income and publicity for the government and professional staff. *Time* magazine called the Dionne quintuplets "the world's greatest news-picture story."[59] The emotional damage to the Dionne family was not acknowledged for many years. Their story is still popular with audiences today, as evidenced by a 1998 television movie. In 1998 the Canadian government paid the three surviving Dionne women approximately $2.8 million dollars to help compensate for the money raised during the years they were on display.[60]

By the late 1930s the increasing availability of premature care in hospitals meant a decline in the number of premature infants available for incubator exhibits. The last major incubator exhibit was held at the New York World's Fair of 1939.[61] The public increasingly viewed hospital births as proper and medically necessary. A baby born in the hospital thus became the responsibility of the hospital staff that could hardly ignore the plight of the premature infant.

The publicity surrounding premature infants and neonatal intensive care in America is really not much different from the attention given to other groups of patients who have mounted campaigns for recognition. AIDS and breast cancer patients and survivors groups have been especially well represented during the 1990s. Premature babies cannot themselves mount a publicity campaign, but every baby has two parents and therefore has two potential advocates. In the years before the Internet and television, the incubator shows sold the idea of premature care to the public. By the 1990s parents of premature infants used the latest technology to advance the cause of prematurity. The March of Dimes switched their focus from polio to the prevention of premature birth and the well-being of those who are born prematurely.

CONGENITAL CARDIAC DEFECTS

Premature babies have a higher risk of many types of birth defects and birth-related problems. Congenital cardiac defects affect both premature and full-term babies, however the defects are often harder to fix in premature infants and cause more difficult preoperative and postoperative problems. Early in the twentieth century babies born with congenital cardiac defects received limited attention. The knowledge, ability, and technology to fix these defects were not available. Some defects were incompatible with life and when a baby with one of these types was born alive, he died shortly thereafter. With other heart defects the baby might survive infancy but succumb during early childhood after several years of decreasing physical and mental abilities. A few did survive until adolescence or early adulthood but the increasing strain on their heart and lungs often led to a proscribed life and early death. A woman with a congenital heart defect who became pregnant was at risk for serious complications including heart failure and death.

Blue Babies

The sixty-two years between 1938 and 2000 transformed the lives of babies born with congenital heart defects like no other time period in history. When a baby is born with a heart that is not formed correctly he is subject to any number of complications. For some they are minor and may include some shortness of breath or possibly a higher susceptibility to infection. For others, the abnormal openings between the heart's chambers, narrowed arterial or venous vessels, persistent fetal structures, misplacement of major vessels, and other problems alone or in combination lead to serious, often life-threatening problems. Most of those with moderate to severe defects were dead before they reached adolescence. The most serious heart defects prevent the pumping of fully oxygenated blood from the heart to the body. This results in the bluish tinge to the babies' skin and the term "blue babies" was often used to describe these patients. One particular condition, tetralogy of Fallot, is most frequently associated with the term. Tetralogy of Fallot is a group of four heart defects that together result in too much blood going to the lungs and too little oxygenated blood going to the body. Untreated it leaves the patient susceptible to infection and can lead to increasingly severe heart failure. Life expectancy varies but without surgery is nearly always limited.

In August 1938 the first surgical procedure to alleviate a cardiac defect was done by Dr. Robert Gross. The patient was an eight-year-old child who had a patent ductus arteriosus (PDA). This duct connected the aorta to the pulmonary artery during fetal life and did not close shortly after birth as it does in the majority of babies. When it does not close properly too much blood can circulate to the lungs causing a variety of problems including congestive heart failure. Dr. Gross tied off the PDA, thus allowing the child's blood supply to circulate correctly.[62] The early pediatric cardiologists and surgeons concentrated on helping older children with severe limitations due to their heart defects. Their bodies were bigger, making operating on the heart easier. Doctors also believed that an older child could withstand the rigors of anesthesia and surgery better than a baby.

In 1944 Dr. Helen Taussig, a cardiologist, Dr. Alfred Blalock, a surgeon, and Mr. Vivien Thomas, a surgical assistant, designed and carried out an operation to shunt venous blood to the lungs without going through the heart. This procedure, known thereafter as the Blalock–Taussig shunt, was performed at Johns Hopkins Hospital in Baltimore. The doctors originally performed it on children suffering from tetralogy of Fallot and thereby allowed an increased amount of oxygenated (red) blood to circulate to the body. Results were dramatic and children often turned pink right in the operating room. The procedure was not at first performed on babies, but it did provide hope for their parents.

Over the course of the next several decades increased understanding of the physiology of all heart and lung functions in both the fetus and neonate allowed physicians and surgeons to develop specific interventions for a variety of heart defects. The Blalock–Taussig shunt is a palliative procedure, or one that does not correct a defect but helps manage the symptoms caused by the defect. As surgeons became more comfortable with the procedure and its benefits they began to use it for smaller children and babies. Physicians developed other shunts to alleviate immediately life threatening defects. By the 1990s surgeons used the Blalock–Taussig shunt less often because they were able to do a complete repair of the tetralogy of Fallot defects during infancy. Doctors still use the shunt when an infant is very small and very cyanotic (blue) or has some other complication requiring the complete repair to be delayed. The shunt is removed when the defect is corrected.[63]

The Blalock–Taussig shunt procedure is closed heart surgery as there is no need for surgeons to enter the heart itself. Open-heart surgery debuted in the 1950s, again for older children. In order to correct a defect within the heart it must be stopped and the blood temporarily oxygenated outside of the body. Medical personnel built mechanical cardio-pulmonary bypass machines and used them for the first time in the mid-1950s. Some of the first patients were children or young adults with congenital cardiac defects. Despite the initial success of the operations, a high mortality rate prompted further investigation into the effect on the heart and lungs of untreated cardiac defects. Because excessive blood flow through a defect can cause pressure related trauma in the lungs surgeons developed a new palliative procedure called pulmonary artery banding. During surgery a doctor placed a band on the pulmonary artery to decrease the amount of blood flowing to the lungs and limit any damage.

With surgery by the age of two, residual lung and vessel damage could be limited.[64]

The development of new medical and surgical techniques to correct cardiac defects continued at a feverish pitch during the 1960s. Improvements in diagnostic technology, monitoring before and after surgery, blood tests, and new cardiac drugs all helped decrease mortality related to the defects. Surgeons developed procedures to treat defects that were always fatal within days or weeks of life. Transposition of the great arteries (TGA) is one example. TGA is fatal if not treated because it means there is no way to mix oxygenated and unoxygenated blood. Simply put the pulmonary artery and aorta are switched and two closed circulation loops result. Unoxygenated blood returning to the heart is pumped back to the body without going to the lungs. Oxygenated blood returning from the lungs is pumped back to the lungs. In 1966, Dr. William Rashkind developed a palliative procedure. He used a cardiac catheter to create a hole in the atria to allow mixing of blood. This allowed the baby time to grow and become better able to withstand the rigors of corrective surgery. At that time corrective surgery involved redirecting the blood so that the aorta performed as the pulmonary artery and vice versa. In the 1970s after documentation of many serious postoperative complications with this procedure, surgeons devised a method to switch the arteries back to their proper positions. By the early 1990s this became the standard treatment for infants with TGA. The procedure could be done within the neonatal period and the mortality rate for TGA dramatically decreased. Today, instead of certain death, infants with TGA can generally look forward to a normal life.[65]

Hypoplastic Left Heart Syndrome

Cardiac transplantation also debuted in the 1960s, mainly for adults. Not until the mid-1980s with the introduction of antirejection medicines did transplantation become successful. Heart transplants in infants are one way of treating a lethal defect known as hypoplastic left heart syndrome (HLHS). HLHS involves several complex defects; however the main problems are the missing or severely proscribed left ventricle and a severely underdeveloped aorta. Without the left ventricle the heart is unable to pump blood to the body and without the aorta there is no way for any blood to get out of the heart. Mortality is 100 percent when untreated. Most babies with HLHS look normal and healthy at birth but within three to four days of life fetal structures that allow some mixing and circulation of the blood from the right ventricle begin to close. Before the 1980s most of the babies died quickly before they received medical attention while others lived a week or slightly longer. Parents of babies with HLHS diagnosed before death were offered comfort care only.

Heart transplantation became possible for infants in the 1980s and is used to replace defective and deformed hearts due to HLHS and other causes. Despite increasing success since the 1980s drawbacks to transplantation remain. The baby must be kept alive until a heart is located and harvested. This can take weeks or months. Cardiologists and surgeons can administer drugs to maintain circulation for relatively short periods of time although the drugs also have potentially serious side effects. Once listed on the national organ procurement list, the baby and family must wait for another baby with an appropriately sized and otherwise healthy heart to die. This wait can be tortuous for families. Transplantation should ideally be done before six months of age; otherwise the medical interventions keeping the baby alive begin to fail. Once transplantation takes place medications to prevent rejection must be taken for the rest of the patient's life that have serious side effects themselves.[66]

Before transplantation became a reality, surgeons sought to develop procedures to palliate HLHS. The most successful built on the success of earlier shunt procedures. Dr. William Norwood, initially at Children's Hospital, Boston, and later at the Children's Hospital of Philadelphia was one of the first surgeons to take on this challenge and many doctors used his Norwood Procedure to palliate HLHS during the last two decades of the twentieth century. The complex procedure involves rerouting blood away from the nonfunctional left side of the heart and to the lungs for oxygenation before circulating to the body. There were two to three surgeries involved for most infants, the first at birth, another several months later, and a third, if necessary, at two to four years of age.[67]

Debate among physicians and other health care professionals continued throughout the 1990s regarding the best choice of surgery for infants with HLHS. In some centers most babies with the defect were put on the transplant list. In others the Norwood procedure was the first option. Parents often made the decision in haste and with limited understanding. In hospitals where doctors preferred transplantation, they would perform the Norwood procedure when a baby's condition deteriorated while waiting for a donor heart. Until the 1990s physicians often gave parents the choice of doing nothing except making the baby comfortable until death. In certain circumstances, such as when a baby was too unstable to move to a pediatric cardiac center, this option remained viable at the close of the century.[68]

CONGENITAL HEART DEFECTS AT THE END OF THE TWENTIETH CENTURY

Survival after congenital heart surgery improved steadily during the second half of the century. The development of prenatal ultrasound testing allowed diagnosis of defects before birth. A mother-to-be could plan to give birth closer to or in a center equipped to care for her newborn. Parents also had more time to learn about and plan for the birth and care of the baby.

Within one generation the risk of dying has gone from 100 percent to less than 10 percent for some defects. For other defects the risk is even lower, approaching 1–2 percent. Dr. Gross's revolutionary surgery in 1938 is now a relatively simple procedure. In many cases it is not even necessary as medication delivered to the infant intravenously often closes off the extra blood vessel. Dr. Blalock's and Dr. Taussig's shunt of 1944 has been modified as experience demonstrated the necessity. New materials and technologies have added choice to some decisions about treatment. The expansion of neonatal intensive care has also played a role. The increase in knowledge about newborns, both premature and born at term, and the willingness of pediatricians, cardiac surgeons, cardiologists, nurses, and parents to work together has lifted the threat of death and replaced it with hope for most of these babies.

The decision to operate on a newborn or young infant remains a difficult one for most people. While many defects are not immediately life-threatening, a few are and over the years have been found to be most amenable to correction during the first days or months of life. Even for non-life-threatening defects early surgery decreases the risk of heart and lung damage caused by the defect itself. Babies born with additional congenital diseases or malformations are often at higher risk of surgical complications. In these cases individual decisions regarding the timing of cardiac surgery are necessary.

The long-term outlook for babies born with congenital cardiac defects brightened considerably during the twentieth century. However some still die before their first birthday. The majority of these succumb within the first month. Death may occur before surgery due to the effects of the defect itself, or because of postoperative complications including infection and major organ failure. Babies requiring more than one surgical procedure, such as those with HLHS, may survive one operation only to die before, during, or immediately after a second.

Once it was demonstrated that surgery could palliate and correct infant hearts, attention turned to assessing outcomes in survivors. While surgery offered a chance at life the future remained unknown. Babies with relatively simple, isolated, and completely correctable defects could be expected to live a normal life span with few, if any, limitations. Those with more complex defects, including tetralogy of Fallot and HLHS that involve several different defects at the same time, could expect a more complicated course.

Anytime a person needs multiple surgeries the risk of complications increase. Infants who required a palliative procedure before the corrective surgery fell into this category.[69] Surgical risks are real for any patient despite the safety measures in place and include uncontrollable bleeding and death during and immediately after the operation. Other problems can include drug reaction, high or low blood pressure, breathing difficulties, and any number of individual reactions that cause the baby's condition to destabilize. Long-term problems such as infection (endocarditis) that can occur years after the surgery, disrupted heart rhythms that require pacemakers or defibrillators, heart failure, and coronary artery disease have been documented.[70]

Neurological complications can also follow open heart surgery. Blood clots that travel to the brain, bleeding in the brain, and decreased blood oxygen levels can cause permanent brain damage. Many clinical studies have demonstrated an increased risk of neurodevelopmental deficits among infants who had heart surgery before one year of age. The overall risk has decreased with increased experience, better techniques, and shorter cardio-pulmonary bypass times, but is still a problem that physicians and parents need to consider.[71] More studies will be needed to determine the continued significance of neurologic deficits following cardiac surgery. People who survived surgery for the most complicated heart defects were only beginning to reach adulthood by 2000. The lifelong implications of their surgery are yet to be determined.[72]

CONCLUSIONS

At the beginning of the twentieth century many people labeled babies born prematurely, with congenital cardiac defects, or both, weak or congenitally debilitated. Little could be done to help them. But as the century progressed the increased attention showered on all babies benefited them as well. Attention to preemies came earlier than it did for those with cardiac defects and it developed over a longer period of time. The exhibition of premature infants in incubator shows and articles written in newspapers and magazines presented parents, and the general public, with something that was previously hidden from view. These infants, tiny, frail, and underdeveloped yet portrayed as "fighters" rather than "weaklings," could with the appropriate care, survive to live a normal life. The portrayal of these infants as survivors rather than victims enabled the public to respond by labeling them as cute, desirable, and worthy of life-saving care. They demanded change and doctors, public health personnel, and hospitals responded.

Individuals with an interest in premature babies used this new interest to develop new techniques, new machines, and new facilities to care for them. When the first permanent premature unit opened in 1922 it signaled the beginning of a new era. In the 1930s, despite the terrible financial and social problems of the Great Depression, premature care expanded and doctors found even more ways to ensure survival of ever smaller babies. By the mid-century mark premature infant care was established as a societal obligation.

Throughout the second half of the century the publicity about premature babies increased steadily along with the ability to care for them. In 1963 Jacqueline Kennedy, wife of President John F. Kennedy, gave birth to a son several weeks early. The baby died a few days after birth due to hyaline membrane disease. For the postwar generation this birth and death of a popular president's baby brought the issue of prematurity to the forefront of popular and professional interest. Between the mid-1960s and late 1990s continued advancements pushed the limits of viability back so that almost any baby born alive had a chance for survival. Multiple births continued to be quite popular with accounts of quintuplets, sextuplets, septuplets, and even octuplets receiving attention from the print and broadcast media. Success stories were common; little attention was given to those who died or suffered long-term complications of prematurity.

Babies with heart defects had to wait for medical advances that helped adults and older children first. Beginning in the 1940s palliative measures helped some babies live until they were old enough to withstand surgery. By the 1980s surgeons routinely operated on infants. Long-term outcomes for these babies wait the twenty-first century as the first are only now reaching adulthood. But for many the disability previously associated with serious cardiac defects is something they only read about. Their lives have not only been saved, but perhaps more important, enhanced.

The changes in the care of premature infants and infants with congenital heart defects have been truly inspirational over the course of the twentieth century. Nonetheless there is room for improvement. Ethical dilemmas are inherent in matters of life and death. Even when a medical treatment or procedure goes exactly right a poor outcome might result. The fact that the patients are infants and unable to give informed consent is a matter that will never go away. Should the parents have the final say in decisions about treatment? And if not them, who? What responsibility does society have to a baby whose life is saved but is neurologically devastated? Access to expensive and extensive care is another issue that confounds families and professionals alike. One recent study found racial disparities in mortality data for cardiac defects. Although all babies with defects experienced a decline in mortality between 1979 and 1997 the decline for black babies was slower and mortality rates remained higher than white babies. The reasons for these disparities need to be identified and steps taken to correct them.[73]

By the late 1990s both neonatal intensive care and cardiac intensive care units were available for babies in almost every area of the country. Specialist and subspecialist pediatricians, pediatric nurses, respiratory therapists, social workers, physical and occupational therapists, nutritionists, and a host of others responded to the needs of babies and the demands of their parents and the public. The babies are no longer victims to be pitied. Parents too refused to be pitied and expect to be involved in every aspect of their baby's care. At the beginning of the twenty-first century research and innovations continue to transform the lives of these babies and their families. Once thought better off dead, they now have the potential for healthy, long, and possibly even notable lives.

NOTES

1. "When Your Baby Is Premature—Advice for New Parents from Preemie-L Parents." *Preemie-L FAQ's and Advice Sheets*, (n.d.), http://www.preemie-l.org/.

2. Much of the information regarding the history of premature infant care in the United States was previously published in my PhD dissertation, Elizabeth Ann Reedy, *Ripe Too Early: The Expansion of Hospital Based Premature Infant Care in the United States, 1922–1950* (PhD dissertation, University of Pennsylvania, 2000).

3. E.H. Ackerknecht, "Incubator and Taboo," *Journal of the History of Medicine* 1 (January 1946): 144–148.

4. Thomas E. Cone, Jr., *History of the Care and Feeding of the Premature Infant* (Boston, MA: Little, Brown and Company, 1985), 9–10, 18–21.

5. Karen Offen, "Depopulation, Nationalism, and Feminism in Fin-de-Siecle France," *American Historical Review* 89 (1984): 648–676; Richard Meckel, *Save the Babies: American Public Health Reform and the Prevention of Infant Mortality, 1850–1929* (Baltimore, MD: Johns Hopkins University Press, 1990), 101–102; and Jeffrey P. Baker, *The Machine in the Nursery* (Baltimore, MD: Johns Hopkins University Press, 1996), 45–50, 78–79, 84–85, 93–94.

6. Pierre Budin, *The Nursling: The Feeding and Hygiene of Premature and Full-Term Infants*, trans. William J. Malloney (London: Caxton Publishing Company, 1907).

7. Baker, *The Machine in the Nursery*, 152–174.

8. Amy A. Armour, "Hints for Maternity Nurses," *Trained Nurse and Hospital Review* 53 (August 1914): 89–90; Jennings C. Litzenberg, "Long Interval Feeding of Premature Infants," *American Journal of Diseases of Children* 4 (1912): 391–409; N.O. Pearce, "Review of Recent Literature on the New-Born," *American Journal of Diseases of Children* 18(1) (July 1919): 51–68; and Cone, *History of the Care and Feeding of the Premature Infant*, 52–53.

9. Julius H. Hess and Evelyn C. Lundeen, *The Premature Infant: Medical and Nursing Care*, 2nd ed. (Philadelphia, PA: J.B. Lippincott Co., 1949).

10. Betty Lachman, telephone interview with author, October 27, 1998, Chicago, Illinois; Natale P. Solway, "The Story of the Infants' Aid Society," in Evelyn C. Lundeen and Ralph H. Kunstadter, *Care of the Premature Infant* (Philadelphia, PA: J.B. Lippincott Company, 1958), 306–309; and Sarah Gordon, ed., *All Our Lives: A Centennial History of Michael Reese Hospital and Medical Center, 1881–1981* (Chicago: Michael Reese Hospital, 1981), 88. The Society also reportedly paid the nurses' salaries. Julius H. Hess and I. McKy Chamberlain, "Premature Infants—A Report of Two Hundred and Sixty-Six Consecutive Cases," *American Journal of Diseases of Children* 34 (1927): 571–584.

11. Julius H. Hess, *Premature and Congenitally Diseased Infants* (Philadelphia, PA: Lea and Febiger, 1922), Part I and II, Chapters 5, 6, 7, 8, 9.

12. Lila J. Napier, "Method of Caring for Premature and Underweight Babies at the Lying-In Hospital, New York City," *Bulletin of the Lying-In Hospital of the City of New York* 13 (1927): 132–134; and Hess and Chamberlain, "Premature Infants—A Report of Two Hundred and Sixty-Six Consecutive Cases," 571–584.

13. D.S. Pulford and W.J. Blevins, "Premature Infant, Birth Weight 680 Grams, with Survival," *American Journal of Diseases of Children* 36 (1928): 797–798; Aaron Capper, "The Fate and Development of the Immature and of the Premature Child," *American Journal of Diseases of Children* 35 (February 1928): 262–275; Hess and Chamberlain, "Premature Infants—A Report of Two Hundred and Sixty-Six Consecutive Cases," 571–584; and Aaron Capper, "The Fate and Development of the Immature and of the Premature Child," *American Journal of Diseases of Children* 35 (March 1928): 443–491.

14. Napier, "Method of Caring for Premature and Underweight Babies at the Lying-In Hospital, New York City"; William N. Bradley, "The Care of the Premature Baby," *Medical Journal and Record* 124 (August 18, 1926): 222–225; "Simplifying the Nursing Care for Premature Babies," *Trained Nurse and Hospital Review* LXXVIII (June 1927): 633; and Ralph M. Tyson and Edward F. Burt, "Continuous Temperature Records of Premature Infants," *American Journal of Diseases of Children* 38 (1929): 944–952.

15. Charles Chapple Papers. MSS 2/0207-01, Series 2.2, Folder 5. Historical Collections, College of Physicians, Philadelphia, PA.

16. William P. Buffum and George F. Conde, "The Use of Oxygen in the Care of Feeble Premature Infants," *Journal of Pediatrics* 4 (1934): 326–330. Alexander M. Burgess and Alexander M. Burgess, Jr., "A New Method of Administering Oxygen," *New England Journal of Medicine* 207 (1932): 1078–1082. Burgess and Burgess describe piping oxygen into a box placed over a patient's head. They were able to achieve oxygen concentrations of 40–50 percent. In the case of babies, they advised placing the box completely over the baby.

17. Anne Y. Peebles, "Care of Premature Infants," *American Journal of Nursing* 33 (1933): 866–869; Buffum and Conde, "The Use of Oxygen in the Care of Feeble Premature Infants," 326–330; Daniel A. Wilcox, "A Study of Three Hundred and Thirty Premature Infants," *American Journal of Diseases of Children* 52 (1934): 848–862; and Julius H. Hess, "Premature Infants—A Report of Sixteen Hundred and Twenty-Three Consecutive Cases," *Illinois Medical Journal* 67 (1935): 14–25. Quote is from Hess, 18.

18. Hess and Chamberlain, "Premature Infants—A Report of Two Hundred and Sixty-Six Consecutive Cases," 578–579; Beatrice M. Clutch, "Feeding Premature Infants," *American Journal of Nursing* 25 (1925): 549–550; and D.S. Pulford and Blevins, "Premature Infant, Birth Weight 680 Grams, with Survival," 797–798.

19. Julius H. Hess, *Infant Feeding—A Handbook for the Practitioner* (Chicago: American Medical Association, 1923), 54–63.

20. Marsh W. Poole and Thomas B Cooley, "The Care of Premature Infants," *Journal of Pediatrics* 1 (July 1932): 16–33; E.A. Wagner, "One Year of Prematures at the Cincinnati General Hospital," *Journal of Medicine* 14 (March 1933): 13–16; Peebles, "Care of Premature Infants," 866–869; C.H. Webb, "Concentrated Feedings in the Nutrition of Premature Infants," *Southern Medical Journal* 27 (1934): 608–613; Ralph M. Tyson, "The Problem of the Premature Infant," *New York State Journal of Medicine* 34 (1934) 811–818; Wilcox, "A Study of Three Hundred and Thirty Premature Infants," 848–862; Hess, "Premature Infants—A Report of Sixteen Hundred and Twenty-three Consecutive Cases," 14–23, Harry Lowenburg, "The Management of Premature Infants," *Archives of Pediatrics* 52 (1935): 313–324; and Abraham Tow, "The Care and Feeding of the Premature Infant: With Special Reference to Simple Milk Mixtures," *Medical Clinics of North America* 20 (1936): 951–960. Tyson used Similac at the Lying-In Charity in Philadelphia and Webb mentions the use of SMA in a presentation to the Southern Medical Association in Richmond, Virginia.

21. Tow, "The Care and Feeding of the Premature Infant," 954; Marcus B. Einhorn, "The Premature Infant, A Statistical Study," *New York State Journal of Medicine* 40 (1940): 1380–1384; Thomas M. Lamb, "Factors Influencing the Mortality Rate of Premature Infants," *Brooklyn Hospital Journal* 1 (1939): 69–78; Julius H. Hess, "The Premature Infant—Early General and Feeding Care," *Illinois Medical Journal* 74 (1938): 506–514; L.T. Meiks, "The Premature Infant," *American Journal of Nursing* 37 (1937): 457–462; Evelyn C. Lundeen, "The Premature Infant at Home," *American Journal of Nursing* 37 (1937): 466–470; and "Nursing Care of Newborn Infants, Excerpts from Children's Bureau Publication 292, Standards and Recommendations for Hospital Care of Newborn Infants, Full-Term and Premature," *American Journal of Nursing* 43 (1943): 560–563.

22. Janet Golden, *A Social History of Wet Nursing in America: From Breast to Bottle.* (New York: Cambridge University Press, 1996); Lydia Furman, Gerry Taylor, Nori Minich, and Maureen Hack, "The Effect of Maternal Milk on Neonatal Morbidity of Very Low-Birth-Weight Infants," *Archives of Pediatric and Adolescent Medicine* 157 (2003): 66–71; Sharon Dell and Teresa To, "Breastfeeding and Asthma in Young Children," *Archives of Pediatric and Adolescent Medicine* 155 (2001): 1261–1265; Anne L. Wright and Richard J. Schanler, "The Resurgence of Breastfeeding at the End of the Second Millennium," *Journal of Nutrition* 131 (2001): 421S–425S; and Thomas M. Ball and Anne L. Wright, "Health Care Costs of Formula-Feeding in the First Year of Life," *Pediatrics* 103 (1999): 870–876.

23. Gerald M. Oppenheimer, "Prematurity as a Public Health Problem: US Policy from the 1920s to the 1960s," *American Journal of Public Health* 86 (1996): 870–878.

24. Ethel C. Dunham and Jessie M. Bierman, "The Care of the Premature Infant," *Journal of the American Medical Association*115 (1940): 658–662.

25. Oppenheimer, "Prematurity as a Public Health Problem," 870–879.

26. Hess, "Premature Infants—A Report of Sixteen Hundred and Twenty-Three Consecutive Cases," 1423. Hess reported in 1935 that intracranial hemorrhage was present in over 40 percent of the infants autopsied after death in his unit. Approximately 11 percent of the unit's graduates demonstrated symptoms. Of these sixty-nine were followed and twenty-seven developed physical injuries related to the central nervous system. Nine of the twenty-seven were classified as mentally retarded.

27. T.L. Terry, "Extreme Prematurity and Fibroblastic Overgrowth of Persistent Vascular Sheath behind Each Crystalline Lens, Preliminary Report," *American Journal of Ophthalmology* 25 (1942): 203–204.

28. T.L. Terry, "Fibroblastic Overgrowth of Persistent Tunica Vasculosa Lentis in Premature Infants, Etiologic Factors," *Archives of Ophthalmology* 29 (1943): 54–65; Kate Campbell, "Intensive Oxygen Therapy as a Possible Cause of Retrolental Fibroplasia: A Clinical Approach," *Medical Journal of Australia* 2 (1951): 48–50; V. Mary Crosse and Philip Jameson Evans, "Prevention of Retrolental Fibroplasia," *Archives of Ophthalmology* 48 (1952): 83–87; Arnall Patz, "The Role of Oxygen in Retrolental Fibroplasia," *Pediatrics* 19 (1957): 504–524; Loren P. Guy, Jonathan T. Lanman, and Joseph Dancis, "The Possibility of Total Elimination of Retrolental Fibroplasia by Oxygen Restriction," *Pediatrics* 17 (1956): 247–249; Leroy E. Hoeck and Edgar De La Cruz, "Studies on the Effect of High Oxygen Administration in Retrolental Fibroplasia—Nursery Observations," *American Journal of Ophthalmology* 35 (1952): 1248–1252; and V. Everett Kinsey, "Retrolental Fibroplasia—Cooperative Study of Retrolental Fibroplasia and the Use of Oxygen," *Archives of Ophthalmology* 56 (1956): 481–543. For an overview of the RLF story see William A. Silverman, *Retrolental Fibroplasia: A Modern Parable* (New York: Grune and Stratton, 1980).

29. Patz, "The Role of Oxygen in Retrolental Fibroplasia," 504–524; Mary Ellen Avery and Ella H. Oppenheimer, "Recent Increase in Mortality from Hyaline Membrane Disease," *Journal of Pediatrics* 57 (1960): 553–559; G.C. Robinson, J.E. Jan, and C. Kinnis, "Congenital Ocular Blindness in Children, 1945–1984," *Archives of Pediatrics and Adolescent Medicine* 141(12) (December 1987): 1321–1324; P.B. Campbell, M.J. Bull, F.D. Ellis, C.Q. Bryson, J.A. Lemons, and R.L. Schreiner,"Incidence of Retinopathy of Prematurity in a Tertiary Newborn Intensive Care Unit," *Archives of Ophthalmology* 101(11) (November 1983): 1686–1688; The Committee for the Classification of Retinopathy of Prematurity, "An International Classification of Retinopathy of Prematurity," *Archives of Ophthalmology* 102(8) (August 1984): 1130–1134; D.R. Brown, J.R. Milley, U.J. Ripepe, and A. W. Biglan, "Retinopathy of Prematurity. Risk Factors in a Five-Year Cohort of Critically Ill Premature Neonates," *Archives of Pediatrics and Adolescent Medicine* 141(2) (February 1987): 154–160; Walter M. Fierson, Earl A. Palmer, Albert W. Biglan, John T. Flynn, Robert A. Petersen, and Dale L. Phelps, "Screening Examination of Premature Infants for Retinopathy of Prematurity," *Pediatrics* 100 (1997): 273–274; and Gary C. Brown, Melissa M. Brown, Sanjay Sharma, William Tasman, and Heidi C. Brown, "Cost-Effectiveness of Treatment for Threshold Retinopathy of Prematurity," *Pediatrics* 104 (1999): 47–52.

30. Murdina MacFarquhar Desmond, *Newborn Medicine and Society: European Background and American Practice (1750–1975)* (Austin, TX: Eakin Press, 1998), 170–171, 198.

31. Ibid., 209.

32. Lynn Singer, Toyoko Yamashita, Lawrence Lilien, Marc Collin, and Jill Baley, "A Longitudinal Study of Developmental Outcome of Infants with Bronchopulmonary Dysplasia and Very Low Birth Weight," *Pediatrics* 100(6) (December 1997): 987–993; H.M. Hennes, M.B. Lee, A.A. Rimm, and D.L. Shapiro, "Surfactant Replacement Therapy in Respiratory Distress Syndrome. Meta-Analysis of Clinical Trials of Single-Dose Surfactant Extracts," *Archives of Pediatrics and Adolescent Medicine* 145(1) (January 1991): 102–104; and Rachel M. Schwartz, Anastasia M. Luby, John W. Scanlon, and Russel J. Kellogg, "Effect of Surfactant on Morbidity, Mortality, and Resource Use in Newborn Infants Weighing 500–1500 g," *New England Journal of Medicine* 330(21) (May 26, 1994): 1476–1480.

33. Julius H. Hess, "A City-wide Plan for the Reduction of Deaths Associated with and due to Prematurity," *Journal of Pediatrics* 6 (1935): 104—121; and Cone, *History of the Care and Feeding of the Premature Infant*, 62–63. The American Academy of Pediatrics (AAP) passed their resolution on June 7, 1935, in New York City.

34. Lilly M.S. Dubowitz, Victor Dubowitz, and Cissie Goldberg, "Clinical Assessment of Gestational Age in the Newborn Infant," *Journal of Pediatrics* 77 (July 1970): 1–10.

35. M.C. Haeusler, P. Konstantiniuk, M. Dorfer, and P.A. Weiss, "Amniotic Fluid Insulin Testing in Gestational Diabetes: Safety and Acceptance of Amniocentesis," *American Journal of Obstetrics and Gynecology* 179(4) (1998): 917–920; and M. Kucuk, "Tap Test, Shake Test and Phosphatidylglycerol in the Assessment of Fetal Pulmonary Maturity," *International Journal of Gynaecology and Obstetrics* 60(1) (1998): 9–14.

36. Joyce A. Martin. Brady E. Hamilton, Stephanie J. Ventura, Fay Menacker, and Melissa M. Park, "Births: Final Data for 2000," *National Vital Statistics Report* 50(5) (February 12, 2002): 15–18; and Kathryn A. Sowards, "What Is the Leading Cause of Infant Mortality? A Note of the Interpretation of Official Statistics," *American Journal of Public Health* 89 (1999): 1752–1754.

37. S.E. Jewell and R. Yip, "Increasing Trends in Plural Births in the United States," *Obstetrics and Gynecology* 85(2) (1995): 229–232; Diane Holditch-Davis, Dia Roberts, and Margarete Sandelowski, "Early Parental Interactions with and Perceptions of Multiple Birth Infants," *Journal of Advanced Nursing* 30(1) (1999): 200–210; Robert L. Goldenberg and Dwight J. Rouse, "Prevention of Premature Birth," *New England Journal of Medicine* 339(5) (1998): 313–320; and L.A. Schieve, Herbert B. Peterson, Susan F. Meikle, Gary Jeng, Isabella Danel, Nancy M. Burnett, and Lynne S. Wilcox, "Live-Birth Rates and Multiple-Birth Risk Using In Vitro Fertilization." *Journal of the American Medical Association* 282(19) (1999): 1832–1838.

38. Stephen N. Wall and John Colin Partridge, "Death in the Intensive Care Nursery: Physician Practice of Withdrawing and Withholding Life Support," *Pediatrics* 99(1) (January 1997): 70; Mark Sklansky, "Neonatal Euthanasia: Moral Considerations and Criminal Liability," *Journal of Medical Ethics* 27 (2001): 5–11; and Jaideep Singh, John Lantos, and William Meadow, "End-of-Life After Birth: Death and Dying in a Neonatal Intensive Care Unit," *Pediatrics* 114(6) (December 2004): 1620–1626.

39. Susan Schindehette, "Coming Up Roses," *People Weekly*, December 8, 1997, 54–60; Linda Kulman, "Cigars All Around," *U.S. News and World Report*, December 1, 1997, 14; Michael D. Lemonick and Jeffrey Kluger, "It's A Miracle," *Time*, December

1, 1997, 34–39; John McCormick and Barbara Katrowizt, "The Magnificent Seven," *Newsweek*, December 1, 1997, 58–62; Claudia Kalb, "Families: The Octuplet Question," *Newsweek*, January 11, 1999, 33; and "Question Time," *People Weekly*, January 11, 1999, 72.

40. Baker, *The Machine in the Nursery*, 93–94.

41. Ibid., 86–106; and William A. Silverman, "Incubator-Baby Side Shows," *Pediatrics* 64(2) (1979): 127–141.

42. Jan Bass, "First Infant Incubators in America Premiered in Omaha," *Omaha Magazine*, February 1998, 66.

43. Baker, *The Machine in the Nursery*, 93–94.

44. Ibid., 135; and Bernadine Courtright Barr, "Entertaining and Instructing the Public: John Zahorsky's 1904 Incubator Institute," *Social History of Medicine* 1 (August 1995), 17–36.

45. Barr, "Entertaining and Instructing the Public," 17–36; and John Zahorsky, "The Baby Incubators on the 'Pike.' A Study of the Care of Premature Infants in Incubator Hospitals Erected for Show Purposes." *St. Louis Courier of Medicine* 31(6) (1904): 345–358; 32(2) (1905): 65–80; 32(3) (1905): 152–166, 32(4) (1905): 203–219, 32(5) (1905): 265–275; 32(6) (1905): 334–343, 33(1) (1905): 1–9, 33(2) (1905): 65–71, 33(3) (1905): 137–143, 33(4) (1905): 211–218.

46. Barr, "Entertaining and Instructing the Public," 17—36; Zahorsky, "The Baby Incubators on the 'Pike'"; and Bass, "First Infant Incubators in America Premiered in Omaha," 66; Silverman, "Incubator-Baby Side Shows," 127—141; and Baker, *The Machine in the Nursery*, 86–106.

47. Silverman, "Incubator-Baby Side Shows," 127–141.

48. Arthur Brisbane, "The Incubator Baby and Niagara Falls," *Cosmopolitan*, September 1901, 509–516. Premature babies were compared to Niagara Falls and the forces of nature. Brisbane criticized a mother of a German baby for taking the infant out of the incubator before it was advisable. He described the physician as wise, inferring that the mother should defer to professionals in this situation.

49. Baker, *The Machine in the Nursery*, 97–98.

50. The incubator show in San Francisco was also placed among Midway entertainment. Unlike other shows, this one was free to the public. Information obtained from photocopy of "Plan of Treasure Island—site of Golden Gate International Exposition." Courtesy of Carlberg Jones, San Francisco, CA, and William B. Jones, M.D., Hickory, NC

51. Baker, *The Machine in the Nursery*, 96–99; Silverman, "Incubator-Baby Side Shows," 135; and "Incubator Babies—14 Rescued as Block on Atlantic City Boardwalk Burns," *The New York Times*, July 6, 1927, 8.

52. "A geographical map of the Century of Progress Exposition … faithfully executed and drawn in a carnival spirit by Tony Sarg." The baby incubators were listed first in the list of attractions. Century of Progress Collection, Section 16, Box 13, Folder 16-197, Main Library, Special Collections, University of Illinois at Chicago (hereafter referred to as UIC library); and Century of Progress Collection, Section 16, Box 13, Folder 16-196, UIC library. The building was captured in a picture taken from afar that showed a huge crowd around the building and flowing down the Midway.

53. Official Guidebook, World's Fair, 1934, 109. Century of Progress Collection, Section 16, Box 13, Folder 16-193, UIC library.

54. "Seeing a Century of Progress with the Riggs Reporter," 1933, Riggs Optical Company—Guidebook. Century of Progress Collection, Section 16, Box 13, Folder 16-193, UIC library.

55. Cone, *History of the Care and Feeding of the Premature Infant*, 46–47; and Silverman, "Incubator-Baby Side Shows," 137. Evelyn Lundeen, the head nurse of the premature center at Michael Reese, was interviewed by Silverman before her death in 1963. Despite misgivings about the carnival-like atmosphere, Lundeen praised the care the infants received.

56. Henry L. Woodward and Bernice Gardner, *Obstetric Management and Nursing* (Philadelphia, PA: F.A. Davis Company, 1942), 681; "Nursing Care of Newborn Infants, Excerpts from Children's Bureau Publication 292, Standards and Recommendations for Hospital care of Newborn Infants, Full-Term and Premature"; and Sister Mary Pulcheria Wuellner, "Safe Nursing Care for Premature Babies," *American Journal of Nursing* 39 (November 1939): 1198–1202. Wuellner suggested allowing parents to view their infants through a glass partition.

57. "Tiny Baby Fights to Live," *The New York Times*, December 8, 1932, 44; "1 3/4-Pound Baby Now Normal," *The New York Times*, December 25, 1933, 5; "Baby Weighing 19 Ounces Is Reported Thriving," *The New York Times*, August 14, 1934, 5; "One-Pound Baby Dies," *The New York Times*, November 15, 1934, 12; "Gives Birth to 1 1/2-Pound Baby," *The New York Times*, February 23, 1935, 13; "15-Ounce Baby Fed Now between Meals," *The New York Times*, February 9, 1936, 28; "Baby Weighs Pound 13 Ounces," *The New York Times*, August 2, 1936, 1; "Tiny Hartford Baby Wins Fight for Life," *The New York Times*, December 7, 1936, 3; "One-Pound Baby Girl Fighting for Life," *The New York Times*, March 13, 1937, 21; "28-Ounce Baby Off Whisky Diet," *The New York Times*, March 27, 1937, 17; "Nine-Ounce Infant Loses Bid for Life," *The New York Times*, March 27, 1937, 30; "24-Ounce Baby a New Napoleon," *The New York Times*, August 15, 1937, 24; "24-Ounce Baby Is 'Gaining,'" *The New York Times*, September 12, 1937, 26; "1-Pound, 11-Ounce Baby Lives," *The New York Times*, April 4, 1938, 19; "Tiny Baby Gains Weight," *The New York Times*, May 23, 1938, 19; "Baby of 2 1/4 Pounds Survives," *The New York Times*, July 17, 1938, 2; "21-Ounce Baby Born at Brooklyn Hospital," *The New York Times*, June 18, 1939, 9; "Bellevue Staff Wins Fight for Baby's Life," *The New York Times*, October 8, 1940, 28; "27-Ounce Boy Born in England," *The New York Times*, August 14, 1940, 29; "Race to Save Baby Fails," *The New York Times*, February 17, 1937, 23.

58. Cone, *History of the Care and Feeding of the Premature Infant*, 64–66.

59. *Time*, January 11, 1937, as quoted in Cone, *History of the Care and Feeding of the Premature Infant*, 64.

60. *Million Dollar Babies*. Made for television movie broadcast on CBS, June 1998. Bernard Zuckerman Productions, Cinar Films. Based on the novel *Time of Their Lives—The Dionne Tragedy* by John Nihmey and Stuart Foxman. This movie cast a negative light on the publicity and circus-like atmosphere that sprung up around the quintuplets. The Canadian government and Dr. A.R. Dafoe, the local physician, were blamed for exploiting the quintuplets for profit. The parents' quest to regain custody of their children is dramatized. When the quintuplets were about five years old, they were returned to their parents' care; however their father apparently continued to display them at the request of the government. The last scene of the movie shows the girls performing with him at a war bond rally. The *Saturday Evening Post* (*SEP*) in May 1938 published articles describing Dr. Dafoe and the "miracle" of the quintuplet's birth and survival. Frazier Hunt, "Little Doc," *Saturday Evening Post* 210, May 7, 1938, 18–19, 48,

50, 52–53; 210, May 14, 1938, 18–19, 90, 97–98, 101–102; 210, May 21, 1938, 20–21, 72, 74–75, 77–78; 210, May 28, 1938, 18–19, 34, 36–37, 40; and Associated Press "Once Used by Government, Dionne Quints Recoup a Loss," *Philadelphia Inquirer*, March 7, 1998, 1. The Ontario government paid the three surviving sisters $2.8 million dollars to compensate for the money earned during their eight years on display.

61. Baker, *The Machine in the Nursery*, 105.

62. Jacqueline A. Noonan, "A History of Pediatric Specialties: The Development of Pediatric Cardiology," *Pediatric Research* 56(2) (2004): 298–306; and Robert M. Freedom, James Lock, and J. Timothy Bricker, "Pediatric Cardiology and Cardiovascular Surgery, 1950–2000," *Circulation* 102 (2000): IV-58–IV-68.

63. *American Heart Association*, "Tetralogy of Fallot," 2006, http://www.americanheart.org.

64. Noonan, "A History of Pediatric Specialties," 299–300.

65. Ibid., 302; and Freedom, Lock, and Bricker, "Pediatric Cardiology and Cardiovascular Surgery, 1950–2000," IV-62.

66. Pamela C. Jenkins, Michael F. Flanagan, James D. Sargent, Charles E. Canter, Richard E. Chinnock, Kathy J. Jenkins, Robert N. Vincent, Gerald T. O'Connor, and Anna N.A. Tosteson, "A Comparison of Treatment Strategies for Hypoplastic Left Heart Syndrome Using Decision Analysis," *Journal of the American College of Cardiology* 38(4) (2001): 1181–1187; Sean W. O'Kelly, "Hypoplastic Left Heart Syndrome," *British Medical Journal* 314(7074) (1997): 87; M. Chiavarelli, S.R. Gundry, A.J. Razzouk, and L.L. Bailey, "Cardiac Transplantation for Infants with Hypoplastic Left Heart Syndrome," *Journal of the American Medical Association* 270(24) (1993): 2944–2947; and Charles Canter, David Naftel, Randall Caldwell, Richard Chinnock, Elfriede Pahl, Elizabeth Frazier, James Kirklin, Mark Boucek, and Robert Morrow for the Pediatric Heart Transplant Study, University of Alabama at Birmingham, "Survival and Risk Factors for Death After Cardiac Transplantation in Infants, A Multi-Institutional Study," *Circulation* 96(1) (1997): 227–231.

67. U. Theilen and L. Shederdemian, "The Intensive Care of Infants with Hypoplastic Left Heart Syndrome," *Archives of Disease in Childhood* 90 (2005): 97–102; and Jenkins et al., "A Comparison of Treatment Strategies for Hypoplastic Left Heart Syndrome Using Decision Analysis," 1181–1187.

68. Ibid., 1181; W.D. Caplan, T.R. Cooper, J.A Garcia-Prats, and B.A. Brody, "Diffusion of Innovative Approaches to Managing Hypoplastic Left Heart Syndrome," *Archives of Pediatrics and Adolescent Medicine* 150(1996): 487–490; and Deborah Soetenga and Kathleen A. Mussatto, "Management of Infants with Hypoplastic Left Heart Syndrome. Integrating Research into Nursing Practice," *Critical Care Nurse* 24(2004): 50, 52, 54–56, 58–60, 62–65.

69. H. Dittrich, C. Bührer, I. Grimmer, S. Dittrich, H. Abdul-Khaliq, and P.E. Lange, "Neurodevelopment at 1 Year of Age in Infants with Congenital Heart Disease," *Heart* 89 (2003): 436–441.

70. Cynthia D. Morris, Mark D. Reller, and Victor D. Menashe, "Thirty-Year Incidence of Infective Endocarditis After Surgery for Congenital Heart Defect," *Journal of the American Medical Association* 279(8) (1998): 599–603; Noonan, "A History of Pediatric Specialties," 298–306; and Freedom, Lock, and Bricker, "Pediatric Cardiology and Cardiovascular Surgery, 1950–2000," IV-58–IV-68.

71. Jeffrey H. Kern, Veronica J. Hinton, Hancy E. Nereo, Constance J. Hayes, and Welton M. Gersony, "Early Developmental Outcome After the Norwood Procedure

for Hypoplastic Left Heart Syndrome," *Pediatrics* 102(5) (1998): 1148–1152; Caroline Caroline C. Menache, Adré J. du Plessis, David L. Wessel, Richard A. Jones, and Jane W. Newburger, "Current Incidence of Acute Neurologic Complications After Open-Heart Operations in Children," *Annals of Thoracic Surgery* 73 (2002): 1752–1758; Dittrich et al., "Neurodevelopment at 1 Year of Age in Infants with Congenital Heart Disease"; and Noonan, "A History of Pediatric Specialties," 298–306.

72. Noonan, "A History of Pediatric Specialties," 304; and Morris, Reller, and Menashe, "Thirty-Year Incidence of Infective Endocarditis After Surgery for Congenital Heart Defect," 601–603.

73. Roumiana S. Boneva, Lorenzo D. Botto, Cynthia A. Moore, Quanhe Yang, Adolfo Correa, and J. David Erickson, "Mortality Associated with Congenital Heart Defects in the United States, Trends and Racial Disparities, 1979–1997," *Circulation* 103 (2001): 2376–2381.

The Economics of Infancy

"... the trouble with children is that they are not returnable."
—Quentin Crisp, 1966

In a country where the "impulse buy" is something nearly everyone does on a frequent basis, we still believe that with major purchases we like to take our time, shop around for good deals, compare prices on the Internet, and become informed before putting out a lot of money for a house, car, or vacation. Raising a baby for one year can easily cost more than a car or vacation. Yet, despite the ability to practice reliable birth control, many American babies were conceived by chance and poor and uneducated women were much more likely to experience a mistimed or unwanted pregnancy.[1]

A birth is often celebrated with gifts and purchases of clothes, furniture, food, toys, and other items. Some gifts are wonderful and practical. Others are beautiful and meaningful, but function only as mementos. For many new parents gifts can offset some of the initial cost of having a baby; however once the gifts stop, and the baby grows, the money flows.

By the end of the twentieth century well-prepared parents required a long list of "essential" products to greet the birth of their infant. One particular baby (mine!) was born in 1999. She needed a cradle to sleep in for the first weeks (family heirloom), a crib to sleep in thereafter (approx. $300.00), disposable diapers ($9.00–$11.00 for a package of two to three dozen; required about two

packages a week in the beginning), clothing (prices varied, initial approxima-
tion $100.00 + many gifts), a car seat (approx. $200.00), a stroller (approx.
$150.00), miscellaneous other linens and clothes (prices varied, some gifts),
a baby tub for washing (gift), breast-feeding needs ($40.00 to rent a breast
pump), bottles and formula after breast-feeding failed (formula costs approx.
$25–$30.00 per week in the beginning; bottle costs approx. $50.00), and var-
ious other items including toys and books. Before she was two weeks old we
had gone through more than $1000.00 and that figure does not include hos-
pitalization and medication costs for the birth. Some of these costs could have
been lower. We could have chosen a cheaper crib, although the lowest prices
we saw hovered around $100.00. A stroller could also have been purchased
cheaper, although this one was far from the most expensive model available.
The car seat, diapers, and a few items of clothing were probably the only thing
absolutely necessary for a baby born in July. The car seat is required by law in
all states for any baby riding in an automobile. We were fortunate to receive
many gifts from friends and family that lessened the burden of supplying the
needs and desires of a late twentieth-century baby.

Most American families are able to provide the basic necessities and even
some extras for their babies. While some babies may sleep in custom-made
cribs with the highest quality linens, others do just as well with used furniture
and bargain quality sheets, towels, and clothes. For babies themselves, the
price paid for clothing, surroundings, and toys just does not matter. As long
as they are safe, warm, fed, and dry, they are generally happy. However, there
are some Americans who have never been able to provide even these basic
needs for their babies. There are many private charities, both large and small,
throughout the country that have historically provided families with these
basic needs. Some of these privately run organizations are religion-based while
others are operated by lay people eager to share some of their own riches. Some
examples include the American Red Cross, Catholic Charities, Lutheran World
Relief, America's Second Harvest, and Habitat for Humanity. Smaller, locally
based charities operate in many communities nationwide. In this chapter I
will not attempt to describe the myriad ways private charities helped their
fellow citizens throughout the twentieth century. There are simply too many
groups, some of which operate on a long-term basis while others assemble in
response to specific needs within an individual community. I will examine the
major publicly funded efforts aimed at minimizing or even erasing the effects
of economic hardship on the American baby. These public welfare programs
have become increasingly important in the twentieth century.

Wealth is a relative term. For many people a big house, a fancy car, and exotic vacations signify abundance. For others, a place of shelter and enough food to prevent starvation is all that is needed. Most of us fall somewhere in between these extremes and many of our life choices dictate where we fall in terms of wealth. Babies do not get to choose. Their well-being is in the hands of their parents or guardians. Throughout history babies whose parents had more money generally fared better than those whose parents had less money. Health and illness had distinct ties to wealth—the babies of the poor suffered more frequent, more serious, and more fatal illnesses. During the twentieth century Americans made many attempts to alter this dynamic. Some were successful, others were not. By the end of the century, while all babies were faring better, it was plain that babies of the richest Americans continued to have an easier life than those of the poorest citizens.

Over the course of the twentieth century the United States of America became the economic leader of the world. This happened despite the Great Depression, several other stock market crashes, two world wars and numerous other military conflicts, and the ups and downs of various industries and businesses. The United States was also able to use its economic might to help people around the globe overcome human and natural disasters and modernize societies. At home most, but certainly not all, Americans found their standard of living rising throughout the century, especially in the years after World War II. For young families this often meant job stability for fathers and the ability to provide food, clothing, and education for their children.

The rise of the middle class and increased money available for discretionary spending changed the outlook for all American citizens. As fewer people learned to sew, homemade clothing for anyone, including babies became rare. Layettes, or a set of clothing and blankets specifically for the newborn, were deemed necessary. Cribs, rather than baskets or drawers, were considered the optimal place for an infant to sleep. Prams, once reserved for the offspring of the wealthy, evolved into coaches and strollers as they were adopted by the middle and lower classes. By the late 1990s the brand of stroller and the price paid for it conveyed status or lack thereof on the infant riding inside almost as much as the brand of automobile driven by the infant's parents. The type and amount of toys available for infants is astounding. Toys to promote appropriate development, toys for pure playing, toys to sleep with, toys to chew on, toys for boys, toys for girls, and gender-neutral toys are all available for purchase. Many of the toys seem to be marketed for the amusement of adults because as any parent can attest, babies often prefer to play with the box!

The costs of having and raising a baby in 1901 varied a great deal and depended on many things, including the parents' social class, income level, and geographic area. Maintaining social status was important then as well and certainly some parents considered this when planning for their new baby. First babies were more expensive as parents needed to purchase, borrow, or make all supplies necessary. Climate played a part as well, as those born in colder areas required more warmth.

In 1905 *The New York Times* reported on the cost of clothing a middle class American baby. The story emphasized the need for a baby to "... make an appearance in keeping with its contemporaries." The most important articles of clothing were said to be night slips at $2.50 each, day slips at $4.00 each, flannel skirts at $5.00–$6.00 each, dresses at $5.00–$10.00 each, sacks at $2.00 each, wrappers at $4.00–$12.00 each, and socks at $0.75–$1.50 per pair. Considering that a baby would need more than one of each item the story calls the American baby "an expensive luxury." Even with no brothers and sisters to provide hand-me-down clothing, the story states that "perhaps, anyway, if the baby is to be properly brought up, as an investment for old age, a paid-up policy, the price is not so high after all."[2] Given the *Times'* suggestion of six to eight of each of the garments listed, this layette would cost, using the lower prices for each item, between $139.50 and $186.00. Average income for a middle-class family in 1903 was estimated as approximately $1500.00 and in 1908 as $1800.00.[3] Thus approximately 10 percent of a middle-class family's income would be needed to purchase the recommended items of clothing. Mothers were assured that although the outfitting of the first baby in the family was expensive, the reuse of clothing for subsequent babies would lower the overall cost. In fact, "... a large family [would] cost less in proportion than a small one."[4]

By 1996 the United States Department of Agriculture estimated that the annual cost to families for a child from birth to age two was approximately $5,670.00 for a family with a before-tax income of less than $34,700.00, $7,860.00 when the before-tax income was between $34,700.00 and $58,300.00, and $11,680.00 for families with incomes greater than $58,300.00. In the lowest income group the average salary was $21,600.00. Thus the cost of a baby for this family represented approximately 26 percent of their total yearly income. The middle-income group spent an average of 17 percent of their income and the upper income group spent approximately 13 percent of their income. There are regional differences. Those in urban areas of the West spent the most and those in rural areas spent the least.[5]

An old saying tells us that money cannot buy happiness. While that may be true, money certainly buys many of the necessities of life along with some extras along the way. During the twentieth century American consumer culture developed rapidly, especially after World War II. The line between necessities and extras became blurred and in some cases erased entirely. For babies and their parents separating the truly necessary from the "nice but not an immediate need" became a difficult, if not nearly impossible task.

The economics of infancy is a subject that on the surface appears simple but once the layers are pulled back becomes much more complicated. In an industrialized nation just the process of obtaining food to nourish both mother and baby is often daunting. Breast milk is free, so the pundits say, so why would economics interfere? But as we know, the quality and quantity of breast milk is dependent on a mother who is well-nourished herself. Food for the mother requires money and thus a steady income. Society often looks down on a mother who returns to work shortly after the birth of her baby, but at the same time often condemns those who require financial assistance. By the 1930s, after several aborted attempts to assist the poor, the severe economic depression pushed the federal government to permanently enter the field of financial assistance for destitute families.

GOVERNMENTAL INTERVENTIONS

Early in the twentieth century parents had a baby and generally supported it themselves. Perhaps they received monetary help from relatives or in desperate situations from local charitable organizations. Some local governments supported almshouses for the poor and destitute but babies were usually not welcome in them. A few public, private, and church-affiliated infant asylums were located in some of the major cities and accepted babies unwanted or abandoned by their parents. These institutions were not hospitals and while they were originally set up with good intentions, some quickly deteriorated and in many the mortality rate for abandoned infants exceeded 50 percent.[6] Lying-in hospitals for poor mothers were found in most major American cities in the nineteenth century. They existed into the twentieth century until acute care hospitals assumed responsibility for the delivery of most babies. In Philadelphia the Lying-In Charity for Attending Indigent Women in Their Homes opened in 1832 and by the early twentieth century became a maternity hospital for the poor. In 1923 it associated with Pennsylvania Hospital, the nation's first hospital. This institution and others like it provided free care and moral guidance for those single women "led astray." These hospitals invited missionaries to visit mothers and their babies and assumed a paternalistic attitude toward single mothers. Other lying-in hospitals only grudgingly, and for purely financial reasons admitted unmarried women. Many babies born in lying-in hospitals were placed in foster care or adopted and their mothers hired to serve as wet nurses for babies of more affluent families.[7]

The economic difficulties faced by many mothers were easily ignored by the middle and upper classes in the United States until Progressive Era reformers, riding the success of environmental reforms, took notice during the 1900s. By 1909 they garnered attention from the highest levels of government with the White House Conference on Dependent Children. The U.S. Children's Bureau was a direct result of this conference. During the 1910s some states passed laws granting pensions to mothers who had lost their husbands, most often to death but also to prison or mental institutions. In 1921 the Sheppard–Towner Act was passed by Congress as a result of reform efforts and although it was not renewed in 1929 it did set the stage for the inclusion of infant and child welfare in the reform initiatives of President Roosevelt's administration during the depths of the Great Depression. In the 1950s private companies began to pay for health insurance for their employees which led to increased access to health care for those babies whose fathers held jobs in a participating business. In the 1960s the civil rights movement helped bring about President Johnson's War on Poverty. Medical care, thanks to Medicaid, was provided for infants whose parents were unable to afford it. The rising cost of living along with changing roles for women and single women who no longer routinely gave their babies up for adoption led to more mothers working and needing infant day care. All of these issues have had a significant impact on American babies and will be discussed below.

MOTHER'S PENSIONS

By the turn of the twentieth century it was apparent in the United States that official policies requiring the break up of families because of poverty were bad policies. In 1909 the first White House Conference on Children represented the culmination of efforts by influential women social workers and Progressive reformers to bring official attention to the needs of infants and children. Politically the time was right for the cause as President Theodore Roosevelt was eager to expand the federal government's role in protecting children's lives.

The idea for mother's pensions in the early twentieth century rose out of concern that infants' and children's health and well-being suffered when the family income was lost. Often this happened when the male head of the family died, or for reasons ranging from imprisonment to mental illness and abandonment, could not or would not financially support his wife and children. The "ideal" family as depicted by middle-class reformers consisted of a working father and a mother who did not work and whose main job was the maintenance of a suitable home and the care and upbringing of the children. Many widowed or deserted mothers had to work to maintain even a basic standard of living. In the late nineteenth century well-intentioned reformers, believing that minor children left home alone or with inappropriate caregivers would grow into a life of crime, took the impoverished children from their homes and placed them in institutions or in foster care. When impoverished mothers could not prove their ability to provide for their children, their youngsters were often placed for adoption with new families. While these actions were taken in the best interests of the children, there were obvious problems. The children suffered not only the loss of their fathers, but were forced to give up their mothers as well. Often siblings were separated and sent to distant places. In 1909 the White House Conference on Children declared foster care more suitable than institutional placement for impoverished babies and young children. While many foster families were loving and nurturing, some were found wanting. In some situations fraud was a problem—some families received subsidies for caring for foster children yet spent little of it on these children. It was also difficult to find enough homes in which to place needy children. Thanks to these criticisms and new theories of child development that focused on the role of mothers, reformers began to push for care of children in their own homes. For "deserving" women and their legitimate children, payment in the form of a pension could keep the children at home with enough money for food and shelter. In addition, pensions that kept mothers out of the workforce were popular with those in the middle and upper classes who objected to women working at all. Pensions eliminated the need to pay institutions or foster parents, both of which were more costly options. Viewed at times as pensions, grants in aid, or payment for services otherwise paid by the court system to third parties, the idea grew and in 1911 Illinois was the first state to pass a law enacting the policy.[8]

By 1913 nineteen states had passed laws enacting mothers' pensions and by 1921 nearly all states and the territories of Alaska and Hawaii had passed similar legislation.[9] However, pensions were not universal. Participation by counties within a state was optional. Eligibility rules and the amount of compensation provided varied greatly. Applicants were expected to adhere to residency rules (they had to reside one to five years in the locality in which they applied for a pension), and either be citizens or apply for citizenship. State and county law and social workers' discriminatory practices resulted in more aid distributed to widows than to unmarried, deserted, or divorced women. Widows of skilled and professional men received more aid than widows of unskilled men. In some areas, native-born white women with Northern European ancestry were more likely to receive aid than immigrants from Mexico and Southern and Eastern Europe. African-American women were less likely to receive aid than white women in some states, while in others they were not eligible at all. Even those who met eligibility requirements could lose part or all of their pensions if investigators determined their home or their child rearing abilities were unsuitable. In many states, work requirements soon appeared when funding sources dried up and fear of cheating caused early proponents of the pensions to change their views on mothers staying at home. Many states allowed outside work; some required it. Generally, mother's pension recipients were expected to work just three days a week to allow for appropriate time at home with their children. Still, the pensions, along with wages, often did not cover the expenses of a mother and her children living in the twentieth century. Mother's pension recipients remained dependent on family and other forms of charity.[10]

The requirements of the mothers' pensions programs highlighted the difficulties faced by the working and lower class mothers and their offspring. Among the middle class motherhood was revered and the image of the self-sacrificing mother was widespread. Many reformers and those in charge of mothers' pensions typically came from the middle class and often pushed their own beliefs and biases on those they were trying to help. The concept of the program was a good one, but too many were excluded from it because they did not meet white middle-class standards. Many poor mothers and babies did not get pensions because of their marital status, ancestry, race, or their methods of keeping house and raising their children. Sadly, even those who received aid usually found it insufficient in amount.

THE U.S. CHILDREN'S BUREAU

Lillian Wald, a nurse, and Florence Kelley, a college-educated woman, were the catalysts behind the 1909 White House Conference on Dependent Children and the subsequent establishment of the U.S. Children's Bureau. Wald is famous for her pioneering efforts with the urban poor in New York

City. Kelley, whose background includes leftist political connections, marriage and separation, and children who were boarded out, was the paid executive for the National Consumers' League for more than thirty years.[11] Both women came to the cause of infant and child welfare through their work with poor and destitute women, many of whom were also mothers. Wald, Kelly, and their supporters viewed child and women's welfare as one and the same—mothers were responsible for the children and thus women's welfare was "inextricably connected to that of their children."[12]

The Children's Bureau, first proposed in 1903 and authorized as a governmental entity in 1912, was initially a political compromise. Those who objected to the formation of the bureau worried that it would lead to the prohibition of child labor or interfere with states' rights and/or the rights of the individual and of parents. Acknowledging the poor health and overall well-being of many of the nation's children, the Congress created the Bureau because, as historian Kriste Lindenmeyer points out, while they "... found it easy to ignore the problems of children, it was difficult for them to actually vote against babies and children" especially in a presidential election year. Julia Lathrop, the first chief of the Children's Bureau, decided on infant mortality as the first major issue the new bureau would address.[13]

The Children's Bureau first engaged in fact-finding and in providing advice to mothers. Statistics collected by the bureau revealed that there was indeed an infant mortality crisis in the country. While high rates of infant death had been acknowledged in medical and social welfare circles, infant mortality had never been analyzed in a systematic manner. When mothers wrote to the Children's Bureau for advice and assistance, Bureau personnel also collected many firsthand accounts of the struggles of poor families.[14] The staff of the bureau compiled statistics on many aspects of infant life and noted the large difference in infant death rates between those born to rich families and those born to poor families. An impoverished baby was twice as likely as a well-off one to die in infancy or childhood.[15] These statistics painted a grim picture of infant life in the United States and led the Children's Bureau to call directly for intervention on a national scale.

SHEPPARD–TOWNER ACT

The Sheppard–Towner Act of 1921 was the culmination of reform efforts begun late in the nineteenth century and continued under the auspices of the

Children's Bureau in the 1910s. By the late 1910s it was obvious that the poor health of many of the nation's mothers and children required some form of intervention. Senator Morris Sheppard of Texas, along with his colleague in the House of Representatives, Horace Towner, introduced the Maternity and Infancy Act. Proponents of the bill included infant welfare workers, various women's groups, and mothers in general who saw hope not only for their babies but for themselves. One of the arguments used by the women to support the bill was the fact that during World War I the number of women who died in childbirth was similar to that of soldiers killed in battle. In addition, many potential recruits for that war had been found unfit for service due to the lasting effects of infant and childhood illnesses. Women had also achieved victory in their battle to vote and some believe that the fear of women using their new franchise to vote out of office politicians opposing Sheppard–Towner Act ultimately ensured its passage. Despite opposition from the American Medical Association (AMA) and conservative politicians who believed it would lead the country into socialism, the Act passed both houses of Congress and was signed into law by President Warren G. Harding on November 23, 1921.[16]

Like many bills enacted by Congress before and since, the Sheppard–Towner Act was pared down from its original format. It provided federal matching grants to states for health education programs aimed at improving the health of babies, children, and mothers. States were given the right to turn down the money although forty-one out of forty-four states eventually did take their share of funds. The yearly appropriation to states was cut by more than half that originally requested and a five-year limit on funding was included. Instruction of individuals and groups in infant and child care, distribution of printed literature to mothers, teachers, and midwives, development of standards and procedures for maternity homes, and collection of data about maternal and infant morbidity and mortality were the major tasks undertaken with Sheppard–Towner funding. Although individual states varied somewhat in the manner in which they carried out the activities, the general focus on the prevention of infant and maternal morbidity and mortality was the same.[17]

There are many reasons cited for the ultimate demise of the Sheppard–Towner Act and most deal at least indirectly with money. It was initially passed as a temporary measure and as such needed to be renewed on a regular basis. This required ongoing political lobbying and debating within the halls of Congress. Physicians, and their increasingly powerful professional organization, the AMA, campaigned vigorously for the Act's defeat in the late 1920s. Specialty practice in the fields of obstetrics and pediatrics continued to grow and many practitioners began to view health education and preventative programs as the purview of the physician. Obstetricians were in the process of transforming childbirth from a home to hospital event. Pediatricians were also increasing their involvement with babies and children, in the hospital and in the community. Public health nurses, who in many cases ran the health education and prevention agencies funded by Sheppard–Towner, were not permitted to treat sick patients. The nurses referred them to physicians. Yet nevertheless physicians often viewed the Sheppard–Towner nurses as potential competitors in the increasingly lucrative practice of medicine. Thus physicians who once disdained preventive care claimed it as their own and accused the government of intruding on their abilities to diagnose, treat, and cure patients. By financing the agencies set up under the auspices of the Sheppard–Towner Act, the government was also accused by the AMA of limiting individual physicians' abilities to earn an appropriate salary.[18]

Another formidable opponent was the Roman Catholic Church which ran and financed many charitable organizations similar to those set up by Sheppard–Towner. Fear of increasing federal intrusions into family lives led most Church leaders to oppose the Act's renewal. Political realities added to the problems faced by the proponents of the Act. By the mid-1920s the number of fiscal conservatives in Congress had increased and none were interested in maintaining or increasing funding for the program. The Revenue Act of 1926 had given the conservatives a taste of victory in their battle to decrease government spending and promote a capitalist economy. Lingering fears of socialism from the post–World War I years also strengthened the arguments of conservatives who no longer felt a political need to assuage women voters.[19]

In the end Sheppard–Towner was not defeated; it was allowed to expire on June 30, 1929. The House of Representatives did not pass the measures necessary for additional funding and a filibuster in the Senate prevented debate on the floor.

Sheppard–Towner had many positive outcomes. Most importantly, infant mortality decreased significantly. Families reached by Sheppard–Towner programs received up-to-date health and child care information. Well baby checkups reassured many mothers that their infants were developing normally. The checkups also identified other babies with health problems and referred them, perhaps earlier than otherwise would have happened, for appropriate care. Early attention to developmental or medical problems is extremely important to the future well-being of an infant. The number of babies dying from gastrointestinal diseases (the number one cause of infant death in the United

States at the time) plummeted almost 50 percent. Financially the Sheppard–Towner Act did provide a precedent for increasing governmental involvement in women and children's health.

However, in other respects the Act was a failure. The Children's Bureau and other reformers had sought to improve the lives of all women and children. They campaigned for legislation that would ensure education, financial assistance, and physical care regardless of the ability to pay. Dependent on Congress to pass laws the Children's Bureau and other reformers settled for an inadequately funded program that did provide much needed information to mostly rural families but failed to provide the means necessary to permanently improve the lives and well-being of all the nation's women, infants, and children.[20] The advent of the Great Depression shortly after the Act's demise once again focused attention on women and infants. When the Roosevelt administration sought means of providing a financial "safety net" for families faced with economic devastation, they could hardly ignore the babies.

SOCIAL SECURITY

The Great Depression of the 1930s hit Americans hard. Lost jobs, wiped out savings accounts, and grim prospects for the future cast many families into poverty and despair. When Franklin D. Roosevelt was elected president in 1932 he promised Americans a "New Deal" to prevent the destitution that so many experienced after the stock market crash of 1929. The Social Security Act of 1935 would be part of the answer. Initially designed as a safety net for senior citizens, it eventually evolved into a plan with something for nearly everyone considered needy. Over the years the definition of needy, and the amount of support available varied, but the program itself continued and expanded.[21]

Two major portions of the Social Security Act dealt with infants and children. Title IV provided grants to states for aid to dependent children and Title V provided grants to states for maternal and child welfare programs. Throughout the rest of the century both of these portions of the Social Security Act would be amended, added to, and changed. In 1996 Title IV was substantially changed to redefine the eligibility rules and provide time limits for federal assistance. Both Title IV and Title V still exist today.

Under Title IV, initially labeled Aid to Dependent Children (ADC), and later Aid to Families with Dependent Children (AFDC), states would administer monetary payments to mothers of dependent children in all parts of the state. No localities could opt out as happened with mothers' pensions. The federal government provided matching grants to the states to fund the program. Initial payments for dependent children were not to exceed $18.00 per month for the first child in a family and $12.00 per month for each additional child. Dependent children were defined as under age sixteen and "deprived of parental support or care by reason of the death, continued absence from the home, or physical or mental incapacity of a parent . . ."[22]

Title IV represented a continuation of the concept of mothers' pensions. Within three years national regulations allowed it to reach more than double the number of children reached by mothers' pensions. However, a lower amount of money was assigned to children than to any other groups covered by the Social Security Act including the needy aged and the needy blind. Eligibility was determined by the individual states. Mothers often found it necessary to work, as the amount of assistance provided through AFDC was inadequate in most cases to make ends meet. Working mothers were penalized however as their earnings were then deducted from the amount of assistance they received. A man living in the home of an AFDC mother and children was assumed to be supporting them. Thus the home became unsuitable and aid to the mother and children could be denied. Southern states also found ways to discriminate against and deny assistance to both African-American and Mexican-American mothers and their children.[23]

During the second half of the twentieth century politicians, lobbyists, social workers, and private citizens spent a great deal of time on the topic of welfare reform. For some the problem was too much governmental assistance to families. For others it was not enough. At some point though most citizens could agree that babies and children suffered when their parents lived in poverty. It was also apparent to most people that what began in the 1930s as an attempt to help people survive a serious economic depression had become a program by the 1960s that was beset by bureaucratic red tape, confusing rules, and contradictory policies. It is not within the scope of this book to detail all the issues surrounding welfare programs in the United States. However two events, thirty years apart, did result in significant changes to the welfare programs for babies.

When President Lyndon Johnson initiated the "War on Poverty" in 1964 he hoped to ensure that all Americans would have enough to eat and a place to sleep at night. Medicare for the elderly helped to ease the expense of growing old while Medicaid helped the youngest citizens, among others, receive basic health care. Medicaid insured that the advances in medicine such as immunizations and antibiotics reached the poor as well as the rich and thus played an important part in the decline in many previously debilitating and fatal childhood diseases. Programs such as Head Start for young children, and food stamps for those unable to afford adequate food, were created and helped lower the poverty level in the United States by the 1970s.

By the 1990s calls for major reform to the welfare system were loud and constant. In 1996, President Bill Clinton signed the Personal Responsibility and Work Opportunity Reconciliation Act (Welfare Reform Act). This legislation set up the Temporary Assistance for Needy Families (TANF) program which replaced AFDC and a job and basic skills program. TANF's major purposes include providing assistance so that children can remain in their own homes, promoting and requiring job preparation and work, promoting marriage and two-parent families, and preventing out-of-wedlock pregnancies. One significant change, aimed specifically at chronic welfare users, was the imposition of a five-year time limit for federally funded assistance to families. The law also imposes residency and educational requirements on minor parents in exchange for eligibility for aid.[24] The impact of these changes on babies is yet to be fully understood.

FOOD STAMPS AND WIC

Two other federally funded programs that have had direct economic effects on babies are Women, Infants, and Children (WIC) and food stamps. The food stamp program began in the 1930s as part of the New Deal but was relatively small until 1970 when Congress expanded the program and relaxed eligibility rules. WIC began in 1974 and is a federal grant program dependent on annual funding authorizations by Congress. Both programs are aimed at eliminating hunger and malnutrition. Breast-feeding mothers are able to buy nourishing food that helps maintain the quantity and quality of their breast milk. Infant formula is also available through these programs. WIC targets low-income women and children deemed to be nutritionally at risk. Pregnant women, breast-feeding mothers up to the baby's first birthday, non-breast-feeding women until the baby is six months old, infants and children up to age five are eligible if they meet the financial, residential, and nutritional criteria. In addition to nutritious food, WIC provides clinics where mothers and babies receive education and counseling as well as health screenings and referrals to medical and social services as appropriate. Mothers must apply for WIC and be certified. Recertification is done every six months. Food stamps are available to all people meeting the eligibility criteria, including older children, men, and women of all ages. There are work requirements as well as income standards.[25]

There are problems associated with both programs. While the majority of people receiving WIC and/or food stamps can be expected to abide by the rules and regulations pertinent to the programs, there are always some who seek to take advantage of them. However, the long-term benefits of these programs for babies and children must be weighed against the instances of fraud. Babies and children fed nutritionally sound diets grow better, learn better, and are more likely to become wage-earning adults who have the ability to provide for themselves.

Title V of the Social Security Act passed in 1935 effectively reinstated many of the provisions of the ill-fated Sheppard–Towner Act. Money was to be used to run a specific agency or bureau for child hygiene, and for "demonstrations, conferences, and examinations." As with Sheppard–Towner, infants or children were to be referred for definitive treatment of identified medical problems. Title V did not attempt to cover all women and children. It focused on the poor and disadvantaged. The medical profession received the authority to determine the appropriate health promotion activities. State and local medical groups were given the right to review and accept or reject all plans under Title V which helped suppress the kind of opposition that helped kill Sheppard–Towner. The success of the Social Security Act prompted the Children's Bureau to lobby, during the late 1930s, for increased funding for mothers and infants before and after birth. In 1938 a National Health Bill was introduced by Senator Robert Wagner of New York. It sought to improve medical care in general through the construction of new health care institutions and through the provision of health and disability insurance. The AMA strongly opposed this bill and successfully prevented it from ever reaching the floor of the Senate. Title V received additional funding in the Social Security Act amendment of 1939 without any additional provisions for care.[26]

Throughout the rest of the century the idea of national, or universal, health care coverage was resurrected on an irregular basis. Steady and strong resistance on the part of the AMA and many private insurance companies was always present. Attempts to introduce legislation on the matter were thwarted. The last major attempt to introduce universal health care occurred in 1993 when President Bill Clinton appointed a committee to formulate a plan. The plan was not voted on by the Congress and the attempt failed.

PRIVATE MEDICAL INSURANCE

By the 1950s many major American businesses offered health insurance plans to their employees. Initially many plans were free of charge to the employee and their immediate family members. Blue Cross and Blue Shield are the most well-known plans and have paid for countless doctor visits, hospitalizations, surgeries, medicines, and other medical needs. In the 1980s Health Maintenance Organizations (HMOs) appeared in an effort to halt the ever-increasing medical care costs. HMOs emphasized prevention and forced traditional insurance companies to do likewise. The costs of medical care continued to spiral upward however and many employers found it impossible to continue to offer the insurance for free. Employees began to pay some of the premiums and also were asked to pay money upfront, a co-payment, when visiting doctors or hospitals. Even with these changes some employers found insurance to be prohibitively expensive and dropped their programs. Purchasing private health insurance individually was financially impossible for many families, even those who made too much money to qualify for Medicaid. An increasing segment of the American population therefore lived without the means to provide even basic medical care to their families. For babies this situation was critical.

Children's Health Insurance Programs (CHIP)

As the cost of health care spiraled upward, the number of uninsured and underinsured Americans continually increased. Parents who were ineligible for Medicaid or unable to pay for their own health care insurance premiums were often forced to put off routine health checkups and preventive care for their babies and children. When the children became sick, their parents often waited to seek medical care until the illness was more serious and thus harder, and more expensive to treat. While universal health care for all citizens had been repeatedly rejected in the United States once again babies and children were singled out for specific help.

In 1997 the Social Security Act was amended once again. Title XXI, State Children's Health Insurance Programs (CHIP) established low-cost insurance programs designed to cover children up to age eighteen (nineteen in some areas). Federal grants provide financial assistance to states meeting program requirements. A variety of outpatient and inpatient services for children are covered and though details differ by state, many are quite similar and all must adhere to federal guidelines. In Pennsylvania, immunizations, routine check-ups and screenings, prescription medicines, emergency care, up to ninety days of hospitalization per year, mental health care, substance abuse treatment, rehabilitation, and home health care are all covered. Qualified families receive CHIP free or for a prorated monthly payment. There are no deductibles and no co-payments. Families qualify based on the number of household members and the total household income.[27]

These programs are available in all states and help assure that babies and children are receiving the recommended preventive care as well as illness and injury treatment. While many state plans are termed simply CHIP, others have different names such as Kids Connection in Nebraska, ALL Kids in Alabama and Illinois, hawk-i in Iowa, Denali KidCare in Alaska, and PeachCare for Kids in Georgia.[28]

WORKING MOTHERS, SINGLE MOTHERS, AND THE AVAILABILITY OF DAY CARE

Mothers have always worked and for many the term "working mothers" is an oxymoron. In contemporary usage it is defined as mothers who work outside the home, for pay. As discussed above, these mothers have been both praised and condemned. Mothers who work to keep their families off the welfare roles are praised for that, but criticized for leaving their babies and children to be cared for by others. Single mothers who work are criticized for the same things, and for getting themselves in the situation requiring such work and day care in the first place. On the other hand poor mothers who do stay home with the children and rely on state and federal assistance programs are condemned for their perceived laziness. These issues have surfaced repeatedly throughout the twentieth century. The availability of adequate, if not nurturing, day care has also been an ongoing problem for mothers for many years.

Early in the century increasing industrialization drew women out of the home to factories, shops, and offices. Many of these women worked due to financial necessity. For poor women everywhere there were few day care options and those that were available catered to children two years of age and older. Babies were more of a problem. They required more attention than did older children and hence more day care workers. Baby care increased the cost of day care dramatically. Mothers of babies were forced to rely on relatives or friends to care for their infants, or the mothers themselves had to work at home. In most cases, a new mother without access to day care lost her job, which obviously affected the family's economic status. The middle and upper classes often hired nurses or nannies to care for babies in the home thus allowing the mothers to do work for pay or, more commonly, volunteer work. During World War II the federal government, realizing that children were being left alone at home while their mothers worked in war production, set up some day care centers. Once again those children under two were generally excluded.[29]

During the last third of the century society continued to idealize the stay-at-home mother although more and more mothers chose to work outside the home. Day care centers sprung up around the country and state regulations began to standardize the number and qualifications of caregivers. In addition many day care centers began to take infants, although most regulated the age at which they would accept an infant. While some accepted babies as young as two to four weeks of age, others required them to be several months old. Other options for infant day care included nonprofessional baby sitters who may or may not have been certified to care for other people's children, grandparents or other relatives, and nannies or governesses. Most options require payment and mothers must weigh family income against infant care costs. Routine colds and stomach upsets play havoc with any child care routine and often force a parent (often the mother) to take a day off from work, many times without pay.[30]

The expense to the family for day care continued to vary from nothing for a grandparent or other family members to a significant percentage of the family's income for high quality day care or a nanny. The quality of day care varied across the country according to the economic status of the area and the availability of workers or volunteers. Nonetheless, infant day care remained an expensive proposition and for many mothers was simply prohibitive. Unable to make enough money to pay the day care expenses, they decided to, or were forced to, stay home. Large companies in the 1990s began to see this as a problem when highly educated and trained women professionals left the workforce. A few built on-site day care centers, or drop-in centers for sick children, providing another option for their employees. Some of these new centers were free or substantially discounted in cost; others charged similar costs as traditional day care centers.[31]

CONCLUSIONS

During the twentieth century the economic realities of having babies became much more visible in America. For the poorest of families it was this acknowledgement of expenses associated with babies that perhaps made the most difference. Governmental assistance that began as "stop-gap" programs became permanent and in the eyes of some, troublesome entitlement issues. Many of these programs have helped babies considerably. Monetary assistance has allowed access to adequate housing, while access to health care and nutritional assistance programs have saved many infant lives and prevented debilitating illnesses. Increases in the number and quality of day care options have helped parents maintain economic stability for their families. Such programs were not available in 1901 and most did not assume a currently recognizable character until the 1960s. Most government welfare programs have had problems, both real and perceived. Fraud, inadequate funding, poor oversight, and other charges have all been made against welfare programs that aid babies and their mothers. Many of these charges are based in fact while others are due to a lack of understanding or knowledge of the programs. Changes to welfare in the 1990s have attempted to address these problems while not ignoring the true needs of the babies. For the middle and upper classes babies have become even more expensive as parents compete to provide the latest "necessities" for their offspring. Ironically, this competition may have increased the distance between poor and middle-class babies despite the general improvement in the lives of poor babies.

Yes, babies are expensive. But do babies really need three hundred thread count crib sheets to sleep on or sterling silver cups to drink from? No, but they do need enough food to eat, a place to sleep, and someone to love them and keep them warm. While the majority of American babies were able to receive these things from their parents at the end of the twentieth century, some continued to want. As a society that routinely celebrates babies, the United States continued to struggle to develop a way to routinely help those babies whose parents were unable to provide such basic necessities. It is a difficult problem, and complicated by factors such as race and immigration status which will be discussed in the following chapters.

NOTES

1. Lawrence B. Finer and Stanley K. Henshaw, "Disparities in Rates of Unintended Pregnancy in the United States, 1994 and 2001," *Perspectives on Sexual and Reproductive Health* 38(2) (2006): 90–96.

2. "Cost of the American Baby," *The New York Times*, March 26, 1905.

3. Scott Derks, *Working Americans. Volume II: The Middle Class* (Lakeville, CT: Grey House Publishing, 2000), 53, 71.

4. "Cost of the American Baby."

5. Mark Lino, "Expenditures on Children by Families, 1996 Annual Report," U.S. Department of Agriculture, Center for Nutrition Policy and Promotion, Miscellaneous Publication No. 1528–1996, May 1997.

6. Janet Golden, "Introduction," in Janet Golden, ed., *Infant Asylums and Children's Hospitals—Medical Dilemmas and Developments 1850–1920* (New York: Garland Publishing, Inc., 1989); John Zahorsky, "The Baby Incubators on the Pike. A Study of the Care of Premature Infants in Incubator Hospitals Erected for Show Purposes," *St. Louis Courier of Medicine* 32(1) (1905): 1–13; and Janet Golden, *A Social History of Wet Nursing in America, From Breast to Bottle* (Cambridge: Cambridge University Press, 1996), 107–127.

7. Charles E. Rosenberg, *The Care of Strangers: The Rise of America's Hospital System* (Baltimore, MD: Johns Hopkins University Press, 1987), 267–271; Philadelphia Lying-In Hospital, *Annual Reports, 1926, 1928–1941*, Pennsylvania Hospital Archives, Philadelphia, PA; and Golden, *A Social History of Wet Nursing in America*, 87–90.

8. Molly Ladd-Taylor, *Mother-Work: Women, Child Welfare, and the State, 1890–1930* (Urbana, IL: University of Chicago Press, 1994), 135–139; Patricia S. Hart, "A Nation's Need for Adoption and Competing Realities: The Washington Children's Home Society, 1895–1915," in E. Wayne Carp, ed., *Adoption in America—Historical Perspectives* (Ann Arbor: University of Michigan Press, 2002), 140–159; Geraldine Youcha, *Minding the Children: Child Care in America from Colonial Times to the Present* (New York: Scribner, 1995), 276–278, 284–285; and Michael B. Katz, *In the Shadow of the Poorhouse: A Social History of Welfare in America* (New York: Basic Books, 1986), 128–129.

9. Kriste Lindenmeyer, "*A Right to Childhood*," in *The U.S. Children's Bureau and Child Welfare, 1912–1946* (Urbana, IL: University of Chicago Press, 1997), 154. By 1931 all states had pension laws except Georgia and South Carolina.

10. Lindenmeyer, "*A Right to Childhood*," 152–157; Ladd-Taylor, *Mother-Work*, 148–159; Steven Mintz, *Huck's Raft: A History of American Childhood* (Cambridge, MA: Belknap Press of Harvard University Press, 2004), 179–180; Bobbie Green Turner, *Federal/State Aid to Dependent Children Program and Its Benefits to Black Children in America, 1935–1985* (New York: Garland Publishing, Inc., 1993), 57–60; and Katz, *In the Shadow of the Poorhouse*, 129.

11. Linda Gordon, *Pitied but Not Entitled* (New York: Free Press, 1994), 88–90; and Ladd-Taylor, *Mother-Work*, 76–77. For more on Florence Kelley, see Kathryn Kish Sklar, *Florence Kelley and the Nation's Work: The Rise of Women's Political Culture, 1830–1900* (New Haven, CT: Yale University Press, 1997).

12. Gordon, *Pitied but Not Entitled*, 91; and Ladd-Taylor, *Mother-Work*, 80, 82, 88.

13. Lindenmeyer, "*A Right to Childhood*," 9–26, 30–31, 35–37.

14. Mothers wrote many thousands of letters a year to the Children's Bureau during the first two decades of its existence. For an in-depth look and analysis of the letters see Molly Ladd-Taylor, *Raising a Baby the Government Way, Mothers' Letters to the Children's Bureau, 1915–1932* (New Brunswick, NJ: Rutgers University Press, 1986).

15. Lindenmeyer, *"A Right to Childhood,"* 42–51; and Joseph M. Hawes, *Children between the Wars: American Childhood, 1920–1940* (New York: Twayne Publishers, 1997), 51–53.

16. Lindenmeyer, *"A Right to Childhood,"* 80–81; Richard A. Meckel, *Save the Babies—American Public Health Reform and the Prevention of Infant Mortality, 1850–1929* (Ann Arbor: University of Michigan Press, 1990), 200–211; and Ladd-Taylor, *Mother-Work*, 170–174.

17. Lindenmeyer, *"A Right to Childhood,"* 94–100. The three states that did not accept funding were Connecticut, Illinois, and Massachusetts. All three did, however, expand their own efforts on behalf of women and children.

18. Lindenmeyer, *"A Right to Childhood,"* 100–101; Katz, *In the Shadow of the Poorhouse*, 143–145; and Meckel, *Save the Babies*, 215–218.

19. Lindenmeyer, *"A Right to Childhood,"* 102–103; Ladd-Taylor, *Mother-Work*, 188; and Meckel, *Save the Babies*, 214–219.

20. Ladd-Taylor, *Mother-Work*, 186–190; Lindenmeyer, *"A Right to Childhood,"* 103–107; and Meckel, *Save the Babies*, 218–219.

21. Mintz, *Huck's Raft*, 233–236.

22. Social Security Act of 1935, Sections 402 (a), 403 (a), and 406 (a & b), Public Law 74–271.

23. Ladd-Taylor, *Mother-Work*, 197–198; and Gordon, *Pitied but Not Entitled*, 275–277, 293–299; Lindenmeyer, *"A Right to Childhood,"* 194–195; and James T. Patterson, *America' Struggle against Poverty in the Twentieth Century* (Cambridge, MA: Harvard University Press, 2000), 65–68.

24. Office of Family Assistance (OFA), "Fact Sheet," *U.S. Department of Health & Human Services, Administration for Children & Families* (Washington, DC, August 2004), http://www.acf.hhs.gov/opa/gact_sheets/tanf_printable.html.

25. Joshua Winicki, Dean Jolliffe, and Craig Gundersen, "How Do Food Assistance Programs Improve the Well-Being of Low-Income Families?" *Food Assistance and Nutrition Research Report* 26(9) (October 2002): 1–3; Katz, *In the Shadow of the Poorhouse*, 265–266. The Food and Drug Administration maintains a Web site that defines the food stamp program and WIC in detail and the services offered in each case. It is available online at http://www.fns.usda.gov/fsp for food stamps and http://www.fns.usda.gov/wic.

26. Meckel, *Save the Babies*, 220–224.

27. Peter G. Szilagyi, Jane L. Holl, Lance E. Rodewald, Laura Pollard Shone, Jack Zwanziger, Dana B. Mukamel, Sarah Trafton, Andrew W. Dick, and Richard F. Raubertas, "Evaluation of Children's Health Insurance: From New York State's Child Health Plus to SCHIP," *Pediatrics* 105(3) (2000): 687–691; Karen G. Duderstadt, Dana C. Hughes, Mah-P. Soobader, and Paul W. Newacheck, "The Impact of Public Insurance Expansions on Children's Access and Use of Care," *Pediatrics* 118(4) (2006): 1676–1682. Information on the Pennsylvania CHIP program is available online at http://www.chipcoverspakids.com.

28. U.S. Department of Health & Human Services, "Insure Kids Now!" *Health Resources and Services Administration*, (n.d.), http://www.insurekidsnow.gov/.

29. Youcha, *Minding the Children*, 118–124, 243–250, 307–319.

30. Mintz, *Huck's Raft*, 357–359; and Youcha, *Minding the Children*, 132–133.

31. Treasury Working Group on Child Care, *Investing in Child Care: Challenges Facing Working Parents and the Private Sector Response* (Washington, DC: United States Department of the Treasury, 1998), vi–ix, 1–32; and Tara Weiss, "The New Mommy Track: Every Day Mom's Day for Savvy Employers," *Forbes*, January 23, 2007, www.forbes.com/2007/01/22/leadership-work-jobs-lead-careers-cx_tw_0123moms.html.

Racism and the American Baby

"The problem of the twentieth century is the problem of the color-line . . ."

—W.E.B. DuBois, 1900

The twentieth century brought many changes for American babies. It unfortunately did not eliminate racism. For while the abolition of slavery in the 1860s meant that no longer would generations of Americans be born into that horrific institution, the racial divide between black and white Americans seemed only to intensify with the new century.

There has not been much written about the plight of African-American babies in the first half of the twentieth century. They were generally ignored. Part of the blame can be placed on the inadequacy of the birth registration process in place at the time. Officials registered the birth of babies only in certain areas—mainly in major cities and a few smaller but still developed areas of the country. In large areas of rural America there was no official birth registration process and thus babies born in these areas, regardless of their race, were not counted. Because large numbers of African-American babies were born outside the registration areas their numbers are unknown. When the Children's Bureau conducted a study to determine the causes of infant deaths in seven medium to large cities during the late 1910s, the only city where race was discussed was Baltimore. The infant mortality rate (IMR) for black babies there was more than twice of that of white babies. We simply do not know the exact infant birth or mortality rates for this population as a whole and can only extrapolate via those few statistics that are available. Another issue is that the transfer of birth from a home event to a hospital event took longer in rural areas and was not complete until well past the mid-century mark.[1] When legislation required it, hospitals officially recorded births. However, when babies were born at home, especially in isolated rural areas, parents frequently ignored requirements to register infant births.

What is known, however, is that throughout the century black babies lagged behind white babies on most scales of well-being. Their birth weights were lower and their first-year survival rates were lower. All babies, no matter their race, did better overall by the end of the twentieth century, but the differences between African-American babies and white babies continued to increase. In other words, the rate of improvement was slower for African-Americans, resulting in an increasing disparity between the races. In this chapter I will discuss the multiple reasons for these facts and attempt to describe the impact of overt and implicit racism on American babies. Poverty is also a factor in the lives of many Americans, particularly those for whom racism is also a dominant presence.

RACISM AND AMERICAN BABIES IN THE EARLY TWENTIETH CENTURY

During the first half of the century race divided all Americans, including babies. Racism was an unacknowledged truth among the predominantly white population which included most of the politically and economically powerful. After the end of slavery, which had provided most blacks with experience only as farmers and servants, African-Americans, for the most part, remained in the South. Southern white landowners took advantage of the fact that most blacks lacked resources and money and relegated them to tenantry, sharecropping, and domestic servitude. Few managed to acquire land of their own or escape poverty.[2] Even African-Americans who moved to the cities in the early twentieth century were often condemned to low-paying, dead-end jobs in inner city slums. They were denied higher paying, more prestigious jobs by pervasive customs that prohibited blacks from assuming such positions. In her study on the benefits of federal and state aid to dependent black children Bobbie Green Turner (1993) described some of the positions available to black families in 1900. Half of the black workforce at the time consisted of agricultural workers and lower end service workers such as laborers, servants, and waiters. Supervisory positions were reserved for whites.[3]

The financial assistance instituted by the federal and state governments for destitute women and children during the first few decades of the century provided a safety net without which many would have perished. But not all received aid. In many parts of the United States, racist white officials denied mothers' pensions to black women and their babies. Of course, all women had to prove their eligibility for pensions and in some cases they needed to prove not only citizenship, but residence in a particular location for a set amount of time. African-Americans, many of who moved out of the South to northern cities during the second and third decades of the century were rarely able to prove citizenship or residency. Rampant prejudice that questioned their skills as mothers and their sexuality generally ensured that they would not find admittance to programs such as mother's pensions or other mother's aid programs.[4]

The migration of black Americans from the southern states to northern cities increased dramatically after World War I. In search of better jobs, less discrimination, and improved lives for their families, blacks took jobs in the new factories of Detroit, Chicago, Pittsburgh, Philadelphia, New York, and other, smaller, cities across the Northeast states. Discrimination continued. Blacks were often given the most menial jobs, forced into segregated living conditions, and, as economic conditions tightened in the late 1920s, lost their jobs to white workers laid off from higher paying jobs.[5]

Salaries for African-Americans lucky enough to have jobs in the 1920s and 1930s lagged behind those of whites in similar positions. In Chicago during the Depression in the mid-1930s the average salary for a black family was less than half that of the average native-born white family. In some cities more than 70 percent of African-American adults were unemployed and those that were employed were denied white-collar jobs and often relegated to unskilled labor positions. The children of these people were receiving little, if any, education in substandard facilities. Many American schools were forced to close or curtail hours during the Depression, and this was especially true of those in black communities.[6]

AFRICAN-AMERICAN WOMEN'S EFFORTS ON BEHALF OF BABIES

That all of this discrimination led to poor outcomes for African-American babies is no surprise. Lack of educational and employment opportunities lead directly to poverty. Poverty begets poor health and increased IMRs. Black citizens did not ignore these problems. As early as the 1890s black women organized to help the less fortunate and the youngest members of society.

Most African-American babies were, and are, cared for by their parents in a loving and nurturing manner. When in the late nineteenth and early twentieth centuries white women were coming together to acknowledge the dismal infant mortality statistics in the United States, black women also organized groups to provide help for women and children of their own race. In many ways these groups were similar to the white women's groups. They had political leanings, a focus on mothers and their children, and a belief that the poor were lacking in education as well as money. The differences lay in their approach to problems. Like white women, the African-American women supported marriage and children for women, but they also encouraged women to achieve political rights and professional employment. However, given the racism of white Senators, Congressmen, and others in the power corridors of Washington, DC, black women could not successfully lobby them. Instead they turned to their peers. Fund-raising was not too successful because of the poverty of the black community. Many of the successes of black women's organizations came with the development of mutual aid societies that helped women and families in times of crisis. Church membership also helped. Women's societies associated with the church filled many gaps left by discriminatory practices of governmental and predominantly white reform efforts.[7]

The first group of African-American women to organize was the National Association of Colored Women (NACW), which formed in 1896 and by 1911 reported 45,000 members. Among other projects they set up day care nurseries for infants and small children and kindergartens for older youngsters in various cities across the nation. The NACW was led by several well-known women including Mary Church Terrell, Ida B. Wells, and Mary McLeod Bethune. Bethune, after serving as NACW president in the 1920s, founded the National Council of Negro Women in 1935. During the 1930s she also served in Franklin Roosevelt's administration as director of Negro Affairs in the National Youth Administration. There "she ensured that at least some of the benefits of the expanding U.S. welfare system reached the African American community."[8]

FEDERAL LEGISLATION AND BABIES

The Sheppard–Towner Act of 1921, the first major federal legislation concerning the needs of mothers and children, was supported by a host of women's
groups, including the NACW. The federal Children's Bureau was the main
catalyst behind the passage of the Act and included African-American communities in the implementation of the Act in the various states. However
state officials administered the Act and many allowed bias and discriminatory
practices. The major emphasis of the Act was on educational and preventive
services that white middle-class persons deemed appropriate. There was no
room for traditional folk medicine or for superstitions passed down through
the generations. Lay midwives, many of whom were black in the southern
states, were considered "dirty" and expected to attend educational programs
and attain state licensure. Many did so, but others either ignored the expectations or stopped delivering babies. Some midwives managed to combine the
new scientific methods with the older, more traditional rituals associated with
the birthing process. In some areas of the country, Sheppard–Towner officials
allowed "inferior services to people of color." In Georgia an African-American
nurse was denied the transportation services that her white coworkers received,
thus limiting her ability to do her job in her community.[9]

In the end Sheppard–Towner did not make much of a dent in the dismal
infant mortality statistics for African-American babies. In 1921 108 out of
1,000 live born babies of color died; in 1928 the number had dropped to only
106. While the 1921 statistics may have been optimistic, meaning that the drop
was actually larger than reported, the overall IMR remained much higher than
the 69 out of 1,000 deaths calculated for the entire population. The Sheppard–
Towner Act was not renewed in 1929 but did convince private physicians to add
preventive care to their services. However once private physicians delivered
prenatal and preventive care, it appeared that there was no further need for
the government to do the same. Minorities, especially the poor, could rarely
afford private physicians, and so, with the end of Sheppard–Towner, many
black mothers and babies received inferior or no care.[10]

The Great Depression and the Rise of Public Welfare

The advent of the Great Depression in 1929 eventually gave rise to the
host of federally funded programs as discussed in Chapter 5. Specifically, the
Social Security Act contained prescriptions for services to women and children

unable to provide for themselves. Despite some increased acknowledgement of the wide disparities between white and black Americans, racial differences in access to and eligibility for benefits continued. Segregation continued as a major presence in virtually all American communities. For babies this often meant less access to preventative and medical care, limited housing choices for their families, and fewer options for the procurement of daily necessities such as milk and food.

World War II brought the country out of the Depression and provided work for the vast numbers of unemployed. Black men served with distinction in the armed forces, albeit in segregated units. The desegregation of all military branches after the war brought hope to African-Americans that the days of segregation and discrimination would soon be over. Unfortunately that would not prove true.

RACISM AND AMERICAN BABIES 1950–2000

After the war the migration of southern blacks to the northern cities continued. They were not welcomed warmly. White families fled to the suburbs in waves of fear spread by unscrupulous "block busters" who then sold whites' former homes to blacks for a profit. Discriminatory practices prevented blacks from joining the suburban sprawl. In Levittown, New York, the first large planned suburb in postwar America, a clause in the purchase agreement prevented blacks from buying homes in the development and prevented the original white homeowners from reselling their homes to blacks. Despite a 1948 Supreme Court verdict outlawing such clauses, or covenants, Levittown remained 99.9 percent white in 1960. Levittown was not alone as suburbs across the country remained nearly all white during those years. Thus babies born to African-American families during the "baby boom" of the 1950s entered a world as segregated as the one their parents fought to save during the war. The outlook and health of these babies continued to lag far behind their white counterparts.[11]

Changes to the Social Security Act in the postwar years continued to favor the rise of private medicine and treatment of illness and injury rather than prevention. The Children's Bureau continued to call for increased funding and the expansion of services beyond the limited scope of medical care. Legislation calling for increased access to medical care for the poor and indigent was proposed, but deemed communistic by opponents who rallied support for its defeat. The only laws passed focused on hospital building and medical education. They did little to educate those who needed help most with the routine aspects of baby care. Infant care in the United States was defined according to medical principles and its social, economic, and demographic aspects were ignored. Poor black families in the inner cities, without medical insurance, many of whom lived within blocks of some of the most highly regarded medical centers in the country, were effectively cut off from care.[12]

The civil rights movement of the 1950s and 1960s finally brought national attention to the racial divide in the United States. Major protests across the country, peaceful and violent, led to the end of officially sanctioned segregation, although racism and discriminatory practices continued at all levels of society. In the early 1960s a drop-off in the decline in overall IMRs once again brought governmental attention to the issue.[13]

Beginning with the Kennedy administration, new programs helped those African-American families caught in the snare of poverty provide better food for their babies and health care before, during, and after birth. That health care however consists mainly of treatment of disease and other conditions amenable to medical care. Preventive services increased but the comprehensive programs envisioned by reformers earlier in the century have not been established. Medicaid was available only to those families eligible for Aid to Families with Dependent Children (AFDC). In addition, because the states administer Medicaid, eligibility requirements, amounts of service, and reimbursement rates are all determined individually by each state. Therefore a family eligible in one state could lose all benefits if they move to another state.[14]

By the mid-1970s the generous spirit of the 1960s gave way to the serious realities of an economic recession that included higher prices for many things, job losses, and a general tightening of the nation's collective financial belt. Welfare, of which social security payments to retired people was a part, came to mean to most people payments to those poor families unable to provide for themselves. In other words only those receiving AFDC were said to be on welfare. "Welfare moms" became a derogatory term. In some instances these mothers were accused of having babies just to collect more money from the government. Most of those targeted were African-American despite the fact that more white than black Americans received AFDC.[15] New rules were put in place to limit the extent of welfare payments during the 1980s. By the 1990s calls for dramatic change were heard as the numbers of families receiving AFDC increased, particularly those headed by female single parents. The numbers of teenage mothers were also increasing. Statistics demonstrated that being born to a teenage mother increased the chances of compromised health during the first year of life thus requiring more in terms of health care assistance. Once again there was a decided racial component to the rhetoric on this issue. The Personal Responsibility and Work Opportunity Reconciliation Act of 1996 established the Temporary Assistance for Needy Families (TANF) program which replaced AFDC and imposed limitations and restrictions seen by many people as discriminatory toward African-Americans.[16]

In other areas discrimination affected African-American babies as well. The crack epidemic of the 1980s hit the inner city black population especially hard. Babies born addicted to the illicit drugs their mothers took during pregnancy suffered immensely. Even after they recovered their well-being was far from certain—could they go home with their mothers? Would they need foster care? The AIDS epidemic, originally viewed as a disease of homosexual men, spread across the country and among all racial, sexual, and cultural groups. Once again babies suffered when their mothers were infected through unprotected sex with a man with AIDS, intravenous drug use with contaminated needles, or through blood transfusions. During the 1980s and early 1990s when there was no effective treatment for AIDS these mothers often died when their children were infants or toddlers. At the time babies born to an AIDS-infected mother were at high risk of contracting the disease through placental transmission. Babies could also contract AIDS through blood transfusions. AIDS was quickly spreading in the inner cities among the black population and once again babies were innocent victims. Continuing prejudices against homosexuals and racial minorities meant that the crisis was not addressed readily by the public at large.[17]

Foster home placement and adoption for these babies seemed to be an answer but also ran into racial barriers. Most adoption agencies in the United States did not place black babies or children at all until after World War II. However social workers quickly changed their official views on adoption within the black community and by 1948 adopted a stance that emphasized the welfare of the child no matter the color of his skin. By the mid-1960s transracial adoption was no longer taboo and a few prospective white parents were even requesting black babies. This trend peaked in 1971. Beginning in 1972 the rate of transracial adoptions decreased dramatically as some members of the African-American community, including many African-American social workers, deemed it unacceptable from racial and cultural viewpoints. They believed black babies were better off in black families. The numbers of African-American homes open to adoption remained small. Whether this was due to an unwillingness to adopt or a lack of effort on the part of adoption agencies is a question still debated today. The decline in numbers of acceptable adoptive families, as whites were denied the opportunity to adopt black babies, resulted in the placement of large numbers of babies and children in foster care for long periods of time. In 1994 federal legislation was finally passed that prohibited race, color, or nationality from being used to deny a person the right to adopt.[18] The debate has continued into the twenty-first century however. In recent years a black baby was placed in a white foster home in Pennsylvania where he lived for several years. The foster family that applied to adopt him were thwarted by a technicality and the child was placed with a black family for adoption. Despite court appeals by the foster family the decision was upheld. The court found the child would be better off in the African-American home. For several weeks both families used the local media to lobby support and editorials called for an end to race-based adoptive practices.[19]

INFANT MORTALITY AMONG AFRICAN-AMERICAN BABIES

The IMR of a nation purportedly signals the overall health of the nation and is a harbinger of economic, political, and social stability. At the end of the twentieth century the U.S. IMR lagged behind that of many other industrialized countries. This fact alone does not tell the story of the dramatic decreases in infant mortality that occurred over the course of the century. Also, a single number cannot tell the differences in infant mortality between racial and ethnic groups. However during the twentieth century the U.S. Census Bureau did break down the numbers and published the disparate IMRs among these groups. When these numbers are analyzed it is readily apparent that race plays a major role in the ability of a baby to survive its first year of life.

In 1915 the overall U.S. IMR was 99.9 deaths per 1000 live births. This declined to 29.2 in 1950, 12.6 in 1980, and 6.9 in 2000. Statistical data available prior to 1932 reflects the IMR only among births reported in specific birth registration areas. These areas tended to be the more developed areas of the country thus the statistics cannot be considered inclusive. However they do show major differences between white babies and nonwhite babies. The IMR for nonwhite babies[20] was 333.9 in 1900 compared to 159.4 for white babies. In 1920 the rate had decreased to 149.2 for nonwhites and 87.3 for whites. In 1950 the IMR continued to decline for both whites and nonwhites, but it remained significantly higher among nonwhites.[21] This trend continued throughout the rest of the century. By 2000 the IMR rate for black babies was 14.0 compared to 5.7 for white babies.[22]

While statistics may help identify a problem they do nothing to solve it. During the last quarter of the twentieth century the reasons for the disparity in IMR's between black and white Americans were debated, argued, and studied by a host of interested people. Their conclusions are varied; however most focus on three variables. Prenatal care has been proven to be beneficial to the health and well-being of the mother and the baby. Babies whose mothers receive prenatal care are healthier and heavier than babies whose mothers receive little or no prenatal care. In 1983 one study found that while 79 percent of white mothers-to-be received prenatal care in the first trimester of pregnancy, only 62 percent of black mothers-to-be did so. Although the difference may not seem too large, prenatal care for all should be a goal of any public health campaign. The second reason cited for the racial difference in IMR is the higher percentage of births to high-risk mothers among black women when compared to white women. The mother's age is important as teenagers and those over forty have a higher risk potential. The teenage pregnancy rate among blacks has been high, though it decreased throughout the 1990s that will hopefully result in improved outcomes for babies. A third reason cited as problematic is an increased rate overall of lower birth weights. This is especially true among African-American babies. Birth weight statistics are complicated by the increase in lower birth weights in the population overall that are attributed to the increased use of infertility treatment resulting in multiple births and increased preterm births. Other factors that contribute to birth weight disparities between black and white babies include maternal diseases that are experienced differently by African-American women, and increased stress associated with the lack of appropriate family and social supports. In addition any mother who has delivered one baby prematurely is at high risk for a second preterm birth.[23]

CONCLUSIONS

The IMR among African-American babies did decrease over the second half of the century. By the 1990s the rate of births to teenage mothers of all races was declining, which helped decrease the number of babies born at risk. But the IMR among black babies continued to outpace that of white babies. Black babies were more likely to be born early and into poverty, to be underweight, and to develop illnesses. They were more likely to be born into and reared in single-parent households. While there are elements of personal responsibility in all these issues, the fact that racism plays a part cannot be ignored. While various private and public initiatives to decrease IMRs in the African-American community can be planned and implemented, real differences can only come when racism is eliminated. It may take one individual at a time but it needs to be done.

NOTES

1. Richard A. Meckel, *Save the Babies: American Public Health Reform and the Prevention of Infant Mortality, 1850–1929* (Ann Arbor: The University of Michigan Press, 1990), 111–112; Kriste Lindenmeyer, *"A Right to Childhood"—The U.S. Children's Bureau and Child Welfare, 1912–1946* (Urbana: University of Illinois Press, 1997), 61–62, 121.

2. Priscilla Ferguson Clement, *Growing Pains: Children in the Industrial Age, 1850–1890* (New York: Twayne Publishers, 1997), 72–74, 128–129.

3. Bobbie Green Turner, *Federal/State Aid to Dependent Children Program and Its Benefits to Black Children in America, 1935–1985* (New York: Garland Publishing, Inc., 1993), 55–62; and Robert J. Norrell, *The House I Live in: Race in the American Century* (New York: Oxford University Press, 2005), 25–26, 66.

4. Turner, *Federal/State Aid to Dependent Children Program and Its Benefits to Black Children in America, 1935–1985*, 58, 60–61; and Linda Gordon, *Pitied but Not Entitled: Single Mothers and the History of Welfare* (New York: Free Press, 1994), 38, 47–48.

5. Turner, *Federal/State Aid to Dependent Children Program and Its Benefits to Black Children in America, 1935–1985*, 61–64; and Gordon, *Pitied but Not Entitled*, 112–113.

6. Norell, *The House I Live in*, 89; and Steven Mintz, *Huck's Raft: A History of American Childhood* (Cambridge, MA: Belknap Press of Harvard University Press, 2004), 239–240.

7. Gordon, *Pitied but Not Entitled*, 111–119.

8. Molly Ladd-Taylor, *Mother-Work: Women, Child Welfare, and the State, 1890–1930* (Chicago: University of Illinois Press, 1994), 55–63.

9. Ibid., 180–184; Gordon, *Pitied but Not Entitled*, 88; Lindenmeyer, *"A Right to Childhood,"* 96; Marie Campbell, *Folks Do Get Born* (New York: Rhinehart & Company, 1946), 51–59; Hettie H. Hough and Lucia Murchison, "Care of Premature Babies in South Carolina," *American Journal of Nursing* 46(12) (1946): 846–848; and Theodora Floyd, April 13, 1987, in the Georgia Public Health Oral History Collection. Special Collections, Robert W. Woodruff Library, Emory University, Atlanta, Georgia.

10. Ladd-Taylor, *Mother-Work*, 187, 189.

11. U.S. Department of Justice, "Fair Housing Act," (1968). http://www.usdoj.gov/crt/housing/title8.htm; Philip Nyden, John Lukehart, Michael T. Maly, and William Peterman, "Racially and Ethnically Diverse Urban Neighborhoods," *CITYSCAPE: A Journal of Policy Development and Research* 4(2) (1998): 19–27; Leonard Steinhorn, *By the Color of Our Skin: The Illusion of Integration and the Reality of Race* (New York: Penguin Group, 1999), 37, 96, 98–99; and Norrell, *The House I Live in*, 87, 124–126, 163, 169–170.

12. Meckel, *Save the Babies*, 220–225.

13. Ibid., 228.

14. Ibid., 229–231.

15. U.S. Bureau of the Census, "Mothers Who Receive AFDC Payments: Fertility and Socioeconomic Characteristics," *Statistical Brief* (March 1995), http://www.census.gov/population/socdemo/statbriefs/sb2-95.html. The actual number of African-American mothers receiving AFDC in 1993 was approximately 1.5 million. White mothers receiving AFDC numbered approximately 2.1 million. These numbers represented approximately 25 percent of African-American mothers and 7 percent of white mothers.

16. Personal Responsibility and Work Opportunity Reconciliation Act of 1996, http://thomas.loc.gov/cgi-bin/query/F?c104:1:./temp/~c1049qpEij:e669; Scott Winship and Christopher Jencks, "Understanding Welfare Reform," *Harvard Magazine*, November–December 2004, 33–34; U.S. Department of Health and Human Services, Administration for Children and Families, Office of Planning, Research and Evaluation, Temporary Assistance to Needy Families (TANF), *Third Annual Report to Congress*, August 2000, 1–4; and Michele A. Tingling-Clemmons, "Welfare Reform Two Years Later: Which Way Is Up?" *National NOW Times*, Fall 1998, http://www.now.org/nnt/fall-98/.

17. Randy Shilts, *And the Band Played On—Politics, People, and the AIDS Epidemic* (New York: Penguin Books, 1987), 188, 194–195, 339, 512; and E. Schneider, M.K. Glynn, T. Kajese, and M.T. McKenna, "Epidemiology of HIV/AIDS—United States, 1981–2005," *Morbidity and Mortality Weekly Report* 55(21) (2006): 589–592.

18. E. Wayne Carp, "Introduction: A Historical Overview of American Adoption," in E. Wayne Carp, ed., *Adoption in America: Historical Perspectives* (Ann Arbor: University of Michigan Press, 2002), 14–16.

19. Benjamin Y. Lowe, "Adoption Policies Baffle Family," *Philadelphia Inquirer*, April 3, 2006; Claude Lewis, "Why Is Race Still a Factor in Adoption?" *Philadelphia Inquirer*, April 12, 2006; and Kathleen Brady Shea and Lini S. Kadaba, "He's Healthy ... Happy," *Philadelphia Inquirer*, April 27, 2006.

20. The terms "white" and "nonwhite" were used by the U.S. Census in early twentieth-century reports. "Black," "white," and "hispanic" were used later in the century. "Nonwhite" sometimes included "Mexican" and other times did not.

21. Donna L. Hoyert, Mary Anne Freedman, Donna M. Strobino, and Bernard Guyer, "Annual Summary of Vital Statistics: 2000," *Pediatrics* 108(6) (2001): 1241–1255; S. Iyasu and K. Tomashek, "Infant Mortality and Low Birth Weight Among Black and White Infants—United States, 1980–2000," *Morbidity and Mortality Weekly Report* 51(27) (2002): 589–592; and National Office of Vital Statistics, "Table 8.22, Infant Mortality Rates by Race: Birth-Registration States, 1915-1950," in *Marriage, Divorce, Natality, Fetal Mortality, and Infant Mortality Data Volume II* (1950), 164–169.

22. Hoyert et al., "Annual Summary of Vital Statistics: 2000," 1247.

23. Reynolds Farley and Walter R. Allen, *The Color Line and the Quality of Life in America* (New York: Russell Sage Foundation, 1987), 47–52; and Iyasu and Tomashek, "Infant Mortality and Low Birth Weight among Black and White Infants," 589–592.

Population and Immigration

"All of our people all over the country—except the pure-blooded Indians—are immigrants or descendants of immigrants, including even those who came over here on the 'Mayflower.'"
—Franklin D. Roosevelt, November 4, 1944

The population of any country rises and falls along a continuum. Individually, babies are born whether the economy is good or bad, the climate is hot or cold, or when food is plentiful or scarce. Overall increases in population in a country occur when people feel good enough about their surroundings purposely to bring more than the average number of babies into the world and when people emigrate to that country from elsewhere in the world. The ability to thwart death in a society leads to more people living longer and the twentieth century's focus on improving infant lives certainly helped produce that result. Decreases in population occur when people have babies at less than the average rate, when immigration slows down, stops, reverses, or when deaths outpaces births and immigration. Between 1900 and 2000 the population of the United States grew from 76 million to 281 million. There were fewer babies born in the 1930s than in any other decade, probably due to the effects of the Great Depression. The "baby boom" began in 1946, when World War II ended and lasted until the early 1960s. This unprecedented increase in the number of babies born produced one of the largest generations of Americans ever. By the

1970s this increase in births was over although there was a "mini baby boom" in the 1990s that helped boost population growth by a higher percentage than was the case in the 1970s and 1980s.[1] In the latter years of the century fears of overpopulation and its effects on the economy and the environment centered on immigrants and their perceived higher than average birthrate. Illegal immigration became, by 2000, a major issue across the country. In this chapter both the effects of the rises and falls in the birthrate and the effects of immigration on babies in America will be discussed.

POPULATION FLUCTUATIONS

On the surface rises and falls in the numbers of babies born in the nation would not appear to have much of an impact on an individual baby. Most babies are happy as long as they are fed, warm, and loved. Problems develop when there are too many babies for the available resources in a community. When there is not enough food, babies can go hungry. Even a breast-fed baby depends on the nutrition of the mother. Inadequate housing means that some families live in overcrowded conditions or, in some cases, are homeless. When families are not able to provide adequate food and housing, babies are affected, often even more so than adults.

Babies in communities where their numbers are declining can also be negatively affected even though there are fewer of them. Resources are often spread over a larger area in these cases. A pediatrician may not be readily available in case of an emergency, or even a simple question from new parents. Families may have to travel great distances to access medical care. When babies have developmental problems, early intervention programs, mandated by federal and state governments, are available but again, may require parents or guardians to cart their babies a long distance. Travel to secure medical care can alter family dynamics and even income as parents juggle jobs, other family members' needs, and the demands of a baby.

On a more positive note, increases in the number of babies cannot be ignored. Local communities will encourage the development of businesses, including food stores, toy stores, and day care centers. Planning boards will be motivated to assess the infrastructure for up-to-date resources such as schools that will be needed to educate the babies as they grow. Socially parents will have more sources of support. Hearing of other parents' sleepless nights and feeding problems can help a parent feel less isolated. A baby may begin to learn to interact early on with other babies, children, and adults. Friends and classmates are almost assured as the baby grows.

On the other hand, fewer babies in a community may mean increased attention from adults. Parents with just one child may have more energy to devote to him. Fewer babies can lead to fewer children in the schools, resulting in smaller class sizes and increased attention from teachers. In a community with limited resources fewer babies to care for eases the worries associated with financial difficulties and troubled economic times such as happened during the Great Depression of the 1930s.

During the twentieth century America experienced, as a whole, a steadily increasing number of citizens. At times the increase in population was greater than at others but at no time did it drop. Individual states, cities, towns, and rural areas experienced and recorded both gains and losses. During the Great Depression many families left their communities and headed to other areas of the country in an attempt to find work and relief. The rapid influx of people into larger cities and states such as California strained the resources available for families and their babies in those places.

As previously discussed, babies seemed to be everywhere in the 1950s and 1960s. Infancy and early childhood became, for many, a healthy and happy time. The growth in the number of babies spurred the development of an infant and young child focus in the country that redefined family and community for the rest of the century. The baby boom was followed by a significant drop off in the number of babies born during the 1970s and early 1980s, often referred to as the "baby bust". The late 1980s and 1990s saw a slight resurgence in the number of babies, but nowhere near the numbers seen in the 1950s.[2] Most babies born in the United States during the twentieth century were considered innocent and deserving of all the resources a modern society could supply. But some were not as revered. When babies were born to parents thought to be a negative influence on society their birth was not celebrated. Immigrants at the beginning and the end of the century experienced most of this negative reaction.

IMMIGRATION

In the early 1900s there were concerns voiced by some of the most prominent men in the nation about the decrease in the number of babies born to native-born American citizens. They lamented that the newer immigrants flooding in from Southern and Eastern Europe were reproducing at higher than average rates, which would soon, it seemed to those in power, lead to a social, economic, political, and cultural upheaval.[3] If the words "Southern and Eastern Europe" were replaced by "Mexico, Central America, and Asia" the above sentence could read the same for the late 1990s and early 2000s. A preoccupation with the number of babies born in America to immigrant parents extends beyond economists, census takers, and government planners to the average citizen wondering what his or her own future will look like.

America is a nation of immigrants and has, for most of her history, relied on immigrants to populate urban and rural areas alike. Before World War I, immigration was virtually unchecked—almost anyone (except Chinese laborers who were excluded by a law passed in 1882) who could get here was allowed in if free of certain diseases and with some prospects of getting a job.[4] According to the U.S. Constitution's fourteenth amendment any baby born on American soil was automatically a citizen and with all the appropriate rights and privileges. In the first years of the twentieth century when new immigrants appeared to be procreating with abandon and filling the streets with babies, the overall native white American birthrate was actually declining. This decline had begun during the middle years of the nineteenth century and did not appear affected by calls for increased childbearing by President Theodore Roosevelt and other leaders. By the 1910s the concern was even greater among many Americans of northern European ancestry.[5] With new understandings of the sciences of genetics and biology, a few men and women turned to the teachings of eugenics for a solution to the immigration "problem."

DESIRABLE OR UNDESIRABLE? EUGENICS AND PROCREATION

The "science" of eugenics grew out of a few professionals' interest in encouraging desirable characteristics while discouraging, or even eliminating, undesirable characteristics. The definitions of desirable and undesirable were somewhat fluid and generally depended on the views of proponents of eugenics in any given community. Francis Galton, an English scientist who is considered the founder of eugenics, compared it to the breeding conducted by farmers on animals and horticulturists on plants. He suggested that, based on his own research, accomplished people generally were descended from other accomplished people while the undesirables in the population had inferior ancestors.

He argued that desirable persons should be encouraged to marry each other and bear children. Undesirable persons should be forced into celibacy. In this way, Galton believed, the entire human race would be improved.[6]

In the United States eugenics was studied and supported by a wide variety of people. Charles Davenport, a biologist from Harvard and the University of Chicago popularized the concept in the 1900s. He obtained funding from the Carnegie Institution of Washington and set up a laboratory to study evolution. He collected data on hundreds of families and cited patterns of inheritance in cases of mental illness, criminal behavior, limited income, and mental deficiencies. He also maintained that different races, including not only blacks, but also people of Polish, Irish, Italian, and Jewish descent, were inferior to the white Protestant citizens who were mainly born in the United States. He supported immigration but only of those deemed free of undesirable characteristics. Unlike some of his colleagues in Britain and the United States, Davenport did not initially support forced sterilization of the so-called unfit. Instead, he advised segregating them during their reproductive years. Preventing procreation by these people would, in his view, eventually save the states the money they ordinarily spent on institutional care.[7]

During the early 1910s eugenics became even more popular in England and the United States. Articles in the press and lectures by experts to a variety of citizen groups encouraged the belief in the powers of eugenics to strengthen not only individuals, but the greater society. World War I proved a problem for eugenicists as desirable and undesirable young men were on the front lines and many of both groups died during battle. Those unfit for service were still at home. The worry of many was that young women would marry these "unfit" men and bear babies with inherited characteristics that would result in a generation of children weaker than their forebears. At the end of the war a renewed interest in eugenics in the United States was supported by money from influential men such as John D. Rockefeller, Jr., and George Eastman. State fairs began to promote fitter family contests to highlight those families possessed of an impeccable family history devoid of unsavory characteristics. Good looks helped also. In Philadelphia at the Sesquicentennial Exposition a board with flashing lights supposedly tallied the amount of money spent on the care of persons with bad heredity.[8]

The field of eugenics was feted by both conservative and liberal Americans and British as well as people from many other European nations and from Russia, Japan, and Central America. Many of the people supporting eugenics were upper middle-class men and women. They also were mainly white, Protestant, and educated professionals.[9] By the mid-1920s eugenics had reached the peak of its popularity and influence.

For babies the issue most often came down to whether they should be conceived or not, depending on the would-be parents' heredity. While most proponents of eugenics began their quest for an improved human race by calling for forced celibacy of identified misfits the idea of mandatory sterilization soon became popular. Mandatory sterilization was legal in several states in the early twentieth century, mainly for those persons, men and women, accused of sexual delinquency or moral degeneration and/or feeblemindedness. Many of these laws were broadly criticized by members of the legal community and some were declared unconstitutional by 1918.[10]

In Virginia eugenic supporters concerned about the courts' attempts to outlaw forced sterilization took up the case of seventeen-year-old Carrie Buck. Diagnosed as a "moral imbecile" she was sent to the Virginia Colony for Epileptics and Feebleminded in Lynchburg, Virginia. Her mother, Emma had been an inmate there for several years and was considered feebleminded. Before entering the colony Carrie gave birth to a daughter. An intelligence test identified Carrie's mental age as nine years old, giving her the classification of a "moron." Her mother's mental age was reported to be slightly less than eight years old. Based on two consecutive generations of mental retardation, eugenicists sought to certify Carrie's infant daughter as feebleminded in order to force Carrie's sterilization. The daughter, Vivian, was assessed at seven months of age to be below average in mental capabilities. A lawsuit filed by a court appointed guardian for Carrie went to the Virginia Supreme Court and then to the U.S. Supreme Court. The court ruled that sterilization of Carrie and others like her was constitutional and necessary to prevent an inordinate increase in the number of mentally incompetent babies being born. Carrie was subsequently sterilized.[11] Many more young men and women were sterilized after Carrie, in Virginia and other states, and prevented from bearing babies.

Sterilization procedures grew in number throughout the 1920s and 1930s. World War II and the atrocities of the Nazi concentration camps dampened the prewar enthusiasm for forced sterilization and the number performed annually declined. In the 1960s many states repealed the laws for forced sterilization, but allowed for voluntary sterilization of mentally retarded and other undesirable persons. In some cases these people were not allowed to leave institutions or to marry until they "volunteered" for sterilization. By the 1970s increased knowledge of the genetic role in disease had some scientists and politicians again calling for sterilization laws, or at the very least, mandatory genetic screening for would-be parents. Mandatory sterilization laws were not passed, however there have been several cases where the term "voluntary" was not explained fully to young women or their parents before sterilization took place.[12] Genetic screening has become routine in many obstetrical practices; genetic testing has also evolved quickly to diagnose disease in the fetus during early pregnancy. In 2002 the Commonwealth of Virginia officially apologized for the sterilization of Carrie Buck and the thousands of other men and women sterilized in the name of eugenics.[13]

While sterilization laws prohibited people like Carrie Buck from bearing any babies, other parents suffered the impact of the eugenic movement when they gave birth to a baby with one or more defects. During the 1910s a few physician supporters of eugenics turned to euthanasia as a way to deal with the undesirable babies born to parents deemed unsuitable for procreation. The first case to cause headlines across the country occurred in Chicago in 1915. In *The Black Stork* historian Martin Pernick reviewed and analyzed this long-forgotten story.[14]

On November 12, 1915, Harry Haiselden, a physician and surgeon practicing in Chicago, was called to see a baby boy born with serious physical defects including a missing neck and ear, shoulder and chest malformations, and an imperforate anus. A supporter of eugenics, Haiselden examined the baby and determined that although the imperforate anus could be repaired, the other defects would leave the baby mentally and physically disabled. He advised the parents, Mr. and Mrs. Bollinger, to let the baby die. They agreed and the baby died on November 17. Two weeks later another baby was born with hydrocephalus (water on the brain). Despite their physician's belief that surgery would save the baby's life the parents refused treatment. Haiselden was traveling, but was contacted and, without seeing the baby himself, supported the withholding of any treatment. The baby died a week later. Over the next few years several other cases were reported in Chicago and around the country where infants born with physical and possibly mental defects were allowed to die rather than be treated. Parents wrote to Haiselden to support them and to ask for help in allowing their own children to die. Baby Bollinger's case and many of the others were publicized by Haiselden himself. Reporters were allowed in the hospital to view the dying babies and interview the mothers. Haiselden became famous in eugenic circles and even to the public at large. His supporters included Lillian Wald, Clarence Darrow, and even Helen Keller. Newspapers in Chicago, Detroit, Baltimore, Washington, DC, Philadelphia, and New York endorsed him. Critics, including prominent physicians, Jane

Addams of Hull House and Julia Lathrop of the Children's Bureau, quickly went on record to denounce Haiselden and called for the treatment of all infants. Competing newspapers in cities across the nation, including Chicago, wrote editorials in support of the critics.[15]

Haiselden subsequently wrote and starred in a movie, titled *The Black Stork*, which fictionalized the Bollinger story and promulgated the theories of eugenics. The beginning of the movie featured men and women with supposedly hereditary defects and the troubles they faced. In the main section of the film two scenarios are acted out. In one Haiselden played a physician whose warnings against fatherhood were ignored by a young man when he married and his wife became pregnant. The baby was born with severe birth defects and although surgery might have saved his life, the physician refused to operate. The mother receives a vision from God depicting the horrific life her son would lead and soon accepts the physician's decision. The baby dies and the baby is seen going to heaven in the arms of Jesus. The second scenario involved a young woman whose mother had epilepsy. She heeds the doctor's warning and refuses to marry her sweetheart. At last she discovers that the woman she thought was her mother was really her stepmother and she could marry without fear of passing on epilepsy to her children. She weds and subsequently gives birth to a healthy, chubby, and very fit baby. *The Black Stork* premiered in 1916 and was shown, under a different name from 1918 until the early 1940s. A revised edition was released in 1927 to update the story somewhat for a more modern audience but the pro-eugenics theme remained.[16]

The 1910s saw the release of many films dealing with health-related issues. A number of other pro-eugenics films were made before and after *The Black Stork*. Anti-eugenics films were also made and ridiculed the idea that science could overpower romantic love.[17] Haiselden never acted again. America's entrance into World War I took his story off the front pages. He left Chicago in April 1919 for Cuba where he died several months later.[18] Although investigations suggested criminal charges be brought for his actions he was never prosecuted. Haiselden only lost his membership in the Chicago Medical Society because he contacted the media to secure attention to his work.[19]

The number of babies allowed, or helped, to die because of real and perceived disabilities will probably never be known. Some, born at home, may never have come to the attention of physicians or surgeons equipped to treat them. Other physicians, with the implied if not written consent of the parents, certainly allowed babies to die. As Pernick points out active and passive infanticide has always been practiced. Ancient Greeks and Romans could legally practice infanticide. Despite laws prohibiting the practice that were in effect as early as the fourth century it remained a legitimate alternative for those babies identified as "monsters" or "changelings." Infanticide regained some popularity in the late nineteenth century for babies thought to be a burden to their families and communities.[20] Harry Haiselden was not the first physician to allow babies to die; but he was the first to garner national attention to his efforts.

Later in the twentieth century allowing defective babies to die again made headlines. In one particular case, an infant identified only as Baby Doe, was born in 1982 and diagnosed at birth with Down Syndrome and esophageal atresia, a condition that involves the termination of the infant's esophagus, or feeding tube, before it reaches the stomach. A physician told the parents that if the baby had surgery it had only a 50 percent chance of survival and that even if the baby lived, it would always be disabled, dependent, and medically needy. The physician opined that the baby should be allowed to die without treatment. The parents agreed despite the disagreement voiced by several other hospital physicians. A lawsuit ensued, however the baby died a few days after birth. Immediately controversial, the decision to allow the baby to die ignited the simmering debate over the rights of babies, their parents, and physicians. When another case in 1983 again prompted headlines more calls came for legislative action to protect babies. Laws requiring treatment for all babies were disallowed by the courts. However Congress, in 1984, rewrote the definition of child abuse to include the withholding of medical treatment for infants with birth defects. More than twenty years later the resultant federal regulations remain controversial as physicians and parents struggle to define the best course for individual babies.[21]

THE END OF THE FIRST WAVE OF MASSIVE IMMIGRATION

By the end of World War I the great waves of immigrants from Western Europe dwindled. In 1921 Congress passed a quota law that severely limited the number of immigrants allowed into the United States from countries other than those in Northern Europe and placed an overall limit on the number of immigrants entering the United States each year. The 1924 Immigration Act made permanent the quota system based on national origins. Again, the system favored those from Northern and Western Europe and disadvantaged those from Southern and Eastern Europe who had been so much criticized before. This quota system, with a few adjustments, remained in place until 1952.[22] The proponents of eugenics were relieved as the number of babies born to parents thought unsavory because of their racial and ethnic backgrounds was limited. The 1924 law effectively quieted the issue of immigration.

By the post–World War II era support for eugenics had all but evaporated. Displaced persons from war-torn areas and foreign-born "war brides" of American soldiers and sailors encouraged the public to ask for immigration revisions. Beginning in 1945 several limited laws loosening immigration requirements helped a few relatively small groups of people. In 1952 the various statutes passed since 1924 were consolidated in the Immigration and Nationality Act. This legislation eliminated race as a barrier to immigration, revised and loosened the quota system, admitted more immigrants from Asian countries, and gave preference to foreign-born relatives of American citizens and aliens. The legislation also required immigrants to annually report their addresses to the Immigration and Naturalization Service and set up a central list of all immigrants residing in the United States.[23]

NEW CONCERNS ABOUT IMMIGRATION

The civil rights movement produced more concern about many groups who were apparently disadvantaged, and immigrants were one such group. President Lyndon B. Johnson (1963–1968) tackled civil rights issues and tried to improve the United States through his Great Society program. In 1965 legislation passed by Congress and signed by President Johnson finally abolished the quota system. National origin, race, and ancestry were no longer to be used when deciding eligibility for immigration. Although the new law placed a restriction on the total number of immigrants, immediate relatives of American citizens were exempted as were immigrants from the Western Hemisphere. The number of immigrants from Mexico, the Caribbean, Latin America, and Asia soared. Millions also came illegally as economic conditions in Latin American nations worsened and population there increased. Between 1965 and 2000 the U.S. Congress reacted by passing many additional pieces of legislation to modify or change the existing immigration laws. In most cases the laws were tightened. In 1990 the total number of immigrants allowed in each year was increased, but more restrictions were imposed. In 1996 the Welfare Reform Act denied federal and state welfare benefits to most legal aliens. Also in 1996 the Illegal Immigration Reform and Immigrant Responsibility Act added even more restrictions on benefits.[24]

Yet the last decade of the century produced possibly even more concern about immigrants, legal and illegal, and their effect on the country than was true in 1901. Opponents to immigration fault the 1965 legislation for opening up immigration to Mexican and Central American citizens and encouraging the increase in illegal immigration.[25] For some people babies became a focus of anger. Those born before coming to the United States were viewed as problems because of the potential need for welfare services. Those born after the mother entered the country were automatic citizens and could not be deported. Because almost no one wants to separate a baby from its mother, the mother and other relatives seemed to get a free pass.

"A babe is a mother's anchor." —Henry Ward Beecher

Henry Ward Beecher was a Congregational minister who was born in 1813, began preaching in the 1830s and became well known as a leader in the Abolitionist movement to free the slaves. He died in 1887. During one of his many sermons he spoke the words above. He never could have imagined that very similar words would be used in a derogatory manner to describe babies born in America to immigrant women.[26]

"Anchor babies" is a term used by opponents of immigration. It was used in the late twentieth century to describe the babies of illegal immigrants born after their arrival in the United States. The babies were said to anchor their mothers, and families, in the country for good. The term has usually been applied to Mexican immigrants who enter the country illegally over the southwestern border. Babies of such illegal immigrants effectively become political pawns in the great debate over immigration. One side argues for the repeal of the right to citizenship for babies of illegal immigrants born on American soil with the goal of diminishing the appeal of illegal immigration. The other side rejects this approach and argues for immigration policies that address the illegal immigration issue without stripping the right of citizenship from babies.[27]

CONCLUSIONS

At the end of the twentieth century the two main population issues were the declining number of babies born to "native" Americans and the increased immigration of people viewed by some as inferior to the traditionally white middle-class citizen. The "baby bust" of the 1980s and 1990s has led to fears of an overwhelmingly large middle-aged and elderly population without enough young people to support them. On the other hand the rapid rise in the population of the United States has people calling for more access to birth control and the end to immigration as it is currently practiced. Immigration opponents cite concerns for the environment and the inability to provide for an ever-increasing citizenry. The birth of babies is still celebrated, as long as they are born to citizens who are self-supporting. Immigrants who can blend in easier—like those from Northern Europe earlier in the century—are not generally viewed as threats when they give birth. Those of a darker countenance, like Mexicans and others from Central and South America, have a more difficult time being accepted. Like the immigrants from Southern and Eastern Europe a century ago, they must struggle for respect. When they are forced to live in poverty their babies also suffer. At the beginning of the twenty-first century it is unclear how or when the issues associated with immigration will be resolved. The population of the United States is increasing and as it does so the ability to adequately care for babies as individuals and as a nation will be tested. The results will determine the future of the country.

NOTES

1. Frank Hobbs and Nicole Stoops, "U.S. Census Bureau, Census 2000 Special Reports, Series CENSR-4," in *Demographic Trends in the Twentieth Century* (Washington, DC: U.S. Government Printing Office), 7, 11–12; and "Table 1-1 Live Births, Birth Rates, and Fertility Rates, by Race of Child: United States, 1909–1980," in *Vital Statistics of the United States, 1997 Volume 1, Natality* (Hyattsville, MD: National Center for Health Statistics, Centers for Disease Control: 1997).

2. Hobbs and Stoops, "U.S. Census Bureau, Census 2000 Special Reports, Series CENSR-4," A–7.

3. David I. Macleod, *The Age of the Child—Children in America, 1890–1920* (New York: Twayne Publishers, 1998), 10–12, Daniel J. Kevles, *In the Name of Eugenics: Genetics and the Uses of Human Heredity* (New York: Alfred A. Knopf, 1985), 85–90; and Geraldine Youcha, *Minding the Children: Child Care in America from Colonial Times to the Present* (New York: Scribner, 1995), 117.

4. U.S. Census Bureau, *Immigration Legal History* (ILH). Legislation from 1790–1900: 3 and Legislation from 1901–1940: 3, (n.d.), http://www.uscis.gov/files/nativedocuments/legislation.

5. MacLeod, *The Age of the Child*, 10–12; Wendy Kline, *Building a Better Race: Gender, Sexuality and Genetics from the Turn of the Century to the Baby Boom* (Berkeley: University of California Press, 2001), 8–12; Paul L. Lombardo, "Taking Eugenics Seriously: Three Generations of ??? Are Enough?" *Florida State University Law Review* 30 (2003): 191–218; and Kevles, *In the Name of Eugenics*, 72–74.

6. Kevles, In the Name of Eugenics, 4.

7. Ibid., 44–49; and Edwin Black, *War against the Weak—Eugenics and America's Campaign to Create a Master Race* (New York: Thunder's Mouth Press, 2003), 252–258. See also Charles B. Davenport Papers, ca. 1903–1940, Background Note, American Philosophical Society, Philadelphia, PA.

8. Kevles, *In the Name of Eugenics*, 57–63; and American Eugenics Society Records, 1916–1973, Background Note, American Philosophical Society, Philadelphia, PA.

9. Kevles, *In the Name of Eugenics*, 57–69.

10. Ibid., 108–109.

11. Ibid., 110–112; and Michael B. Katz, *In the Shadow of the Poorhouse—A Social History of Welfare in America* (New York: Basic Books, 1986), 183–184.

12. Kevles, *In the Name of Eugenics*, 275–276.

13. William Branigin, "Warner Apologizes to Victims of Eugenics." *The Washington Post*, May 3, 2002, B1.

14. Martin S. Pernick, *The Black Stork* (New York: Oxford University Press, 1996).

15. Ibid., 3–7.

16. Ibid., 5–6, 143–158.

17. Ibid., 129–141.

18. Ibid., 11–12.

19. Ibid., 7–8.

20. Ibid., 19–24.

21. Loretta M. Kopelman, "Are the 21-Year-Old Baby Doe Rules Misunderstood or Mistaken?" *Pediatrics* 115 (2005): 797–802.

22. ILH, Legislation from 1901–1940, Quota Law of May 19, 1921, Immigration Act of May 26, 1924, 3–6; and Legislation from 1941–1960, 1–5.

23. ILH, Legislation from 1941–1960, 2–5; and Black, *War against the Weak*, 202–205, 275.

24. ILH, Legislation from 1961–1980, 1–6; and ILH, Legislation from 1981–1996, 1–7.

25. Leon F. Bouvier and Lindsey Grant, *How Many Americans? Population, Immigration and the Environment* (San Francisco, CA: Sierra Club Books, 1994), 6–7, 20–23, 79.

26. Thomas W. Knox, *Life and Work of Henry Ward Beecher* (Hartford, CT: The Hartford Publishing Company, 1887), 25, 140–141, 305; and Lyman D. Abbot and S.B. Halliday, *Henry Ward Beecher: A Sketch of His Career* (Hartford, CT: American Publishing Company, 1887), 634.

27. Edward Sifuentes, "Minuteman, Contreras debate illegal immigration," *North County Times*, June 22, 2006, http://www.nctimes.com/articles/2006/06/23/news/top_stories/22_30_156_22_06.txt.

Infertility and the Quest
for American Babies

"When you go to the doctor and he tells you that you're not going to be able to have a baby . . . it's like the world comes crashing down on you."

—Doris Del Zio[1]

You grow up, get married, and start a family. For many generations of citizens this American dream appeared to work perfectly. Getting pregnant and giving birth seems easy enough—after all, the mechanics are purely human nature. However, throughout human history, some would-be parents have been thwarted in their desires to have babies. Although we now know that both men and women have infertility problems, in the past women were blamed when a couple did not produce children. Kings and queens required progeny to carry on the royal bloodlines and maintain familial power. Wives who did not "give their husbands a child" (preferably a boy) were shunned, divorced, and even killed. Motherhood was often considered the only way for women to achieve eternal salvation; those who remained childless might hope to gain heavenly favor through other good works, but there were no guarantees.[2] Infertility has many causes, some of which remain unknown.[3] Until the late nineteenth century the only treatments available were patience, prayers, and belief in the powers of a myriad of folk cures. For many people none of this worked and their dreams of becoming parents faded over time. Some were pitied; others thought too selfish to share their lives with children. Most people affected by infertility simply continued on with their lives. Adoption was an alternative in some cases and certainly many children benefited from a loving and nurturing adoptive home.[4]

On July 25, 1978, a baby girl was born in Manchester, England, and named Louise Brown. She was heralded around the world as the first "test tube baby." She was healthy and happy and represented the beginning of the end to the answer to infertility to many men and women in England, the United States, and elsewhere. The first American test tube baby, Elizabeth Jordan Carr, was born on December 28, 1981. Since then thousands of American babies have been born using reproductive technology. Couples previously without hope of having their children naturally are benefiting from the new technology and raising families of one or more children. In addition to the in vitro fertilization used for Louise Brown, other methods have been used including refined and improved fertility drugs, microsurgery techniques to open blocked fallopian tubes, artificial insemination, and a variety of other simple and complex means. Men, who account for up to 40 percent of infertility problems among couples, are also treated, although there has not been as much progress in treating men for infertility as there has been in treating women for infertility. Some male infertility issues remain untreatable. Unfortunately for some men and women, there is no identifiable cause of infertility, nor any cure.[5]

While infertility remains the most compelling reason for reproductive assistance measures, other reasons surfaced during the 1980s and 1990s. Single women without a boyfriend or husband sought medical help when they wanted to have a child but faced an expiring "biological clock." Sperm donors provided the requisite sperm and doctors helped the women achieve their dream. Some women, who were unable to carry a baby to full term, turned to surrogate mothers. Oftentimes relatives, but sometimes strangers, surrogates provided a womb for the baby of another woman and man to grow in until birth. The surrogate relinquished the baby at birth to the parents. During the 1990s lesbians and gay men also turned to reproductive technology to aid their desires to have families of their own.[6] By the end of the century it seemed that anyone wanting a baby could have one given the right technology and the means to pay for it. Unfortunately the technologies do not work for everyone, although the percentages of successful pregnancies achieved through assistive reproduction have been increasing.

A RIGHT TO HAVE BABIES?

The stunningly rapid advances in reproductive technology since the 1960s left many physicians, scientists, ethicists, politicians, religious leaders, and parents overwhelmed and often confused. Ethical dilemmas cropped up immediately. Was it ethical, or even legal, to interfere with the natural process of human reproduction? How would the babies born as a result of such treatment grow and develop? Would they be "normal"? Who would decide when to proceed with fertility treatments and were there any people who should be excluded from receiving them? Who would pay for the treatments? What would happen to embryos created in the lab but not implanted into a mother's womb?[7]

Only a few of these questions have answers. Louise Brown had no known birth defects and by all accounts grew and developed normally. She had a sister a few years later, also a "test tube" baby, who in the late 1990s became the first of these children to give birth herself, without any fertility assistance. In her late twenties Louise was engaged to be married and was looking forward to bearing her own children.

The ethical questions remain contentious in the United States. Politicians regularly argue the merits of one point of view over another while the general public struggles to understand the myriad methods of treatment and the positives and negatives of each. For most people infertility remains a mystery until and unless they are affected by it personally.

HISTORIC PERSPECTIVES ON INFERTILITY

Before the twentieth century little, if anything, could be done about infertility. Religious belief played a major role in the lives of American families and the lack of offspring was often seen as the "will of God."[8] This attitude was similar notion to that of parents of babies who died at birth or during infancy. Not until after the Civil War, and the increasing medicalization of many human conditions, did infertility begin to receive outside attention. Various surgical techniques were developed in an attempt to fix the perceived problems and physicians began to consider the effects of illnesses such as gonorrhea on infertility. Male infertility was also "discovered" during these years and ascribed to many issues, including venereal disease (correctly) and masturbation (incorrectly).[9] In 1895 one surgeon began to transplant portions of ovaries from fertile women into infertile women. Despite more than ten years of practice, only one baby was born after transplantation and the procedure was abandoned.[10] That women voluntarily underwent such an untested procedure at a time when death due to infection and other surgical mishaps was very high demonstrates the desperation many felt when unable to conceive.

By the beginning of the twentieth century, while infertility was recognized as a problem for women (and some men), there were very few options available to those who sought them. Patent medicines were touted as the answer for many women but were as ineffective for infertility as they were for many of the other diseases and conditions they purportedly relieved.[11] During the first half of the century most infertile women and men were forced to do what their ancestors had done—hope and pray for a baby. In a society where marriage and motherhood were expected for young women, those who did not conceive soon after their weddings became frustrated.

There was some hope however. Physicians began experimenting with artificial insemination as early as the 1850s. Physicians would wait while a married couple had sexual intercourse, then shortly after they finished, withdraw fluid from the woman's vagina and inject it into her uterus. Since no one understood the precise timing needed in regard to ovulation, nor the scope of fertility problems, the procedure was rarely successful.[12] Artificial insemination by donor (AID) was successful as early as 1884 when a Philadelphia physician inseminated a woman with the sperm of an attractive male medical student, without the knowledge of the woman or her husband. When the news came out several decades later the procedure became more common despite generally negative public response. Concerns arose regarding the donor—was he of the same ethnic, racial, and cultural backgrounds as the prospective parents? This was very troubling in the early twentieth century when miscegenation was a serious issue. Legal issues also arose. AID could lead, legally in some states, to charges of adultery and thus suitable grounds for divorce. Children born after AID could also be legally considered illegitimate. Both adultery and illegitimacy could be claimed even when the husband gave his written consent for his wife to undergo AID. During the second half of the twentieth century the legal issues became less important as society became more receptive to AID. The numbers of children conceived and born via this method increased to approximately 20,000 every year.[13]

Physicians responded to female sterility with other surgical procedures; unfortunately most were ineffective at best and frequently ill-advised as well.

During the latter half of the nineteenth century sterility was often believed to be the result of mechanical problems and physicians operated on many women in an attempt to devise procedures that would solve the problem of infertility. Ovaries were removed and cervixes were clipped in what were essentially experimentations without what we would today consider informed consent of the patient. Very few pregnancies occurred after the operations and they were eventually abandoned.

Adoption was an alternative used by many infertile couples in an era when single mothers and their babies were shunned because birth outside marriage was considered taboo. After World War II parents increasingly preferred to adopt infants rather than older children, perhaps to hide the fact that they were not the biological parents. Prior to the twentieth century adoption often was not legalized and thus records do not accurately reflect the extent of this practice. Legal statutes began to appear in the middle of the nineteenth century. Welfare agencies were rarely authorized to remove babies of single mothers or babies thought to be at risk due to poverty of their biological parents from these parents. Sometimes welfare officials justified their reluctance to remove babies from their impoverished biological parents with the argument that the single mother or family should be responsible themselves for the baby. Foster parenting was encouraged. After some time in an approved foster home babies whose biological parents had brought their home up to the standards set by the welfare agency had their babies removed from foster care and returned to them. Becoming a foster parent was not as attractive as adoption to childless couples seeking a permanent family of their own.[14]

During the late nineteenth and twentieth centuries public and private agencies provided assistance to expectant mothers willing to place their infants or children for adoption. Private adoptions, generally with the intervention of a lawyer, also occurred frequently. Until later in the twentieth century it was customary for the birth mother to give up all rights to the baby shortly after birth. Laws preventing the disclosure of birth and adoption information to the baby or the birth mother severed any possibility of future contact. In the later part of the twentieth century adults adopted as children have achieved legal victories allowing them to access adoption and birth records. In most cases the information obtained is nonidentifying; however, many adoptees have had reunions with birth mothers and fathers.[15] While adoption provided safe and happy homes for many babies and fulfilled the wishes of infertile couples for a family of their own, it did not solve the underlying problem of infertility. Nevertheless, stories continue to be told of women who conceived naturally after deciding to adopt, presumably because when they ceased to worry about conception they relaxed, thus allowing conception to occur.[16]

Assisted reproduction reached several major milestones early in the twentieth century. The expansion of knowledge about infertility corresponded with the advancement of the practices of obstetrics and gynecology. As physicians gained respect and authority they were able to examine the reproductive organs of women (and men) in much greater detail than ever before. The identification of sexually transmitted diseases, especially gonorrhea, as causes of infertility helped explain many cases. Gonorrhea was found to cause sterility in men who often passed on the infection to their wives causing pain and suffering. Gonorrhea was not curable until the 1940s with the availability of penicillin, but its identification as a problem in both men and women was a breakthrough and "focused scientific attention on the biology of reproduction and the physical impediments to conception."[17]

The identification of hormones as key to the process of reproduction in humans occurred in the early twentieth century. By the 1930s scientists were aware that women required certain amounts of estrogen to conceive a baby and progesterone to maintain a pregnancy. Without the appropriate amounts of either, pregnancy could either not occur at all, or was doomed to fail. In men, sperm production depended on the appropriate amount of testosterone. Throughout the 1930s and 1940s scientists worked first to extract hormones from humans and when that proved difficult to produce synthetic hormones. Fertility treatment with synthetic hormones took off and by mid-century in the major cities, infertile couples could find physicians willing to use them.[18] Over the next several decades doctors refined infertility treatment using hormones and it became more successful for those whose infertility could be traced to hormonal problems.

By the 1970s the numbers of infertile couples seemed to be increasing. It was unclear whether the increase was due to an actual increase in infertility or an increase in the numbers of people seeking treatment for infertility. It was clear that the number of physicians willing and able to treat at least some causes of infertility was increasing. Success rates were never high and even in the best practices rarely exceeded 25 percent. Surgery, all but abandoned by the 1940s, was safer but no more successful. Psychological reasons for infertility were proposed and accepted by many professionals as well as by the general public. Doctors advised women to quit their jobs, hire help for housework, and generally learn to relax if they had trouble conceiving a baby. Male infertility was increasingly treatable through hormone therapy as well as surgery. It remained, however, difficult to persuade some men that they could be the source of the couple's infertility problem.[19]

In vitro fertilization (IVF) had its beginnings in the 1940s when a Harvard University professor, Dr. John Rock, announced the successful fertilization of four donated human eggs. He lacked the facilities and knowledge to do any-more at that point, yet he did not lack volunteers for further experimentation. Hundreds of infertile women, when they heard of Rock's success, wrote to him offering their uteruses to further his work and hopefully provide them a baby.[20]

IVF faced many obstacles. The physical conditions necessary for it to be successful are difficult to achieve, yet seem simple when compared to the moral, ethical, and legal questions IVF raised in the United States and around the world. In 1973 Doris Del-Zio was poised to become the first American woman to have an embryo, created in the laboratory from the fertilization of her egg with her husband's sperm, implanted into her uterus. The procedure was being done in secret and before the embryo could be implanted it was destroyed by authorities at Columbia Presbyterian Medical Center in New York City. For the Del-Zio's this was the end of their hopes of having a child together. (Doris had one child from a previous marriage and John had two children, also from a previous marriage.) Columbia's objections centered on the procedure itself, the credibility of the researchers, and the legality of the procedure. They were afraid, since the procedure was not yet legal in the United States, that all federally funded research projects underway at Columbia were at risk if the University allowed the Del-Zio IVF to proceed. The Del-Zio's eventually sued the physician responsible for the destruction of their embryo. The jury found for them, but awarded far less money than they requested. Less than ten years later, the physician, Raymond Vand Wiele, was appointed the head of a new IVF clinic at Columbia Presbyterian Medical Center.[21]

HOPES AND FEARS

For many Americans the idea of a "test tube" baby conjured up images of all the monster movies they had ever watched. Surely playing with nature would result in bad things. At the same time dreams of a future where everyone who wanted a baby could have one, and congenital diseases would be only a bad memory, held the promise of a better life for all. National pride was also at stake—if anyone should be the first to produce a "test tube" baby surely it should be a fellow American. After all, American ingenuity had won a world war and since then had given Americans the highest quality of life on Earth.

Even in the 1970s, when the use of ovulation-stimulating drugs and hormones had been accepted for several decades, the fear of producing a baby with devastating birth defects was too much for many hospitals to contemplate. The 1970s was an era when issues such as informed consent, ethical considerations of treatments, and liability for previously unknown complications of treatments all became hot topics in hospital board rooms. In order to design a research study on human beings, scientists had to prove that they had considered all of the possible complications and repercussions of their proposed treatments, experimented on animal subjects, and had procedures in place to obtain written, informed consent from all human subjects. While this may seem second nature today, at the time, having to justify the proposed research to relative strangers was a change for most scientists. In the past research was carried on, for the most part ethically, out of the spotlight until scientists could publicly announce results that improved the health and well-being of humans. But recent revelations of scientific mistakes and misdeeds made the process of medical research much more public and much more emotionally charged.[22] Public and private funding sources also increased the complexity of their applications to reflect the increased concern for public safety. Thus researchers in the United States who had been working on infertility for decades had to justify their research in new ways just as they were getting to the process of IVF.

These concerns led to the almost complete ban on IVF research in the United States by the late 1970s. In addition, the 1973 Supreme Court decision to uphold *Roe v. Wade*, guaranteeing American women the right to an abortion, galvanized anti-abortion activists. The process of IVF would almost certainly result in embryos left over once the strongest were implanted into the patient's uterus. These embryos would then be disposed of—either actively killed or passively allowed to die. Some believed this practice resembled abortion. Several states considered this fetal research unethical and banned it. In 1975 the federal government temporarily suspended all funding for IVF until the meeting of the newly formed National Ethics Advisory Board in January 1978.[23]

With the Americans effectively out of the race, the focus of IVF shifted to other countries. Australia, India, and England all had scientists closing in on the goal of a baby born via IVF. Drs. Robert Edwards and Patrick Steptoe worked in the north of England and despite the official misgivings of the British government were able to secure enough private funds and public approval from their local hospital to continue their research. It ultimately resulted in a pregnancy for Lesley and Gilbert Brown of Bristol, England. Mrs. Brown had blocked fallopian tubes. She had several operations attempting to open them but each operation failed. In late 1977 her pregnancy via IVF was confirmed and she gave birth to a healthy baby girl on July 25, 1978. Louise Brown's birth made headlines around the world. Steptoe and Edwards had filmed the birth to prove their claim that Mrs. Brown's fallopian tubes had been removed and that IVF had been used. The fear that IVF would create a baby with horrible defects was put to rest. By all accounts Louise was a healthy, happy, and above all apparently normal baby.[24]

In the United States, the National Ethics Advisory Board finally met to discuss IVF and, after more bureaucratic red tape, allowed the opening of IVF clinics although the government offered them no funding. In Norfolk, Virginia, the first American IVF clinic opened on March 1, 1980, at the Eastern Virginia Medical Center, despite the objections of right-to-life groups. The first American test tube baby was born in Virginia on December 28, 1981. Elizabeth Carr was the fifteenth IVF baby born worldwide. The federal government funding ban remained in place. However, private funding sources made money available and within two years several large, private, institutions had opened IVF clinics and were routinely using IVF to achieve successful pregnancies.[25]

INFERTILITY SINCE THE MID-1980s

Infertility remains an issue for American parents today. Diagnostic techniques have developed tremendously and can pinpoint the cause of infertility, be it male or female, with astonishing accuracy. In some cases, couples go through testing only to find out that no one knows what is causing their inability to conceive. This is probably the most frustrating answer infertile couples can hear. For the majority of people there are options. Surgery to correct physical abnormalities is often a first course when no other problems are known to exist. Hormone therapy, either alone or in conjunction with IVF and its many similar procedures, is also commonplace today.

Intracytoplasmic sperm injection (ICSI) has been available since the early 1990s as a treatment for male infertility. This procedure "involves the injection of a single sperm into an egg."[26] ICSI has been controversial. There is some evidence that genetic diseases or chromosomal abnormalities that caused male infertility in the first place can be transferred to the resulting baby. More studies are needed to confirm or reject these findings. Parents are urged to take advantage of genetic counseling.[27]

For many parents the availability of infertility treatments has been a blessing—their families simply would not exist if not for some sort of treatment. The fear that babies born after IVF would be monsters virtually disappeared by the 1990s. IVF was common and almost everyone knew of someone who was experiencing infertility and either using IVF or contemplating using it. In 1982 physicians in the United States had two statements ready for press release once the first American IVF baby was born. One would announce the birth of a healthy baby and focus on the promise of the technology for other infertile couples. The other press release was written in case the first birth after IVF resulted in a baby with significant birth defects.[28] Fortunately Elizabeth Carr was born healthy and had an apparently healthy childhood.[29] By the 1990s early concerns about IVF babies seemed quaint. But as with any technology there were potential problems.

COMPLICATIONS

One area of concern for babies born after the use of any type of assisted reproductive technique is the increased number of twin, triplet, and other higher order multiple births. Statistics accumulated over the past twenty years indicate a definite increase in the number of multiple births and a significant relationship between this increase and the use of artificial means of inducing or creating pregnancies. The likelihood of birthing more than one baby rises with increased maternal age both for those using assisted reproductive techniques and for those who have a naturally conceived pregnancy.[30] In the late 1990s there were a few highly publicized cases of women carrying seven and eight babies. The babies were born prematurely and experienced stays in neonatal intensive care units. Several of the babies experienced long-term effects of premature birth including cerebral palsy.[31]

When more than one baby is conceived and carried by a mother, the risk of problems skyrockets. Identical twins (the result of one fertilized egg dividing into two embryos) and fraternal twins (two fertilized eggs) have always occurred naturally. Triplets are seen naturally much less frequently, but they are not rare. Twins, and more so triplets, put a much greater strain on the mother's entire body system and these pregnancies often result in premature birth with all its potential problems. Even twins and triplets carried to term tend to be smaller than the average newborn. Quadruplets (four), quintuplets (five), sextuplets (six), and so on, have a very difficult time in utero and premature birth is quite likely.

There are several reasons for the increased numbers of multiple births among fertility patients. Women taking fertility drugs tend to produce more than the normal one egg per cycle. When more than one egg is fertilized, a multiple pregnancy can occur. Women who undergo IVF or another assisted fertility technique take drugs purposely to induce the maturation of multiple eggs at the same time. These eggs are harvested and when fertilization takes place more than one embryo usually results. Because not all embryos may implant, it has been the practice of IVF clinics to implant two or more embryos at a time. If more than one implants successfully, a multiple pregnancy occurs. Twins are generally not too much of a problem; however, when three or more embryos implant women and their husbands or partners are faced with tough decisions. In Europe, some countries have legally mandated that IVF clinics transfer no more than three embryos at a time. In the United States there is no legal mandate; however, organizations such as the Society for Assisted Reproductive Technology and the American Society for Reproductive Medicine are suggesting that the number transferred be voluntarily limited.[32]

Many physicians today will suggest that a woman "reduce" or abort the extra embryos to bring the pregnancy down to two or three at the most. This decision poses an ethical and moral quandary for many who do not support abortion. Even for those who do, aborting embryos that one worked so hard to produce can be emotionally distressing. Which embryos to abort, for those who decide to do so, is another dilemma. When all appear to be healthy, which ones are chosen to remain? The answers to these questions are intensely personal for the parents involved.[33] Yet the answers are also political in the United States where the right to an abortion is considered inviolable by one side and considered murder by the other side.

PHYSICAL AND DEVELOPMENTAL OUTCOMES

While it appears that the vast majority of babies born to infertile couples utilizing the various forms of assisted reproduction techniques are healthy there is increasing concern that these techniques increase the risk of physical and developmental defects. Some studies suggest that the major problems encountered are due to premature birth, a frequent outcome of multiple pregnancies.[34] Other studies have concluded that babies born after their mothers use certain assisted reproduction techniques including IVF develop birth defects at a higher rate than naturally conceived babies.[35] Obviously much more work is needed to determine the actual prevalence of physical and developmental defects among these babies and to develop techniques to decrease or eliminate any problems found.

OTHER USES FOR ASSISTED REPRODUCTION

Some parents have begun to use assisted reproduction techniques in order to avoid certain genetic diseases and conditions. This field was just beginning to grow in the late 1990s and holds out promise for people not wishing to pass on inheritable and potentially debilitating and sometimes fatal diseases. Preimplantation genetic diagnosis (PGD) involves creating embryos using IVF and, before transferring any embryo to the mother, testing one cell of each embryo for genetic disease. Those embryos free of disease are transferred; those affected are not and are probably discarded.[36] PGD has become controversial. The same technology that allows screening for devastating diseases can also screen for other inherited characteristics and can allow parents to select the sex of their offspring. For many people the screening of embryos for diseases that would cause a painful and circumscribed life is morally acceptable. Selecting embryos that will produce children who are taller than average, have a specific hair color, or other more desirable characteristics is less acceptable. People are less clear about the ethical implications of selecting embryos based on the risk of a possible adult onset disease such as breast cancer.[37]

PGD has also been used to screen embryos for one that would be a genetic match for a sibling suffering from a potentially fatal disease such as cancer. Bone marrow transplantation is often curative for these children, but marrow must be harvested from a person who is an exact genetic match. In the past parents have conceived children in hopes of producing a genetic match for the cancer patient. PGD helps ensure that the child born will match.[38]

Another concern about PGD is that it remains expensive. Health insurance coverage varies greatly and its availability will ultimately be driven by cost-benefit analysis and also, in all likelihood, by political realities. If PGD for desirable characteristics is considered morally unacceptable it may not be covered by health insurance. Without insurance payments only the wealthy will be able to afford it. Those unable to pay will continue to run the risk of bearing children with serious inheritable disease. Moreover, even healthy children born to those who are not rich enough to afford PGD may be left further behind children of the well-to-do who have been selected for their academic, athletic, intellectual, and cosmetic superiority.[39]

CONCLUSIONS

By the end of the twentieth century infertile men and women were able to utilize scientific and medical advances in their quest for babies. Within one generation the number of children conceived through advanced reproductive techniques such as IVF has dramatically increased. These children have grown up and are now beginning their own families. Childlessness has become an option for many people, rather than an unfortunate and emotionally devastating diagnosis. Infertility treatment has become so mainstream that people discuss and debate its merits as easily as they might the weather. For those going through the process of infertility diagnosis and treatment this public familiarity can be a blessing and a curse. As discussed in Chapter 2, advice and opinions are offered whether they are requested or not, and while generally well meaning, can be seen as intrusive. The number of twins and triplets born to those who have undergone infertility treatment has also led to some misunderstandings. In the late 1990s a friend of mine had identical twins, conceived naturally. During her pregnancy, and after the twins were born, many people, friends, and strangers alike assumed that she had had infertility treatments and commented on it. Taken aback, she did not know whether to deny it or to tell the people to mind their own business.[40]

The success rates of the many methods of artificial conception vary widely. The success of more invasive techniques such as IVF are improving, yet depend a great deal on the age and health of the mother-to-be, and on the reasons for the infertility diagnosis. Doctors and clinics publicize their success rates; however, each case needs to be considered separately as well. The definition of success may also vary. Is a pregnancy enough to claim success? A live-born baby? A full-term baby? A healthy baby? And what of the future? The long-term consequences of infertility treatments on the babies conceived and born are only now beginning to be understood. As these children grow, and more babies are born, the answers to how successful infertility treatments are may begin to be answered.

For those Americans who have experienced the birth of a healthy baby because of infertility treatments the future looks bright. The hopelessness they felt when unable to conceive naturally fades away when holding a baby in their arms. The expense, both financially and emotionally, becomes tolerable and perhaps inconsequential. The number of books chronicling infertility issues continues to multiply. Some recount individual experiences while others attempt to make sense of all the resources available to infertile people.[41] Novelists have also written about infertility—although since most people like a story with a happy ending, the stories often end with the heroine getting pregnant and giving birth to a beautiful, healthy, and full-term baby.[42]

Infertility treatment has been a major success in the United States during the twentieth century. It promises more success in the twenty-first century when the ethical and moral questions surrounding it will mature and demand more involved answers. Those unable to have a baby despite years of infertility treatment will look for newer and better designed options to help them on their quest. The American dream of having a baby of one's own will continue to drive this process.

NOTES

1. Doris Del Zio and her husband John attempted to have a baby via in vitro fertilization in 1973 but were thwarted by officials at a New York Hospital. They successfully sued the doctors involved but never had their own children, http://www.pbs.org/wgbh/amex/babies/sfeature/stories_01_1.html.

2. Janet Jaffe, Martha Ourieff Diamond, and David J. Diamond, *Unsung Lullabies: Understanding and Coping with Infertility* (New York: St. Martin's Griffin, 2005), 34–36; Debora L. Spar, *The Baby Business: How Money, Science, and Politics Drive the Commerce of Conception* (Boston, MA: Harvard Business School Press, 2006), 6–11; Marlynn Salmon, "The Cultural Significance of Breast-Feeding and Infant Care in Early Modern England and America," in Rima D. Apple and Janet Golden, eds., *Mothers and Motherhood: Readings in American History* (Columbus: Ohio State University Press, 1997), 24.

3. Spar, *The Baby Business*, 2; and Samuel Smith, Samantha M. Pfeifer, and John A. Collins, "Diagnosis and Management of Female Infertility," *Journal of the American Medical Association* 290(13) (2003): 1767–1770. Causes of infertility are varied. According to the National Institutes of Health (NIH) and the National Library of Medicine (NLM) age is one factor—women older than thirty-five, and even more so those older than forty, have less than a 10 percent chance of getting pregnant each month. Infertility risk also rises when there are (or were) multiple sexual partners, sexually transmitted diseases, a history of pelvic inflammatory disease, testicular defects or diseases in men, mumps in men, chemical exposures, eating disorders in women, anovulation, endometriosis, uterine and/or cervical defects or obstructions, and chronic diseases such as diabetes. Men are thought to be the responsible party in about 30–40 percent of infertility and women in 40–50 percent. 10–30 percent of cases are either shared or due to some unknown cause.

4. For an in-depth analysis of the history of adoption in America see E. Wayne Carp, ed., *Adoption in America: Historical Perspectives* (Ann Arbor: University of Michigan Press, 2002); and E. Wayne Carp, *Family Matters: Secrecy and Disclosure in the History of Adoption* (Cambridge, MA: Harvard University Press, 1998).

5. Stephen F. Shaban, "Male Infertility Overview: Assessment, Diagnosis, and Treatment," *Georgia Reproductive Associates* (2005), http://www.ivf.com/shaban.html; American Society for Reproductive Medicine (ASRM), "*Infertility: An Overview. A Guide for Patients* (Birmingham, AL: ASRM, 2003), 8–9; Natan Bar-Chama, "It's in the Male: Getting a Grip on Male Factor Infertility," *American Fertility Association* (2004–2006), http://www.theafa.org/faqs/afa_itsinthemale.html.

6. The Ethics Committee of the American Society for Reproductive Medicine (ASRM), "Access to Fertility Treatment by Gays, Lesbians, and Unmarried Persons," *Fertility and Sterility* 86(5) (2006): 1333–1335.

7. Robin Marantz Henig, *Pandora's Baby* (Boston, MA: Houghton Mifflin Company, 2004), 64–77.

8. Margaret Marsh and Wanda Ronner, *The Empty Cradle: Infertility in America from Colonial Times to the Present* (Baltimore, MD: Johns Hopkins University Press, 1996), 2.

9. Ibid., 89–96.

10. Ibid., 131–134.

11. Ibid., 105.

12. Spar, *The Baby Business*, 18; and Marsh and Ronner, *The Empty Cradle*, 66–71.

13. Henig, *Pandora's Baby*, 26–29.

14. E. Wayne Carp and Anna Leon-Guerrero, "When in Doubt, Count—World War II as a Watershed in the History of Adoption," in E. Wayne Carp, ed., *Adoption in America*, 210; Carp, *Family Matters*, 11–12, 28–31, 49, 82, 143, 198; and Marsh and Ronner, *The Empty Cradle*, 105–108.

15. Access to adoption records is controlled by state laws in the United States. See Child Welfare Information Gateway, "Access to Adoption Records," *Child Welfare Information Gateway* (2006), http://www.childwelfare.gov/systemwide/laws_policies/statutes/infoaccessacfm. See also Carp, *Family Matters*, 30–31, 102–121, 169–195.

16. Marsh and Ronner, *The Empty Cradle*, 204–205.

17. Spar, *The Baby Business*, 18–19.

18. Ibid., 20–21.

19. Marsh and Ronner, *The Empty Cradle*, 181–202; and Spar, *The Baby Business*, 23–24.

20. Spar, *The Baby Business*, 21–22.

21. See Henig, *Pandora's Baby*, for the complete story of the Del-Zio's quest to conceive a baby and the legal proceedings that resulted after the destruction of their embryo prior to transfer.

22. Henig, *Pandora's Baby*, 82–84; and Marsh and Ronner, *The Empty Cradle*, 238. The Tuskegee Syphilis Study and the Dalkon Shield are two of the instances that prompted tighter control of the research process.

23. Marsh and Ronner, *The Empty Cradle*, 233–234.

24. Henig, *Pandora's Baby*, 133–134, 150–152, 170–173, 262; Spar, *The Baby Business*, 24–26; and Marsh and Ronner, *The Empty Cradle*, 234–238.

25. Marsh and Ronner, *The Empty Cradle*, 238–241; and Henig, *Pandora's Baby*, 130–132, 134–138, 176, 205–212, 217–228.

26. Marsh and Ronner, *The Empty Cradle*, 248.

27. M.G. Kent-First, S. Kol, A. Muallem, R. Ofir, D. Manor, S. Blazer, N. First, and J. Itskovitz-Eldor, "The Incidence and Possible Relevance of Y-Linked Microdeletions in Babies Born After Intracytoplasmic Sperm Injection and Their Infertile Fathers," *Molecular Human Reproduction* 2(12) (1996): 943–950; Mark D. Johnson, "Genetic Risks of Intracytoplasmic Sperm Injection in the Treatment of Male Infertility: Recommendations for Genetic Counseling and Screening," *Fertility and Sterility* 70(3) (1998): 397–411; and P. Devroey and A. Van Steirteghem, "A Review of Ten Years Experience of ICSI," *Human Reproduction Update* 10(1) (2004): 19–28.

28. NOVA, *18 Ways to Make a Baby*, prod. Sarah Holt. Originally broadcast on PBS, October 9, 2001. Transcript at http://www.pbs.org/wgbh/nova/transcripts/2811baby. html.

29. Henig, *Pandora's Baby*, 264.

30. Centers for Disease Control and Prevention, (CDC), "Contributions of Assisted Reproductive Technology and Ovulation-Inducing Drugs to Triplet and Higher-Order Multiple Births—United States, 1980–1997," *Morbidity and Mortality Weekly Report* 49(24) (2000): 535–538; CDC, "Impact of Multiple Births on Low Birthweight—Massachusetts, 1989–1996," *Morbidity and Mortality Weekly Report* 48(14) (1999): 289–292; C. Tallo, B. Vohr, W. Oh, L.P. Rubin, D.B. Seifer, and R.V. Haning, Jr., "Maternal and Neonatal Morbidity Associated with In Vitro Fertilization," *Journal of Pediatrics* 127(5) (1995): 794–800; L.S. Wilcox, J.L. Kiely, C.L. Melvin, and M.C. Martin, "Assisted Reproductive Technologies: Estimates of Their Contribution to Multiple Births and Newborn Hospital Days in the United States," *Fertility and Sterility* 65(2) (1996): 361–366; Meredith A. Reynolds, Laura A. Schieve, Joyce A. Martin, Gary Jeng, and Maurizio Macaluso, "Trends in Multiple Births Conceived Using Assisted Reproductive Technology, United States, 1997–2000," *Pediatrics* 111(5) (2003): 1159–1162; Laura A. Schieve, Herbert B. Peterson, Susan F. Meikle, Gary Jeng, Isabella Danel, Nancy M. Burnett, and Lynne S. Wilcox, "Live-Birth Rates and Multiple-Birth Risk Using In Vitro Fertilization," *Journal of the American Medical Association* 282(19) (1999): 1832–1838; and Tamara L. Callahan, Janet E. Hall, Susan L. Ettner, Cindy L. Christiansen, Michael F. Greene, and William F. Crowley, "The Economic Impact of Multiple-Gestation Pregnancies and the Contribution of Assisted-Reproduction Techniques to Their Incidence," *New England Journal of Medicine* 331(4) (1994): 244–249.

31. Susan Schindehette, "Coming Up Roses," *People Weekly*, December 8, 1997, 54–60; Linda Kulman, "Cigars All Around," *U.S. News and World Report*, December 1, 1997, 14; Michael D. Lemonick and Jeffrey Kluger, "It's A Miracle," *Time*, December 1, 1997, 34–39; John McCormick and Barbara Katrowizt, "The Magnificent Seven," *Newsweek*, December 1, 1997, 58–62; Claudia Kalb, "Families: The Octuplet Question," *Newsweek*, January 11, 1999, 33; and "Question Time," *People Weekly*, January 11, 1999, 72.

32. The Practice Committee of the Society for Assisted Reproductive Technology and the Practice Committee of the American Society for Reproductive Medicine, "Guidelines on Number of Embryos Transferred," *Fertility and Sterility* 86(4) (2006): S51–S52; Susan Mayor, "UK Authority Sets Limit on Number of Embryos Transferred," *British Medical Journal* 328 (2004): 65; and Schieve et al., "Live-Birth Rates and Multiple-Birth Risk Using In Vitro Fertilization."

33. R.J. Wapner, G.H. Davis, A. Johnson, V.J. Weinblatt, R.L. Fischer, L.G. Jackson, F.A. Chervenak, and L.B. McCullough, "Selective Reduction of Multifetal Pregnancies,"

The Lancet 335 (1990): 90–93; Richard L. Berkowitz, Lauren Lynch, Joanne Stone, and Manuel Alvarez, "The Current Status of Multifetal Pregnancy Reduction," *American Journal of Obstetrics and Gynecology* 174(4) (1996): 1265–1272; and Callahan et al., "The Economic Impact of Multiple-Gestation Pregnancies and the Contribution of Assisted-Reproduction Techniques to Their Incidence."

34. Tallo et al., "Maternal and Neonatal Morbidity Associated with In Vitro Fertilization."; T. Bergh, A. Ericson, T. Hillensjö K.G. Nygren, and U.B. Wennerholm, "Deliveries and Children Born After In-Vitro Fertilisation in Sweden 1982–95: A Retrospective Cohort Study," *Lancet* 354 (1999): 1579–1585; and B. Stromberg, G. Dahlquist, A. Ericson, O. Finnström, M. Köster, and K. Stjernqvist, "Neurological Sequelae in Children Born After In-Vitro Fertilisation: A Population Study," *Lancet* 359 (2002): 461–465.

35. Henig, *Pandora's Baby*, 238–242; Sari Koivurova, Anna-Liisa Hartikainen, Mika Gissler, Elina Hemminki, Ulla Sovio, and Marjo-Riitta Järvelin, "Neonatal Outcome and Congenital Malformations in Children Born After In-Vitro Fertilization," *Human Reproduction* 17(5) (2002): 1391–1398, Michele Hansen, Jennifer J. Kurinczuk, Carol Bower, and Sandra Webb, "The Risk of Major Birth Defects After Intracytoplasmic Sperm Infection and In Vitro Fertilization," *New England Journal of Medicine* 346(10) (2002): 725–230; E.R. Maher, L.A. Brueton, S.C. Bowdin, A. Luharia, W. Cooper, T.R. Cole, F. Macdonald, J.R. Sampson, C.L. Barratt, W. Reik, and M.M. Hawkins, "Beckwith-Wiedemann Syndrome and Assisted Reproduction Technology (ART)," *Journal of Medical Genetics* 40 (2003): 62–64; Laura A. Schieve, Sonja A. Rasmussen, Germaine M. Buck, Diana E. Schendel, Meredith A. Reynolds, and Victoria C. Wright, "Are Children Born After Assisted Reproductive Technology at Increased Risk for Adverse Health Outcomes?" *Obstetrics and Gynecology* 103(6) (2004): 1154–1163; and Alfred A. Rimm, Alyce C. Katayama, Mireya Diaz, and K. Paul Katayama, "A Meta-Analysis of Controlled Studies Comparing Major Malformation Rates in IVF and ICSI Infants with Naturally Conceived Children," *Journal of Assisted Reproduction and Genetics* 21(12) (2004): 437–443.

36. Spar, *The Baby Business*, 98; and Kathy L. Hudson, "Preimplantation Genetic Diagnosis: Public Policy and Public Attitudes," *Fertility and Sterility* 85(6) (2006): 1638–1645.

37. Hudson, "Preimplantation Genetic Diagnosis."

38. Ibid.

39. Ibid.

40. Catherine Corcoran, conversation with author, Spring 1999; confirmed December 14, 2006.

41. Patty Doyle Debano, Courtney Edgerton Menzel, and Shelly Dicken Sutphen, *The Conception Chronicles: The Uncensored Truth About Sex, Love and Marriage When You're Trying to Get Pregnant* (Deerfield Beach, FL: Health Communications, Inc., 2005); Jaffe, Diamond, and Diamond, *Unsung Lullabies*; M. Sara Rosenthal, *The Fertility Sourcebook* (Chicago: Contemporary Books, 1995); and Debra Fulghum Bruce and Samuel Thatcher, *Making a Baby: Everything You Need to Know to Get Pregnant* (New York: Ballantine Books, 2000).

42. Barbara Delinsky, *The Woman Next Door* (New York: Simon and Schuster, 2001); and Danielle Steele, *Mixed Blessings* (New York: Dell Publishing, 1992).

Beginning the World Again—American Babies at the Start of a New Century

By what astrology of fear or hope
Dare I to cast thy horoscope!
Like the new moon thy life appears;
A little strip of silver light,
And widening outward into night
The shadowy disk of future years
——Henry Wadsworth Longfellow, *To a Child*

On January 1, 2001, at 12:32 A.M., Eastern Standard Time, a baby girl was born in Biddeford, Maine. According to the *Bangor Daily News*, she was the first baby born in Maine in 2001.[1] Miami welcomed its first baby at 1:01 A.M., while in Chicago, where Baby Iagolo was the first baby in that city in 1901, two babies were born at the stroke of midnight. Moving to the West Coast, San Jose, California, welcomed a baby boy at ten seconds past midnight and in Hawaii a baby boy was born at 12:08 A.M. in an army hospital.[2] These babies, the first few of the more than 4 million born in 2001, represent the future of the United States.[3]

The beginning of a new century, indeed a new millennium, is a chance to celebrate both the past and the future. Between 1901 and 2000, the life of babies in America improved dramatically. The infant mortality rate (IMR), considered a key measure of a nation's overall health, declined from a high of approximately 100 deaths in the first year of life for every 1,000 white babies and 200 per 1,000 black babies born in the United States in 1915 to 6 per one thousand white babies and slightly more than 14 per 1000 black babies in 1998.[4] These figures alone are cause for celebration for they indicate astonishing achievement in a variety of fields. Cultural, social, technological, medical, and political changes occurred that redefined the status of babies and in so doing changed the entire nature of infancy. This is not to say that this all happened in the twentieth century. Many of the physical and cultural advantages enjoyed by twentieth-century babies had their roots in the nineteenth century. Late in that century Progressive Era reformers began to focus their efforts on life in major cities. Babies, as well as all citizens, benefited from their efforts to clean up the water supply and sewer services. Infection rates declined as more and more Americans acquired new knowledge of disease transmission. The increasing importance of and attention to the well-being of infants, already apparent in the middle and upper classes by the 1890s, expanded to the working and lower classes between 1900 and 1930.

Changes affecting all Americans directly and indirectly affected babies throughout the country. Industrial and home safety regulations as well as medical advances helped parents survive their baby's childhood. Maternal death in childbirth declined substantially, leaving fewer babies motherless or orphaned. Between 1950 and 1998, maternal death fell by 90 percent.[5] Improvements in nutrition for all produced healthier babies at birth and enhanced growth and development during the first year of life. Immunizations have saved many lives and in a few cases virtually eliminated once dreaded diseases of infancy and childhood. Other medical breakthroughs include the acknowledgement of infants as physiologically different from older children and adults, the introduction of prenatal care for mothers-to-be, the advancement of premature infant care, the development of surgical procedures that correct once debilitating and even fatal birth defects, and the improved treatment of "typical" diseases including infectious diarrhea and ear infections as well as rare but previously always deadly forms of cancer. Sudden Infant Death Syndrome (SIDS), once a scary and random problem of infancy that defied multiple attempts at prevention, has decreased substantially since the early 1990s. Changing infants' sleep position, from the traditional prone to supine, was a result of long-term research and has saved many infant lives.[6]

CELEBRATING BABIES

Americans became fascinated with babies during the twentieth century. The decline in the fertility rate, begun in the latter part of the nineteenth century, meant smaller families and perhaps more attention to and regard for babies. The baby boom of the 1940s through early 1960s disrupted the decline of the fertility rate but did not stop it. There are more babies born in the United States today than ever before because of the overall increased population, but the fertility rate continues to fall. The birth of any baby is a major event for a family and often celebrated with exuberance.

Early in the century mothers (and fathers, although the emphasis was on mothers) needed prodding to celebrate their babies. For the first time in the 1910s baby contests supported by the U.S. Children's Bureau, rewarded the mothers of the best-looking, healthiest, and most intelligent babies as defined by various "authorities."[7] Baby contests, baby parades, and baby model searches are still held around the country today. Parenting and women's interest magazines urge mothers to send in pictures of their babies for a chance at a cover shot and the resultant fame.[8] "Celebrity" babies are not a new passion either. The birth of the Dionne quintuplets in Canada was front-page news in the United States. Many Americans traveled to Ontario to see them in the exhibition hospital built to house them and bought products that used their names and pictures for purposes of increasing sales.[9] Later in the century multiple births continued to fascinate as the extensive coverage of sextuplets (six) and septuplets (seven) in the 1980s and 1990s demonstrated. Popular magazines and newspapers print frequent stories about the babies of actresses and successful athletes. Babies who survive life-threatening events are also heralded.

Attention to babies has influenced all aspects of life in America. Economically, babies are very good for business. Many parents are eager to possess the latest baby gear and manufacturers are happy to oblige, reinventing many things time and again. Often these items feature improved safety and comfort features; other times they appeal to a desire for the superiority that comes with possessing a new version of almost anything. If a neighbor purchases a battery-operated, multiple-position swing that plays selections of classical music for a baby, can a parent justify keeping the old windup swing handed down from the baby's grandparents?

The increased availability of knowledge about babies has itself spawned business. Advice for new parents abounds. Parents are inundated with information on the latest and greatest ways of raising a baby from the time the mother discovers she is pregnant. In 1901 there was only a limited amount of literature about babies available. By 1920 the amount of information available had increased dramatically and came from books, newspapers, magazines, doctors, social workers, and the government. In the 1950s and 1960s the amount soared again. It would seem that American parents had, by the end of the century, an abundance of knowledge and expertise from which to draw regarding their babies. Yet the sheer volume of information can itself cause anxiety. Even with all the advances of the past century parents today continue to worry about their babies. When babies are portrayed as vulnerable and fragile, it is not surprising that parents fear for a baby's safety. Nearly instantaneous media coverage of any event involving a baby's safety and vulnerability increases the anxiety of parents and promotes the protective nature of all citizens.

Keeping babies safe has always been one of the key tasks of parenthood. In the twentieth century, the increased focus on babies has transferred some of this responsibility to society at large. Safety campaigns attempt to prevent any number of calamities that have a potential impact on babies and children. Safety measures in place for infants by the end of the century included radio frequency alarm bracelets placed on newborns in hospital nurseries to prevent kidnapping, rear-facing car seats required in all fifty states to protect babies in car crashes, and safety standards in some states that regulate crib design to decrease the number of head entrapment and fall injuries. A federal agency, the Consumer Products Safety Commission, works to improve safety and decrease injury from many consumer goods. Infants and children are a major focus of their efforts. But can all threats be identified and thwarted? Do we want to make our children's lives so safe that they never learn the healthful and life-saving aspects of fear?[10] While many Americans see these baby protection initiatives as positive influences, some people view them as governmental intrusions into family life. In previous centuries the rights of parents to raise their children as they saw fit superceded all other views. In the twentieth century parents did not have as much freedom.

CONTINUING PROBLEMS

While most American babies live much more comfortable and healthy lives than their counterparts a century ago, problems remain. As the twentieth century progressed it became apparent that many babies needed governmental assistance to fully benefit from the new ideas and attention to infant care. Poverty, a problem in most societies, has not been eliminated. During the Great Depression of the 1930s the level of federal and state involvement in the lives of babies expanded dramatically and set the tone for the rest of the century. This involvement has greatly benefited many babies over the years. Nutrition programs ensure that they have enough food to eat. Preventive care and medical treatments are available at low or no cost. Babies living in high-risk environments are watched for signs of abuse and neglect. But serious problems with the various programs exist. They are not always administered in a fair and just manner. Paperwork abounds, and even in the computer age system breakdowns and failures occur and babies sometimes "fall through the cracks." Governmental programs cost a lot of money and are financed by all of us through taxes. Most of these programs were conceived of as temporary assistance for the truly needy. Some families, however, remained dependent on governmental assistance for many years. The general public rebelled and during the 1990s called for and received new legislation aimed at returning the system to temporary assistance with incentives to climb out of poverty to a self-sustaining lifestyle. Will this work without sacrificing the gains made in the health and well-being of babies? It is still too soon to tell but it is difficult to imagine America turning its back on babies in the twenty-first century.

How to deal effectively with the impact on babies of racism and immigration is more difficult to imagine. Racism was an unacknowledged truth in 1901, rarely discussed and hidden in laws and widespread practices designed to keep African-Americans from achieving a better life for themselves and their families. By the 1960s many considered racism a national disgrace and it was widely discussed. Unfortunately racism did not end with the century. Changes have been made and black babies in general are also healthier than the average baby in 1901. But many more changes are required before an African-American baby will be offered the same possibilities as others. Even though most Americans are descended from immigrants, immigration presents a recurring threat to some. Babies of immigrants, whether born here or brought here after birth, are affected when their parents' intentions, loyalty, intelligence, and ability to assimilate are questioned. Early in the century reformers, in their quest to improve IMRs and "Americanize" entire families, focused on the babies of recent immigrants. Immigration law expanded and the number of immigrants allowed to enter the country each year became more restricted throughout the century. In the late 1990s concern about immigrants from Mexico and Central

America as well as from Asian nations rivaled concerns about Southern and Eastern European immigrants a century ago.

Neither racism nor immigration problems will go away easily. As much as America celebrates the common citizen it struggles to identify commonality among all its citizens. Babies born in a racist society are affected no matter what their race. Babies are not born with preconceived notions of other races. Like so many other things they learn from the words and actions of their parents and others around them.

One thing we do have in common, no matter where our parents, grandparents, or ancestors originally hailed from, is that we all started life as babies. We were all helpless in the sense that we needed adults to care for us—to feed and clothe us, protect us from danger, and to seek help in our name when necessary. Most of the time parents are able to fulfill those needs. However, sometimes parents are unable to do so, either partially or completely. When this happens babies require assistance to assure their survival. As a society Americans took on that challenge in the twentieth century. Ignoring the needs of the smallest members of society was no longer acceptable. All American babies were deserving of the support of their fellow citizens.

BABIES IN THE TWENTY-FIRST CENTURY

On January 1, 2101, babies will be born and celebrated as the first new Americans of the twenty-second century. What will history say about the infancy of their great grandparents, grandparents, and parents? The ability to predict the future is quite limited for most people and I will certainly not attempt to make specific predictions about babies in the current century. However, we can assume that some patterns will persist. Experts predict that the declining birthrate will continue, although recent immigrants will maintain an overall higher birthrate. This pattern has been repeated since at least the mid-1800s and should not be a surprise to anyone.

One area that should continue to evolve and change is infertility treatment. Technological and medical breakthroughs will probably allow even more women to become mothers in ways that are safer for them and their babies. The ability to collect and store semen and eggs to conceive babies years later has evolved rapidly along with the ability to freeze embryos conceived in the laboratory for future implantations and births. In 2007 there are reports of babies born who were conceived months and even a few years after the deaths of their fathers in the Iraq War. The fathers had deposited semen samples as a safeguard against injury or death. The mothers conceived the babies through artificial means.[11] Efforts are also underway to decrease the risk of multiple gestations and the problems inherent with them while also increasing the likelihood that infertility treatments will result in healthy babies. Ethical, moral, and legal issues related to infertility treatment are also evolving and will hopefully catch up to the technology in a meaningful manner.

It is difficult to imagine what life was like for a baby at the beginning of the twentieth century. It is impossible to generalize, for then, as now, babies' experienced life through the lens of the families into which they were born. Political, economic, and environmental issues all affect American families to greater and lesser degrees. Middle-class and upper-class families provided for their babies without difficulty 100 years ago and no change in that ability is seen for the current century. For the working and lower classes, financial struggle has always been a part of life. A baby deprived of basic necessities will be hard-pressed to enjoy the benefits of twenty-first-century life.

Presidential candidates in the United States often ask potential voters "are you better off today than you were four (or eight) years ago?" In 2000 and 2001 Americans asked themselves that question about the entire century. Were we better off in 2001 than in 1901? It is tempting to think of 1901 as a simpler time for all Americans, including babies. There were few automobiles so there were no concerns about the type and brand of car seat to purchase. More families worked closer to or at home so the long commutes that take parents away from babies and children for many hours a day did not disrupt many families' lives a century ago. No televisions meant more meaningful time with the baby. Or did it? The availability of consumer products that we take for granted today would make parents of 1901 cringe with jealousy. Disposable diapers and a dependable supply of clean water are only two examples that make lives easier for babies and parents today. Cars simplify the transport of babies from place to place and have even been known to lull a cranky baby to sleep.

The twentieth century has often been called the American century and the century of the child. Over the course of 100 years the lives of all American babies have improved. At the 1939–1940 New York World's Fair, a sign at the entrance to the premature infant incubator exhibit read "all the world loves a baby."[12] Today in America most people would agree with that sentiment when asked. We believe that babies mean more to us now than ever before in history, yet our actions as a nation and as individuals do not always support the notion. Most Americans are aware of the inequities in our society. How we choose to address them will undoubtedly affect the lives of all, including babies.

Challenges remain as America ages. The needs of a burgeoning elderly population will compete with the needs of infants and children for interest and material resources. How much of a finite supply of money and personal resources is set aside for babies is an issue that demands attention today.[13] For at least 100 years babies have been a barometer of sorts, allowing us to measure ourselves against other nations and societies. The first year of all our lives influences our health and welfare for our entire lives. We owe it to the babies of tomorrow to ensure that their well-being remains at the top of any list of national priorities.

NOTES

1. "Maine's 1st Baby in 2001 Born to Sanford Pair," *Bangor Daily News*, January 2, 2001, 1.

2. "Welcome to the World of 2001," *Miami Herald*, January 2, 2001, 2B; "Special Deliveries for 2001," *Chicago Sun-Times*, January 2, 2001, 1; Steve Rubenstein, "San Jose Baby's Birth Sets Slew of Records," *San Francisco Chronicle*, January 2, 2001; and Rosemary Bernardo, "Hawaii's First 2001 Baby Checks in Three Days Early," *Honolulu Star-Bulletin*, January 1, 2001.

3. Joyce A. Martin, Brady E. Hamilton, Stephanie J. Ventura, Fay Menacker, Melissa M. Park, and Paul D. Sutton, "Births: Final Data for 2001," *National Vital Statistics Reports* 51(2) (December 18, 2002): 3. "Beginning the World Again" is adapted from "every child begins the world again" in Henry D. Thoreau, *Walden, An Annotated Edition*, ed. Walter Harding (New York: Houghton Mifflin Company, 1995), 25.

4. Bernard Guyer, Mary Anne Freedman, Donna M. Strobino, and Edward J. Sondik, "Annual Summary of Vital Statistics: Trends in the Health of Americans during the Twentieth Century," *Pediatrics* 106(6) (2000): 1307–1317.

5. Ibid., 1307.

6. Ibid., 1313. Placing babies on their backs or sides to sleep resulted in a 40 percent drop in mortality caused by SIDS between 1992 and 1998.

7. See Annette K. Vance Dorey, *Better Baby Contests: The Scientific Quest for Perfect Childhood Health in the Early Twentieth Century* (Jefferson, NC: McFarland & Company, 1999).

8. See, for example the Americanbaby.com photo contest Web site, http://www.americanbaby.com/app/photocontest.

9. Thomas E. Cone, Jr., *History of the Care and Feeding of the Premature Infant* (Boston, MA: Little, Brown and Company, 1985), 64–66; and John Nihmey and Stuart Foxman, *Time of Their Lives—The Dionne Tragedy* (Ottawa, Canada: NIVA Publishing, 1987).

10. Peter N. Stearns, *Anxious Parents, A History of Modern Childrearing in America* (New York: New York University Press, 2003).

11. Gregg Zoroya, "Science Makes Fallen Soldier a Father," *USA Today*, February 12, 2007, http://www.usatoday.com/news/nation/2007-02-11-soldier-child-cover_x.htm.

12. A.J. Liebling, "Patron of the Preemies," *The New Yorker*, 15 (June 3, 1939), 20–24.

13. Guyer et al., "Annual Summary of Vital Statistics," 1316.

Bibliography

Abbot, Lyman D., and S.B. Halliday. *Henry Ward Beecher: A Sketch of His Career.* Hartford, CT: American Publishing Company, 1887.

Ackerknecht, E.H. "Incubator and Taboo." *Journal of the History of Medicine* 1 (January 1946): 144–148.

Adams, S.H. "The Great American Fraud." *Colliers Magazine* (October 7, 1905): 14.

American Academy of Pediatrics, Committee on Pediatric AIDS. "Planning for Children Whose Parents Are Dying of HIV/AIDS." *Pediatrics* 103(2) (1999): 509–511.

American Diabetes Association. "Type 2 Diabetes in Children and Adolescents." *Diabetes Care* 23(3) (2000): 381–389.

American Eugenics Society Records, 1916–1973. American Philosophical Society. Philadelphia, PA.

American Society for Reproductive Medicine (ASRM). *Infertility: An Overview. A Guide for Patients.* Birmingham, AL: ASRM, 2003.

Andrews, Moya L. *Voice Treatment for Children & Adolescents.* Clifton Park, NY: Thomson Delmar Learning, 2001.

Annual Reports, 1926, 1928–1941. Philadelphia Lying-In Hospital, Pennsylvania Hospital Archives. Philadelphia, PA.

Apple, Rima D., and Janet Golden, eds. *Mothers & Motherhood: Readings in American History.* Columbus: Ohio State University Press, 1997.

Armour, Amy A. "Hints for Maternity Nurses." *The Trained Nurse and Hospital Review* 53 (August 1914): 89–90.

Artenstein, Andrew W. "History of U.S. Military Contributions to the Study of Vaccines against Infectious Diseases." *Military Medicine* 170(4) (April Supplement, 2005): 3–11.

"Attachment Parenting International Position Paper Regarding the New Recommendations by the American Academy of Pediatrics." *Attachment Parenting International* (October 12, 2005), http://www.attachmentparenting.org/aappp.

Avery, Mary Ellen, and Ella H. Oppenheimer. "Recent Increase in Mortality from Hyaline Membrane Disease." *The Journal of Pediatrics* 57 (1960): 553–559.

Baker, Jeffrey P. "The Incubator Controversy: Pediatricians and the Origins of Premature Infant Technology in the United States, 1890–1910." *Pediatrics* 87(5) (1991): 654–662.

———. *The Machine in the Nursery*. Baltimore, MD: The Johns Hopkins University Press, 1996.

Baker, S. Josephine. "The Reduction of Infant Mortality in New York City." *American Journal of Diseases of Children* 5 (1913): 151–161.

Ball, Thomas M., and Anne L. Wright. "Health Care Costs of Formula-Feeding in the First Year of Life." *Pediatrics* 103 (1999): 870–876.

Bar-Chama, Natan. "It's in the Male: Getting a Grip on Male Factor Infertility." *American Fertility Association* (2004–2006), http://www.theafa.org/faqs/afa_itsinthemale.html.

Barlow, William E., Robert L. Davis, John W. Glasser, Phillip H. Rhodes, Robert S. Thompson, John P. Mullooly, Steven B. Black, Henry R. Shinefield, Joel I. Ward, S. Michael Marcy, Frank DeStefano, Virginia Immanuel, John A. Pearson, Constance M. Vadheim, Viviana Rebolledo, Dimitri Christakis, Patti J. Benson, Ned Lewis, and Robert T. Chen for the Centers for Disease Control and Prevention Vaccine Safety Datalink Working Group. "The Risk of Seizures after Receipt of Whole-Cell Pertussis or Measles, Mumps, and Rubella Vaccine." *The New England Journal of Medicine* 345(9) (2001): 656–661.

Barr, Bernadine Courtright. "Entertaining and Instructing the Public: John Zahorsky's 1904 Incubator Institute." *Social History of Medicine* (August 1, 1995): 17–36.

Bass, Jan. "First Infant Incubators in America Premiered in Omaha." *Omaha Magazine* (February 1998): 66.

Baughcum, Amy E., Kathleen A. Burklow, Cindy M. Deeks, Scott W. Powers, and Robert C. Whitaker. "Maternal Feeding Practices and Childhood Obesity." *Archives of Pediatric and Adolescent Medicine* 152 (1998): 1010–1014.

Baumgartner, Leona. "Nation-wide Plan for Reduction of Premature Mortality." *Journal of the American Medical Association* 146 (July 7, 1951): 893–896.

Beck, Andrew H. "The Flexner Report and the Standardization of American Medical Education" (Reprinted). *Journal of the American Medical Association* 291(17) (2004): 2139–2140.

Belongia, Edward A., Bradley J. Sullivan, Po-Huang Chyou, Elisabeth Magagame, Kurt D. Reed, and Benjamin Schwartz. "A Community Intervention Trial to Promote Judicious Antibiotic Use and Reduce Penicillin-Resistant Streptococcus pneumoniae Carriage in Children." *Pediatrics* 108(3) (2001): 575–583.

Bergh, T., A. Ericson, R. Hillensjo, K-G Nygren, and U-B Wennerholm. "Deliveries and Children Born After In-Vitro Fertilisation in Sweden 1982–95: A Retrospective Cohort Study." *The Lancet* 354 (1999): 1579–1585.

Berkowitz, Richard L., Lauren Lynch, Joanne Stone, and Manuel Alvarez. "The Current Status of Multifetal Pregnancy Reduction." *American Journal of Obstetrics and Gynecology* 174(4) (1996): 1265–1272.

Black, Edwin. *War against the Weak—Eugenics and America's Campaign to Create a Master Race*. New York: Thunder's Mouth Press, 2003.

Blanchette, Howard. "Comparison of Obstetric Outcome of a Primary-Care Access Clinic Staffed by Certified Nurse-Midwives and a Private Practice Group of

Obstetricians in the Same Community." *American Journal of Obstetrics and Gynecology* 172(6) (1995): 1864–1871.

Bok, Edward. *The Americanization of Edward Bok.* New York: Charles Scribner's Sons, 1921.

Boneva, Roumiana S., Lorenzo D. Botto, Cynthia A. Moore, Quanhe Yang, Adolfo Correa, and David Erickson. "Mortality Associated with Congenital Heart Defects in the United States, Trends and Racial Disparities, 1979–1997." *Circulation* 103 (2001): 2376–2381.

Bouvier, Leon F., and Lindsey Grant. *How Many Americans? Population, Immigration and the Environment.* San Francisco, CA: Sierra Club Books, 1994.

Bradley, William N. "The Care of the Premature Baby." *Medical Journal and Record* 124 (August 18, 1926): 222–225.

Brazelton, T. Berry. *Infants and Mothers: Differences in Development.* New York: Delacourt Press, 1967.

Brisbane, Arthur. "The Incubator Baby and Niagara Falls." *The Cosmopolitan* (September 1901): 509–516.

Brown, D.R., J.R. Milley, U.J. Ripepi, and A.W. Biglan. "Retinopathy of Prematurity. Risk Factors in a Five-Year Cohort of Critically Ill Premature Neonates." *Archives of Pediatrics and Adolescent Medicine* 141(2) (February 1987): 154–160.

Brown, Gary C., Melissa M. Brown, Sanjay Sharma, William Tasman, and Heidi C. Brown. "Cost-Effectiveness of Treatment for Threshold Retinopathy of Prematurity." *Pediatrics* 104 (1999): 47–52.

Brown, Julie C. "The Management of Croup." *British Medical Bulletin* 61 (2002): 189–202.

Bruce, Debra Fulghum, and Samuel Thatcher. *Making a Baby: Everything You Need to Know to Get Pregnant.* New York: Ballantine Books, 2000.

Bruner, Joseph P., Noel Tulipan, Ray L. Paschall, Frank H. Boehm, William F. Walsh, Sandra R. Silva, Marta Hernanz-Schulman, Lisa H. Lowe, and George W. Reed. "Fetal Surgery for Myelomeningocele and the Incidence of Shunt-Dependent Hydrocephalus." *Journal of the American Medical Association* 282(19) (1999): 1819–1825.

Budin, Pierre. *The Nursling: The Feeding and Hygiene of Premature and Full-Term Infants,* trans. William J. Malloney. London: The Caxton Publishing Company, 1907.

Buffum, William P., and George F. Conde. "The Use of Oxygen in the Care of Feeble Premature Infants." *Journal of Pediatrics* 4 (1934): 326–330.

Buhler Wilkerson, Karen. "The Call to the Nurse: Our History from 1893 to 1943." *Visiting Nurse Service of New York,* http://www.vnsny.org/mainsite/about/a_history_more.

Burgess, Alexander M., and Alexander M. Burgess, Jr. "A New Method of Administering Oxygen." *New England Journal of Medicine* 207 (1932): 1078–1082.

Callahan, Tamara L., Janet E. Hall, Susan L. Ettner, Cindy L. Christiansen, Mechael F. Greene, and William F. Crowley. "The Economic Impact of Multiple-Gestation Pregnancies and the Contribution of Assisted-Reproduction Techniques to Their Incidence." *The New England Journal of Medicine* 331(4) (1994): 244–249.

Campbell, Kate. "Intensive Oxygen Therapy as a Possible Cause of Retrolental Fibroplasia: A Clinical Approach." *The Medical Journal of Australia* 2 (1951): 48–50.

Campbell, Marie. *Folks Do Get Born.* New York: Rhinehart & Company, 1946.

Campbell, P.B., M.J. Bull, F.D. Ellis, C.Q. Bryson, J.A. Lemons, and R.L. Schreiner. "Incidence of Retinopathy of Prematurity in a Tertiary Newborn Intensive Care Unit." *Archives of Ophthalmology* 101(11) (November 1983): 1686–1688.

Canter, Charles, David Naftel, Randall Caldwell, David Naftel, Randall Caldwell, Richard Chinnock, Elfriede Pahl, Elizabeth Frazier, James Kirklin, Mark Boucek, and Robert Morrow for the Pediatric Heart Transplant Study, University of Alabama at Birmingham. for the Pediatric Heart Transplant Study, University of Alabama at Birmingham. "Survival and Risk Factors for Death After Cardiac Transplantation in Infants, A Multi-Institutional Study." *Circulation* 96(1) (1997): 227–231.

Caplan, W.D., T.R. Cooper, J.A. Garcia-Prats, and B.A. Brody. "Diffusion of Innovative Approaches to Managing Hypoplastic Left Heart Syndrome." *Archives of Pediatrics and Adolescent Medicine* 150(5) (1996): 487–490.

Capper, Aaron. "The Fate and Development of the Immature and of the Premature Child." *American Journal of Diseases of Children* 35 (February 1928): 262–275.

———. "The Fate and Development of the Immature and of the Premature Child." *American Journal of Diseases of Children* 35 (March 1928): 443–491.

Carp, E. Wayne. *Family Matters: Secrecy and Disclosure in the History of Adoption*. Cambridge, MA: Harvard University Press, 1998.

Carp, E. Wayne, ed. *Adoption in America: Historical Perspectives*. Ann Arbor: The University of Michigan Press, 2002.

Centers for Disease Control and Prevention. "Achievements in Public Health, 1900–1999: Healthier Mothers and Babies." *Morbidity and Mortality Weekly Report* 48(38) (1999): 849–858.

———. "Achievements in Public Health, 1900–1999: Safer and Healthier Foods." *Morbidity and Mortality Weekly Report* 48(40) (1999): 905–913.

———. "Achievements in Public Health: Elimination of Rubella and Congenital Rubella Syndrome—United States, 1969–2004." *Morbidity and Mortality Weekly Report* 54(11) (2005): 279–282.

———. "Impact of Multiple Births on Low Birthweight—Massachusetts, 1989–1996." *Morbidity and Mortality Weekly Report* 48(14) (1999): 289–292.

———. "Contributions of Assisted Reproductive Technology and Ovulation-Inducing Drugs to Triplet and Higher-Order Multiple Births—United States, 1980–1997." *Morbidity and Mortality Weekly Report* 49(24) (2000): 535–538.

———. "FAQs (Frequently Asked Questions) about Measles." *National Immunization Program* (2001), http://www.cdc.gov/nip/diseases/measles/faqs.htm.

———. "HIV and AIDS—United States, 1981–2000." *Morbidity and Mortality Weekly Report* 50(21) (June 1, 2001): 430–434. See also "Erratum: Vol. 50, No. 21," *Morbidity and Mortality Weekly Report* 50(47) (November 30, 2001): 1066.

———. "Rubella—In Short (German Measles)." *National Immunization Program* (2001), http://www.cdc.gov/nip/diseases/rubella/vac-chart.htm.

———. "Vaccinia (Smallpox) Vaccine: Recommendations of the Advisory Committee on Immunization Practices (ACIP)." *Morbidity and Mortality Weekly Report* 50(rr10) (June 22, 2001): 1–25.

———. "Table 1-1. Live Births, Birth Rates, and Fertility Rates, by Race of Child: United States, 1909–1980." In *Vital Statistics of the United States, 1997, Volume I, Natality* (National Center for Health Statistics, August 30, 2006), www.cdc.gov/nchs/data/statab/t991x01.pdf.

———. "Recommended Childhood and Immunization Schedule for Persons Aged 0–18 Years—United States, 2007." *Morbidity and Mortality Weekly Report* 55(51) (January 5, 2007): Q1–Q4.

CDC and National Immunization Program. "Achievements in Public Health, 1900–1999 Impact of Vaccines Universally Recommended for Children—United States, 1990–1998." *Morbidity and Mortality Weekly* 48(12) (1999): 243–248.

CDC and National Immunization Program. "Hib Immunization." *American Academy of Pediatrics* (2006), http://www.cispimmunize.org/ill/ill_main.html.

Century of Progress collection. Main Library, Special Collections. University of Illinois at Chicago.

Chiavarelli, M., S.R. Gundry, A.J. Razzouk, and L.L. Bailey. "Cardiac Transplantation for Infants with Hypoplastic Left Heart Syndrome." *Journal of the American Medical Association* 270(24) (1993): 2944–2947.

Child Welfare Information Gateway. "Access to Adoption Records." Child Welfare Information Gateway (2006), http://www.childwelfare.gov/systemwide/laws_policies/statutes/infoaccessap.cfm.

Clarke, T. Wood. "The Baby in the Small City." *Lady's Home Journal* (July 1914): 61.

Clement, Priscilla Ferguson. *Growing Pains: Children in the Industrial Age, 1850–1890.* New York: Twayne Publishers, 1997.

"Cloth without Looms." *Time* (May 25, 1942) www.time.com/time/printout/0,8816, 766607,00.html.

Clutch, Beatrice M. "Feeding Premature Infants." *The American Journal of Nursing* 25 (1925): 549–550.

Collins, Steve, Nicky Dent, Paul Binns, Paluku Bahwere, Kate Sadler, and Alistair Hallam. "Management of Severe Acute Malnutrition in Children." *The Lancet* 368 (2006): 1992–2000.

Committee for the Classification of Retinopathy of Prematurity. "An International Classification of Retinopathy of Prematurity." *Archives of Ophthalmology* 102(8) (1984): 1130–1134.

Cone, Thomas E. *History of American Pediatrics.* Boston, MA: Little, Brown and Company, 1979.

Cone, Thomas E., Jr. *History of the Care and Feeding of the Premature Infant.* Boston, MA: Little, Brown and Company, 1985.

Cooledge, Evelyn Linda. "The Young Mother's Calendar." *Lady's Home Journal* (December 1904): 30.

Crosse, V. Mary, and Philip Jameson Evans. "Prevention of Retrolental Fibroplasia." *Archives of Ophthalmology* 48 (1952): 83–87.

Davis, Robert L., Piotr Kramarz, Kari Bohlke, Patti Benson, Robert S. Thompson, Johan Mullooly, Steve Black, Henry Shinefield, Edwin Lewis, Joel Ward, S. Michael Marcy, Eileen Eriksen, Frank Destefano, and Robert Chen for the Vaccine Safety Datalink Team. "Measles-Mumps-Rubella and Other Measles-Containing Vaccines Do Not Increase the Risk for Inflammatory Bowel Disease." *Archives of Pediatric and Adolescent Medicine* 155 (2001): 354–359.

Debano, Patty Doyle, Courtney Edgerton Menzel, and Shelly Dicken Sutphen. *The Conception Chronicles: The Uncensored Truth About Sex, Love & Marriage When You're Trying to Get Pregnant.* Deerfield Beach, FL: Health Communications, Inc., 2005.

Delinsky, Barbara. *The Woman Next Door.* New York: Simon & Schuster, 2001.

Dell, Sharon, and Teresa To. "Breastfeeding and Asthma in Young Children." *Archives of Pediatric and Adolescent Medicine* 155 (2001): 1261–1265.

Derks, Scott. *Working Americans. Volume II: The Middle Class.* Lakeville, CT: Grey House Publishing, 2000.

Desmond, Murdina MacFarquhar. *Newborn Medicine and Society: European Background and American Practice (1750–1975).* Austin, TX: Eakin Press, 1998.

Devroey, P., and A. Van Steirteghem. "A Review of Ten Years Experience of ICSI." *Human Reproduction Update* 10(1) (2004): 19–28.

Dietz, William H. "Breastfeeding May Help Prevent Childhood Overweight." *Journal of the American Medical Association* 285(19) (2001): 2506–2507.

Diggins, F.W. "The True History of the Discovery of Penicillin, with Refutation of the Misinformation in the Literature." *British Journal of Biomedical Science* 56(2) (1999): 83–93.

Dittrich, H., C. Buhrer, I. Grimmer, S. Dittrich, H. Abdul-Khaliq, and P.E. Lange. "Neurodevelopment at 1 Year of Age in Infants with Congenital Heart Disease." *Heart* 89 (2003): 436–441.

Donadio, Stephen, Joan Smith, Susan Mensner, and Rebecca Davison, eds. *The New York Public Library Book of 20th-Century American Quotations.* New York: The Stonesong Press, Inc., and the New York Public Library, 1992.

Dorey, Annette K. Vance. *Better Baby Contests: The Scientific Quest for Perfect Childhood Health in the Early Twentieth Century.* Jefferson, NC: McFarland & Company, 1999.

Dubowitz, Lilly M.S., Victor Dubowitz, and Cissie Goldberg. "Clinical Assessment of Gestational Age in the Newborn Infant." *Journal of Pediatrics* 77 (July 1970): 1–10.

Duderstadt, Karen G., Dana C. Hughes, Mah-P Soobader, and Paul W. Newacheck. "The Impact of Public Insurance Expansions on Children's Access and Use of Care." *Pediatrics* 118(4) (2006): 1676–1682.

Dudgeon, J.A. "Immunization in Times Ancient and Modern." *Journal of the Royal Society of Medicine* 73 (1980): 581–586.

Dunham, Ethel C., and Jessie M. Bierman. "The Care of the Premature Infant." *Journal of the American Medical Association* 115 (1940): 658–662.

Dunn, Halbert L., Robert D. Grove, Iwao M. Moriyama, Sam Shapiro, Hugh Carter, Carl C. Dauer, Hazel V. Aune, Frank S. Morrison, and Howard West. "Analysis and Summary Tables with Supplementary Tables for Alaska, Hawaii, Puerto Rico and Virgin Islands." In *Vital Statistics of the United States, 1950,* Vol. 1. Washington, DC: U.S. Government Printing Office, 1954.

Edwards, Kathryn M. "State Mandates and Childhood Immunization." *Journal of the American Medical Association* 284(24) (2000): 3171–3173.

Einhorn, Marcus B. "The Premature Infant, A Statistical Study." *New York State Journal of Medicine* 40 (al 1940): 1380–1384.

Escobar, Gabriel J., Veronica M. Gonzales, Mary Anne Armstrong, Bruce F. Folck, Blong Xiong, and Thomas B. Newman. "Rehospitalization for Neonatal Dehydration." *Archives of Pediatric and Adolescent Medicine* 156 (2002): 155–161.

Ethics Committee of the American Society for Reproductive Medicine. "Access to Fertility Treatment by Gays, Lesbians, and Unmarried Persons." *Fertility and Sterility* 86(5) (2006): 1333–1335.

Farley, Reynolds, and Walter R. Allen. *The Color Line and the Quality of Life in America* New York: Russell Sage Foundation, 1987.

"Fat Babies and Health." *Journal of the American Medical Association* 41 (1903): 37. Reprinted, *Journal of the American Medical Association* 289(14 (2003): 1866.

Felix, Carolyn A., J. Beverly, B.J. Lange, and Judith M. Chessells. "Pediatric Acute Lymphoblastic Leukemia: Challenges and Controversies in 2000." *Hematology* 2000 1 (2000): 285–302.

Fierson, Walter M., Earl A. Palmer, Albert W. Biglan, John T. Flynn, Robert A. Petersen, and Dale L. Phelps. "Screening Examination of Premature Infants for Retinopathy of Prematurity." *Pediatrics* 100 (1997): 273–274.

Finer, Lawrence B., and Stanley K. Henshaw. "Disparities in Rates of Unintended Pregnancy in the United States, 1994 and 2001." *Perspectives on Sexual and Reproductive Health* 38(2) (2006): 90–96.

Freedom, Robert M., James Lock, and J. Timothy Bricker. "Pediatric Cardiology and Cardiovascular Surgery, 1950–2000." *Circulation* 102 (2000): IV-58–IV-68.

Furman, Lydia, Gerry Taylor, Nori Minich, and Maureen Hack. "The Effect of Maternal Milk on Neonatal Morbidity of Very Low-Birth-Weight Infants." *Archives of Pediatric and Adolescent Medicine* 157 (2003): 66–71.

Georgia Public Health Oral History Collection. Special Collections. Robert W. Woodruff Library, Emory University. Atlanta, Georgia.

Gillman, Matthew W., Sheryl L. Rifas-Shiman, Carlos A. Camargo, Catherine S. Berkey, A. Lindsay Frazier, Helaine R.H. Rockett, Alison E. Field, and Graham A. Colditz. "Risk of Overweight among Adolescents Who Were Breastfed as Infants." *Journal of the American Medical Association* 285(19) (2001): 2461–2467.

Glynn, Simone A. "Trends in Incidence and Prevalence of Major Transfusion-Transmissible Viral Infections in US Blood Donors, 1991 to 1996." *Journal of the American Medical Association* 284(2) (2000): 229–235.

Goldberg, Susan. "Parent-Infant Bonding: Another Look." *Child Development* 54(6) (1983): 1355–1382.

Golden, Janet, ed. *Infant Asylums and Children's Hospitals—Medical Dilemmas and Developments 1850–1920.* New York: Garland Publishing, Inc., 1989.

———. *A Social History of Wet Nursing in America: From Breast to Bottle.* New York: Cambridge University Press, 1996.

Goldenberg, Robert L., and Dwight J. Rouse. "Prevention of Premature Birth." *The New England Journal of Medicine* 339(5) (1998): 313–320.

Goodwin, Joanne L. "'Employable Mothers' and 'Suitable Work'—A Reevaluation of Welfare and Wage Earning for Women in the Twentieth-Century United States." *Journal of Social History* 29 (1995): 539–564.

Gookin, Sandra Hardin. *Parenting for Dummies,* ed. Dan Gookin. Foster City, CA: IDG Books Worldwide, Inc., 1995.

Gordon, Linda. *Pitied but Not Entitled: Single Mothers and the History of Welfare.* New York: The Free Press, 1994.

Gordon, Sarah, ed. *All Our Lives: A Centennial History of Michael Reese Hospital and Medical Center, 1881–1981.* Chicago: Michael Reese Hospital, 1981.

Graham, Edwin E. "Infant Mortality." *Journal of the American Medical Association* 51(13) (1908): 1045–1050.

"Great Diaper Battle." *Time* (January 24, 1969).

Griffin, M.R., W.A. Ray, E.A., Mortimer, G.M. Fenichel, and W. Schaffner. "Risk of Seizures and Encephalopathy after Immunization with the Diphtheria-Tetanus-Pertussis Vaccine." *Journal of the American Medical Association* 263(12) (1990): 1641–1645.

Guy, Loren P., Jonathan T. Lanman, and Joseph Dancis. "The Possibility of Total Elimination of Retrolental Fibroplasia by Oxygen Restriction." *Pediatrics* 17 (1956): 247–249.

Guyer, Bernard, Mary Anne Freedman, Donna M. Strobino, and Edward J. Sonkik. "Annual Summary of Vital Statistics: Trends in the Health of Americans during the 20th Century." *Pediatrics* 106(6) (2000): 1307–1317.

Haeusler, M.C., P. Konstantiniuk, M. Dorfer, and P.A. Weiss, "Amniotic Fluid Insulin Testing in Gestational Diabetes: Safety and Acceptance of Amniocentesis." *American Journal of Obstetrics and Gynecology* 179(4) (1998): 917–920.

Hansen, Michele, Jeffifer J. Kurinczuk, Carol Bower, and Sandra Webb. "The Risk of Major Birth Defects After Intracytoplasmic Sperm Infection and In Vitro Fertilization." *The New England Journal of Medicine* 346(10) (2002): 725–730.

Hart, Patricia S. "A Nation's Need for Adoption and Competing Realities: The Washington Children's Home Society, 1895–1915." In E. Wayne Carp, ed., *Adoption in America—Historical Perspectives*. Ann Arbor: The University of Michigan Press, 2002, 140–159.

Hawes, Joseph M. *Children between the Wars: American Childhood, 1920–1940*. New York: Twayne Publishers, 1997.

Hediger, Mary L., Mary D. Overpeck, Robert J. Kuczmarski, and W. June Ruan. "Association between Infant Breastfeeding and Overweight in Young Children." *Journal of the American Medical Association* 285(19) (2001): 2453–2460.

Henderson, John, Kate North, Mancell Griffiths, Ian Harvey, J. Jean Golding, and the Avon Longitudinal Study of Pregnancy and Childhood Team. "Pertussis Vaccination and Wheezing Illnesses in Young Children: Prospective Cohort Study." *British Medical Journal* 318 (1999): 1173–1176.

Henig, Robin Marantz. *Pandora's Baby*. Boston, MA: Houghton Mifflin Company, 2004.

Hennes, H.M., M.B. Lee, A.A. Rimm, and D.L. Shapiro. "Surfactant Replacement Therapy in Respiratory Distress Syndrome. Meta-Analysis of Clinical Trials of Single-Dose Surfactant Extracts." *Archives of Pediatrics and Adolescent Medicine* 145(1) (January 1991): 102–104.

Hernanz-Schulman, Marta. "Infantile Hypertrophic Pyloric Stenosis." *Radiology* 227(2) (2003): 319–331.

Hess, Julius H. "A City-Wide Plan for the Reduction of Deaths Associated with and Due to Prematurity." *The Journal of Pediatrics* 6 (1935): 104–121.

———. *Infant Feeding—A Handbook for the Practitioner*. Chicago: American Medical Association, 1923.

———. *Premature and Congenitally Diseased Infants*. Philadelphia, PA: Lea and Febiger, 1922.

———. "The Premature Infant—Early General and Feeding Care." *Illinois Medical Journal* 74 (1938): 506–514.

———. "Premature Infants—A Report of Sixteen Hundred and Twenty-Three Consecutive Cases." *Illinois Medical Journal* 67 (1935): 14–25.

Hess, Julius H., and Evelyn C. Lundeen. *The Premature Infant: Medical and Nursing Care*, 2nd ed. Philadelphia, PA: J.B. Lippincott Co., 1949.

Hess, Julius H., and I. McKy Chamberlain. "Premature Infants—A Report of Two Hundred and Sixty-Six Consecutive Cases." *American Journal of Diseases of Children* 34 (1927): 571–584.

Historical Collections, College of Physicians, Philadelphia, PA.

Hobbs, Frank, and Nicole Stoops. "U.S. Census Bureau, Census 2000 Special Reports, Series CENSR-4." In *Demographic Trends in the 20th Century*. Washington, DC: U.S. Government Printing Office, 2002, 7, 11–12.

Hockenberry, Marilyn J. *Wong's Nursing Care of Infants and Children*, 7th ed. St. Louis, MO: Mosby, 2003.

Hoeck, Leroy E., and Edgar De La Cruz. "Studies on the Effect of High Oxygen Administration in Retrolental Fibroplasia—Nursery Observations." *American Journal of Ophthalmology* 35 (1952): 1248–1252.

Holditch-Davis, Diane, Dia Roberts, and Margarete Sandelowski. "Early Parental Interactions with and Perceptions of Multiple Birth Infants." *Journal of Advanced Nursing* 30(1) (1999): 200–210.

Holt, L. Emmett. *The Care and Feeding of Children*, 9th ed. New York: D. Appleton and Company, 1912.

Hough, Hettie H., and Lucia Murchison. "Care of Premature Babies in South Carolina." *American Journal of Nursing* 46(12) (1946): 846–848.

"How to Make a Buck." *Time* (July 29, 1957), www.time.com.

Hoyert, Donna L., Mary Anne Freedman, Donna M. Strobino, and Bernard Guyer. "Annual Summary of Vital Statistics: 2000." *Pediatrics* 108(6) (2001): 1241–1255.

Hudson, Kathy L. "Preimplantation Genetic Diagnosis: Public Policy and Public Attitudes." *Fertility and Sterility* 85(6) (2006): 1638–1645.

Hulbert, Ann. *Raising America. Experts, Parents and a Century of Advice About Children*. New York: Alfred A. Knopf, 2003.

Hunt, Frazier. "Little Doc." *Saturday Evening Post* 210 (May 7, 1938): 18–19, 48, 50, 52–53; 210 (May 14, 1938): 18–19, 90, 97–98, 101–102; 210 (May 21, 1938): 20–21, 72, 74–75, 77–78; 210 (May 28, 1938): 18–19, 34, 36–37, 40.

Ingram, H. "Some Simple Helps." *The New York Times, Sunday Magazine* (June 26, 1910): 6.

International Lactation Consultant Association. "ILCA Responds to Policy Statement by AAP Task Force on SIDS." *World Alliance for Breastfeeding Action* (n.d.), http://www.waba.org.my/ilca_sids_response.

Israels, Belle Lindner. *The Child*. New York: Metropolitan Life Insurance Company, 1916.

Iyasu, S., and K. Tomashek. "Infant Mortality and Low Birth Weight among Black and White Infants—United States, 1980–2000." *Morbidity and Mortality Weekly Reports* 51(27) (2002): 589–592.

Jaffe, Janet, Martha Ourieff Diamond, and David J. Diamond. *Unsung Lullabies: Understanding and Coping with Infertility*. New York: St. Martin's Griffin, 2005.

Jenkins, Pamela C., Michael F. Flanagan, James D. Sargent, Charles E. Canter, Richard E. Chinnock, Kathy J. Jenkins, Robert N. Vincent, Gerald T. O'Connor, and Anna N.A. Tosteson. "A Comparison of Treatment Strategies for Hypoplastic Left Heart Syndrome Using Decision Analysis." *Journal of the American College of Cardiology* 38(4) (2001): 1181–1187.

Jewell, S.E., and R. Yip. "Increasing Trends in Plural Births in the United States." *Obstetrics and Gynecology* 85(2) (1995): 229–232.

Johnson, Mark D. "Genetic Risks of Intracytoplasmic Sperm Injection in the Treatment of Male Infertility: Recommendations for Genetic Counseling and Screening." *Fertility and Sterility* 70(3) (1998): 397–411.

Jones, Landon Y. "Swinging 60s? The First Baby Boomer Looks Back—and Forward—On the Eve of a Milestone." *The Smithsonian Magazine* (January 6, 2006), http://smithsonianmag.com/issues/2006/january/presence.

Kalb, Claudia. "Families: The Octuplet Question." *Newsweek* (January 11, 1999): 33.

Katz, David L., Meghan O'Connell, Ming-Chin Yeh, Haq Nawaz, Valentine Njike, Laurie M. Anderson, Stella Cory, and William Dietz. "Public Health Strategies for Preventing and Controlling Overweight and Obesity in School and Work-site Settings." *Morbidity and Mortality Weekly Report* 54(rr10) (October 7, 2005): 1–12.

Katz, Michael B. *In the Shadow of the Poorhouse, a Social History of Welfare in America.* New York: Basic Books, 1986.

Kent-First, M.G., S. Kol, A. Muallem, R. Ofir, D. Manor, S. Blazer, N. First, and J. Itskovitz-Eldor. "The Incidence and Possible Relevance of Y-Linked Microdeletions in Babies Born After Intracytoplasmic Sperm Injection and Their Infertile Fathers." *Molecular Human Reproduction* 2(12) (1996): 943–950.

Kern, Jeffrey H., Veronica J. Hinton, Nancy E. Nereo, Constance J. Hayes, and Welton M. Gersony. "Early Developmental Outcome After the Norwood Procedure for Hypoplastic Left Heart Syndrome." *Pediatrics* 102(5) (1998): 1148–1152.

Kevles, Daniel J. *In the Name of Eugenics: Genetics and the Uses of Human Heredity.* New York: Alfred A. Knopf, 1985.

Kinsey, V. Everett. "Retrolental Fibroplasia—Cooperative Study of Retrolental Fibroplasia and the Use of Oxygen." *Archives of Ophthalmology* 56 (1956): 481–543.

Klaus, Marshall H., and John H. Kennell. *Maternal-Infant Bonding.* St. Louis, MO: Mosby, 1976.

Kline, Wendy. *Building a Better Race: Gender, Sexuality and Genetics from the Turn of the Century to the Baby Boom.* Berkeley: University of California Press, 2001.

Kluger, Jeffrey. *Splendid Solution. Jonas Salk and the Conquest of Polio.* New York: G.P. Putnam's Sons, 2004.

Knox, Thomas W. *Life and Work of Henry Ward Beecher.* Hartford, CT: The Hartford Publishing Company, 1887.

Koivurova, Sari, Anna-Liisa Hartikainen, Mika Gissler, Elina Hemminki, Ulla Sovio, and Marjo-Riita Jarvelin. "Neonatal Outcome and Congenital Malformations in Children Born After In-Vitro Fertilization." *Human Reproduction* 17(5) (2002): 1391–1398.

Kopelman, Loretta M. "Are the 21-Year-Old Baby Doe Rules Misunderstood or Mistaken?" *Pediatrics* 115 (2005): 797–802.

Kuchment, Anna. "Parenting: Ditching Diapers." *Newsweek* (September 26, 2005): 9.

Kucuk, M. "Tap Test, Shake Test and Phosphatidylglycerol in the Assessment of Fetal Pulmonary Maturity." *International Journal of Gynaecology and Obstetrics* 60(1) (1998): 9–14.

Kulman, Linda. "Cigars All Around." *U.S. News & World Report* (December 1, 1997): 14.

Ladd-Taylor, Molly. *Raising a Baby the Government Way. Mothers' Letters to the Children's Bureau, 1915–1932.* New Brunswick, NJ: Rutgers University Press, 1986.

———. *Mother-Work: Women, Child Welfare, and the State, 1890–1930.* Urbana: The University of Illinois Press, 1994.

Lamb, Thomas M. "Factors Influencing the Mortality Rate of Premature Infants." *Brooklyn Hospital Journal* 1 (1939): 69–78.

Latimer, Caroline Wormely. "How Can I Keep My Baby from Crying?" *Lady's Home Journal* (January 1912): 35, 48.

Leavitt, Judith Walzer. *Brought to Bed: Childbearing in America, 1750–1950.* New York: Oxford University Press, 1986.

———, ed. *Women and Health in America,* 2nd ed. Madison: The University of Wisconsin Press, 1999.

Lemonick, Michael D., and Jeffrey Kluger. "It's a Miracle." *Time* (December 1, 1997): 34–39.

Leyendecker, J.C. "No Trespassing." *Saturday Evening Post* (January 3, 1942), cover photo, available at http://www.curtispublishing.com/images/NonRockwell/9420103.jpg.

Liebling, A.J. "Patron of the Preemies." *The New Yorker* 15 (June 3, 1939): 20–24.

Lindenmeyer, Kriste. "A Right to Childhood." In *The U.S. Children's Bureau and Child Welfare, 1912–1946.* Urbana: The University of Illinois Press, 1997.

Lino, Mark. "Expenditures on Children by Families, 1996 Annual Report." In U.S. Department of Agriculture, Center for Nutrition Policy and Promotion, Miscellaneous Publication No. 1528–1996, May 1997.

Litzenberg, Jennings C. "Long Interval Feeding of Premature Infants." *American Journal of Diseases of Children* 4 (1912): 391–409.

Lombardo, Paul L. "Taking Eugenics Seriously: Three Generations of ??? Are Enough?" *Florida State University Law Review* 30 (2003): 191–218.

Lowenburg, Harry. "The Management of Premature Infants." *Archives of Pediatrics* 52 (1935): 313–324.

Lundeen, Evelyn C. "The Premature Infant at Home." *American Journal of Nursing* 37 (1937): 466–470

Lundeen, Evelyn C., and Ralph H. Kunstadter. *Care of the Premature Infant.* Philadelphia, PA: J.B. Lippincott Company, 1958.

Luria, Joseph W., Javier A Gonzalez-del-Rey, Gregg A. DiGiulio, Constance M. McAneney, Jennifer J. Olson, and Richard M. Ruddy. "Effectiveness of Oral or Nebulized Dexamethasone for Children with Mild Croup." Archives of Pediatric and Adolescent Medicine 155 (2001): 1340–1345.

MacDorman, Marian F., and Gopal K. Singh. "Midwifery Care, Social and Medical Risk Factors, and Birth Outcomes in the USA." *Journal of Epidemiology and Community Health* 52 (1998): 310–317.

Macleod, David I. *The Age of the Child: Children in America, 1890–1920.* New York: Twayne Publishers, 1998.

Madsen, Kreesten Meldgaard, Anders Hviid, Mogens Vestergaard, Diana Schendel, Jan Wohlfahrt, Poul Thorsen, Jøn Olsen, and Mads Melbye. "A Population-Based Study of Measles, Mumps, and Rubella Vaccination and Autism." *The New England Journal of Medicine* 347(19) (2002): 1477–1482.

Maher, E.R., L.A. Brueton, S.C. Bowdin, A. Huharia, W. Cooper, R.R. Cole, F. Macdonald, J.R. Sampson, C.L. Barratt, W. Reik, and M.M. Hawkins. "Beckwith-Wiedemann Syndrome and Assisted Reproduction Technology (ART)." *Journal of Medical Genetics* 40 (2003): 62–64.

March of Dimes. "Spina Bifida." *Pregnancy and Newborn Health Education Center* (April 2006), http://www.marchofdimes.com/pnhec/4439_1224.asp.

———. "Uniting to Beat Polio." *About Us* (n.d.), http://www.marchofdimes.com/aboutus/789_821.asp.

Marco, Fernando. "High Survival Rate in Infant Acute Leukemia Treated with Early High-Dose Chemotherapy and Stem-Cell Support." *Journal of Clinical Oncology* 18(18) (2000): 3256–3261.

Marsh, Margaret, and Wanda Ronner. *The Empty Cradle: Infertility in America from Colonial Times to the Present.* Baltimore, MD: The Johns Hopkins University Press, 1996.

Martin, Joyce A., Brady E. Hamilton, Stephanie J. Ventura, Fay Menacker, and Melissa M. Park. "Births: Final Data for 2000." *National Vital Statistics Report* 50(5) (February 12, 2002): 15–18.

Mayor, Susan. "UK Authority Sets Limit on Number of Embryos Transferred." *British Medical Journal* 328 (2004): 65.

McCormick, John, and Barbara Datrowizt. "The Magnificent Seven." *Newsweek* (December 1, 1997): 58–62.

Meckel, Richard A. *Save the Babies: American Public Health Reform and the Prevention of Infant Mortality, 1850–1929.* Ann Arbor: The University of Michigan Press, 1990.

Meiks, L.T. "The Premature Infant." *The American Journal of Nursing* 37 (1937): 457–462.

Menache, Caroline C., Adre J. du Plessis, David L. Wessel, Richard A. Jonas, and Jane W. Newburger. "Current Incidence of Acute Neurologic Complications After Open-Heart Operations in Children." *Annals of Thoracic Surgery* 73 (2002): 1752–1758.

Merriam, William R., and William C. Hunt. "Census Reports." In *Twelfth Census of the United States, Taken in the Year 1901,* Vol. 1. Washington, DC: U.S. Census Office, 1901.

Mersereau, P., K. Kilker, H. Carter, E. Fassett, J. Williams, A. Flores, L. Williams, C. Mai, and J. Mulinare, "Spina Bifida and Anencephaly Before and After Folic Acid Mandate—United States, 1995–1996 and 1999–2000," *Morbidity and Mortality Weekly Report* 53(17) (May 7, 2004): 362–365.

Metropolitan Life Insurance Company. "Helping and Healing People." (n.d.), http://www.metlife.com/Applications/Corporate/WPS/CDA/PageGenerator.

Minino, Arialdi M., Elizabeth Arias, Kenneth D. Kochanek, Sherry L. Murphy, and Betty L. Smith, "Deaths: Final Data for 2000," *National Vital Statistics Reports* 50(15) (2002): 1–120.

Mintz, Steven. *Huck's Raft. A History of American Childhood.* Cambridge, MA: The Belknap Press of Harvard University Press, 2004.

Mintz, Steven, and Susan Kellogg. *Domestic Revolutions, A Social History of American Family Life.* New York: The Free Press, 1988.

Modlin, John F. "Poliomyelitis in the United States, the Final Chapter?" *American Journal of Medicine* 292(14) (2004): 1749–1751.

Morris, Cynthia D., Mark D. Reller, and Victor D. Menashe. "Thirty-Year Incidence of Infective Endocarditis After Surgery for Congenital Heart Defect." *Journal of the American Medical Association* 279(8) (1998): 599–603.

Murphy, M.S. "Guidelines for Managing Acute Gastroenteritis Based on a Systematic Review of Published Research." *Archives of Disease in Childhood* 79 (1998): 279–284.

Murray, Barbara E. "Can Antibiotic Resistance Be Controlled?" *The New England Journal of Medicine* 330(17) (1994): 1229–1230.

Napier, Lila J. "Method of Caring for Premature and Underweight Babies at the Lying-In Hospital, New York City." *Bulletin of the Lying-In Hospital of the City of New York* 13 (1927): 132–134.

National Center for Health Statistics. *Health, United States with Chartbook on Trends in the Health of Americans* (November 2006): 127, http://www.cdc.gov/nchs/data/hus/hus06.pdf#027 and www.cdc.gov/nchs/about/major/dvs/mortdata.htm.

National Office of Vital Statistics. *Marriage, Divorce, Natality, Fetal Mortality, and Infant Mortality Data*, Vol. II (1950): 164–169.

Nihmey, John, and Stuart Foxman. *Time of Their Lives—The Dionne Tragedy*. Ottawa, Canada: NIVA Publishing, 1987, www.time.com.

"No Boiling, No Burps," *Time* (March 17, 1947).

Noonan, Jacqueline A. "A History of Pediatric Specialties: The Development of Pediatric Cardiology." *Pediatric Research* 56(2) (2004): 298–306.

Norrell, Robert J. *The House I Live in: Race in the American Century*. New York: Oxford University Press, 2005.

Nuland, Sherwin B. *The Doctors' Plague. Germs, Childbed Fever, and the Strange Story of Ignác Semmelweis*. New York: W.W. Norton & Company, 2003.

"Nursing Care of Newborn Infants, Excerpts from Children's Bureau Publication 292, Standards and Recommendations for Hospital Care of Newborn Infants, Full-Term and Premature." *The American Journal of Nursing* 43 (1943): 560–563.

Nyden, Philip, John Lukehart, Michael T. Maly, and William Peterman. "Racially and Ethnically Diverse Urban Neighborhoods." *CITYSCAPE: A Journal of Policy Development and Research* 4(2) (1998): 19–27.

"Obstetrics. A Brief History of Obstetrical Care at Pennsylvania Hospital." *Historical Timeline* (n.d.), http://www.uphs.upenn.edu/paharc/timeline/1801/tline10.htm.

O'Connor, Edward M., Rhoda S. Sperling, Richard Gelber, Pavel Kiselev, Gwendolyn Scott, Mary Jo O'Sullivan, Russell VanDyke, Mohammed Bey, William Shearer, Robert L. Jacobson, Eleanor Jimenez, Edward O'Neill, Brigitte Bazin, Jean-Francois Delfraissy, Mary Culnane, Robert Coombs, Mary Elkins, Jack Moye, Pamela Stratton, and James Balsley, for the Pediatric AIDS Clinical Trials Group Protocol 076 Study Group. "Reduction of Maternal-Infant Transmission of Human Immunodeficiency Virus Type 1 with Zidovudine Treatment." *The New England Journal of Medicine* 331(18) (1994): 1173–1180.

Odgen, Cynthia L., Katherine M. Flegal, Margaret D. Carroll, and Clifford L. Johnson. "Prevalence and Trends in Overweight among US Children and Adolescents, 1999–2000." *Journal of the American Medical Association* 288(14) (2002): 1728–1732.

Offen, Karen. "Depopulation, Nationalism, and Feminism in Fin-de-Siecle France." *The American Historical Review* 89 (1984): 648–676.

Office of Family Assistance. "Fact Sheet." In *U.S. Department of Health & Human Services, Administration for Children & Families* (August 2004), www.acf.hhs.gov/opa/gact_sheets/tanf_printable.html.

O'Kelly, Sean W. "Hypoplastic Left Heart Syndrome." *British Medical Journal* 314(7074) (1997): 87.

Oppenheimer, Gerald M. "Prematurity as a Public Health Problem: US Policy from the 1920s to the 1960s." *American Journal of Public Health* 86 (1996): 870–878.

Orenstein, Walter A., and Alan R. Hinman. "The Immunization System in the United States—The Role of School Immunization Laws." *Vaccine* 17(3) (1999): S19–S24.

Palmer, Diana A., and Howard Bauchner. "Parents' and Physicians' Views on Antibiotics." *Pediatrics* 99(6) (1997): e6–e10.

Parashar, Umesh D., Paul E. Kilgore, Robert C. Holman, Matthew J. Clarke, Joseph S. Bresee, and Roger I. Glass. "Diarrheal Mortality in US Infants." *Archives of Pediatric and Adolescent Medicine* 152 (1998): 47–51.

Pasquariello, Jr., Patrick S., senior ed. *The Children's Hospital of Philadelphia Book of Pregnancy and Child Care.* New York: John Wiley, 1999.

Patterson, James T. *America' Struggle against Poverty in the Twentieth Century.* Cambridge, MA: Harvard University Press, 2000.

Patz, Arnall. "The Role of Oxygen in Retrolental Fibroplasia." *Pediatrics* 19 (1957): 504–524.

Pearce, N.O. "Review of Recent Literature on the New-Born." *American Journal of Diseases of Children* 18(1) (July 1919): 51–68.

Peebles, Anne Y. "Care of Premature Infants." *The American Journal of Nursing* 33 (1933): 866–869.

Pernick, Martin S. *The Black Stork.* New York: Oxford University Press, 1996.

Personal Responsibility and Work Opportunity Reconciliation Act of 1996 (August 22, 1996), http://thomas.loc.gov/cgi-bin/query/F?c104:1:./temp/~c104HIrfhm:e19928.

Poland, Gregory A., and Robert M. Jacobson. "Vaccine Safety: Injecting a Dose of Common Sense." *Mayo Clinic Proceedings* 75 (2000): 135–139.

Poole Marsh W., and Thomas B. Cooley. "The Care of Premature Infants." *Journal of Pediatrics* 1 (July 1932): 16–33.

Practice Committee of the Society for Assisted Reproductive Technology and the Practice Committee of the American Society for Reproductive Medicine. "Guidelines on Number of Embryos Transferred." *Fertility and Sterility* 86(4) (2006): S51–S52.

Pulford, D.S., and W.J. Blevins. "Premature Infant, Birth Weight 680 Grams, with Survival." *American Journal of Diseases of Children* 36 (1928): 797–798.

"Question Time." *People Weekly* (January 11, 1999): 72.

Reaman, Gregory H. "Treatment Outcome and Prognostic Factors for Infants with Acute Lymphoblastic Leukemia Treated on Two Consecutive Trials of the Children's Cancer Group." *Journal of Clinical Oncology* 17(2) (1999): 445–455.

Record Group 44. Data Control Group LCS. U.S. Archives, Washington, DC.

Reedy, Elizabeth Ann. *Ripe Too Early: The Expansion of Hospital Based Premature Infant Care in the United States, 1922–1950.* PhD dissertation, University of Pennsylvania, 2000.

Reynolds, Meredith A., Laura A. Schieve, Joyce A. Martin, Gary Jeng, and Maurizio Macaluso. "Trends in Multiple Births Conceived Using Assisted Reproductive Technology, United States, 1997–2000." *Pediatrics* 111(5) (2003): 1159–1162.

Rimm, Alfred A., Alyce C. Katayama, Mireya Diaz, and K. Paul Katayama. "A Meta-Analysis of Controlled Studies Comparing Major Malformation Rates in IVF and

ICSI Infants with Naturally Conceived Children." *Journal of Assisted Reproduction and Genetics* 21(12) (2004): 437–443.

Robbins, K.B., D. Brandling-Bennett, and A.R. Hinman. "Low Measles Incidence: Association with Enforcement of School Immunization Laws." *American Journal of Public Health* 71(3) (1981): 270–274.

Robinson, G.C., J.E. Jan, and C. Kinnis. "Congenital Ocular Blindness in Children, 1945–1984." *Archives of Pediatrics and Adolescent Medicine* 141(12) (December 1987): 1321–1324.

Rosenberg, Charles E. *The Care of Strangers: The Rise of America's Hospital System.* Baltimore, MD: The Johns Hopkins University Press, 1987.

Rosenthal, M. Sara. *The Fertility Sourcebook.* Chicago: Contemporary Books, 1995.

Santosham, Mathuram, Edward Maurice Keenan, Jim Tulloch, Denis Broun, and Roger Glass. "Oral Rehydration Therapy for Diarrhea: An Example of Reverse Transfer of Technology." *Pediatrics* 100(5) (1997): 10–12.

Shaban, Stephen F. "Male Infertility Overview: Assessment, Diagnosis, and Treatment." *Georgia Reproductive Associates* (2005), http://www.ivf.com/shaban.html.

Schieve, Laura A., Herbert B. Peterson, Susan F. Meikle, Gary Jeng, Isabella Danel, Nancy M. Burnett, and Lynne S. Wilcox. "Live-Birth Rates and Multiple-Birth Risk Using In Vitro Fertilization." *Journal of the American Medical Association* 282(19) (1999): 1832–1838.

Schieve, Laura A., Sonja A. Rasmussen, Germaine M. Buck, Diana E. Schendel, Meredith A. Reynolds, and Victoria C. Wright. "Are Children Born After Assisted Reproductive Technology at Increased Risk for Adverse Health Outcomes?" *Obstetrics and Gynecology* 103(6) (2004): 1154–1163.

Schindehette, Susan. "Coming Up Roses." *People Weekly* (December 8, 1997): 54–60.

Schneider, E., M.K. Glynn, T. Kajese, M.T. McKenna. "Epidemiology of HIV/AIDS—United States, 1981–2005." *Morbidity and Mortality Weekly Reports* 55(no.21 (2006): 589-592.

Scheinberg, D.A., G.Y. Minamoto, K. Dietz, J.W.M. Gold, T. Gee, D. Armstrong, J. Garilove, B. Clarkson, N. Chein, L. Reich, D.L. Morse, M. Batt, H.J. Miller, B. Stevko, L.A. Chambers, L. Kunches, and G.F. Grady. "Human Immunodeficiency Virus Infection in Transfusion Recipients and Their Family Members." *Morbidity and Mortality Weekly Report* 36(10) (March 20, 1987): 137–140.

Schwartz, Rachel M., Anastasia M. Luby, John W. Scanlon, and Russell J. Kellogg. "Effect of Surfactant on Morbidity, Mortality, and Resource Use in Newborn Infants Weighing 500—1500 g." *The New England Journal of Medicine* 330(21) (May 26, 1994): 1476–1480.

Shilts, Randy. *And the Band Played On—Politics, People, and the AIDS Epidemic.* New York: Penguin Books, 1987.

Shulman, Stanford T. "The History of Pediatric Infectious Diseases." *Pediatric Research* 55(1) (2004): 163–176.

Silverman, William A. "Incubator-Baby Side Shows," *Pediatrics* 64(2) (1979): 127–141.

———. *Retrolental Fibroplasia: A Modern Parable.* New York: Grune and Stratton, 1980.

"Simplifying the Nursing Care for Premature Babies." *The Trained Nurse and Hospital Review* LXXVIII (June 1927): 633.

Sinclair, Upton. *The Jungle.* Cutchogue: Buccaneer Books, 1906.

Singer, Lynn, Toyoko Yamashita, Lawrence Lilien, Marc Collin, and Jill Baley. "A Longitudinal Study of Developmental Outcome of Infants with Bronchopulmonary

Dysplasia and Very Low Birth Weight." *Pediatrics* 100(6) (December 1997): 987–993.

Singh, Jaideep, John Lantos, and William Meadow. "End-of-Life After Birth: Death and Dying in a Neonatal Intensive Care Unit." *Pediatrics* 114(6) (December 2004): 1620–1626.

Sklansky, Mark. "Neonatal Euthanasia: Moral Considerations and Criminal Liability." *Journal of Medical Ethics* 27 (2001): 5–11.

Sklar, Kathryn Kish. *Florence Kelley and the Nation's Work: The Rise of Women's Political Culture, 1830–1900.* New Haven, CT: Yale University Press, 1997.

Smith, Samuel, Samantha M. Pfeifer, and John A. Collins. "Diagnosis and Management of Female Infertility." *Journal of the American Medical Association* 290(13) (2003): 1767–1770.

Soetenga, Deborah, and Kathleen A. Mussatto. "Management of Infants with Hypoplastic Left Heart Syndrome. Integrating Research into Nursing Practice." *Critical Care Nurse* 24(6) (2004): 46–65.

Sowards, Kathryn A. "What Is the Leading Cause of Infant Mortality? A Note of the Interpretation of Official Statistics." *American Journal of Public Health* 89 (1999): 1752–1754.

Spar, Debora L. *The Baby Business: How Money, Science, and Politics Drive the Commerce of Conception.* Boston, MA: Harvard Business School Press, 2006.

Spock, Benjamin, and Steven J. Parker. *Dr. Spock's Baby and Child Care,* 7th ed. New York: Pocket Books, 1998.

Stearns, Peter N. *Anxious Parents, A History of Modern Childrearing in America.* New York: New York University Press, 2003.

Steele, Danielle. *Mixed Blessings.* New York: Dell Publishing, 1992.

Steinhorn, Leonard. *By the Color of Our Skin: The Illusion of Integration and the Reality of Race.* New York: Penguin Group, 1999.

Stevens, Rosemary. *In Sickness and in Wealth: American Hospitals in the Twentieth Century.* New York: Basic Books, 1989.

Stromberg, B., G. Dahlquist, A. Ericson, O. Finnstrom, M. Koster, and K. Stjernqvist. "Neurological Sequelae in Children Born After In-Vitro Fertilisation: A Population Study." *The Lancet* 359 (2002): 461–465.

Subcommittee on Management of Acute Otitis Media. "Diagnosis and Management of Acute Otitis Media." *Pediatrics* 113(5) (2004): 1451–1465.

"Summer 1957." *Time* (July 29, 1957).

Sun, Min, and Simone Rugolotto. "Assisted Infant Toilet Training in a Western Family Setting." *Journal of Developmental and Behavioral Pediatrics* 25(2) (2004): 99–101.

Sykes, Richard. "Penicillin: From Discovery to Product." *Bulletin of the World Health Organization* 79(8) (2001): 778–779.

Szilagyi, Peter G., Jane L. Holl, Lance E. Rodewald, Laura Pollard Shone, Jack Zwanziger, Dana B. Mukamel, Sarah Trafton, Andrew W. Dick, and Richard F. Raubertas, "Evaluation of Children's Health Insurance: From New York State's Child Health Plus to SCHIP." *Pediatrics* 105(3) (2000): 687–691.

Tallo, C.P., B. Vohr, W. Oh, L.P. Rubin, D.B. Seifer, and R.V. Hanning, Jr. "Maternal and Neonatal Morbidity Associated with In Vitro Fertilization." *Journal of Pediatrics* 127(5) (1995): 794–800.

Task Force on Sudden Infant Death Syndrome. "The Changing Concept of Sudden Infant Death Syndrome: Diagnostic Coding Shifts, Controversies Regarding the

Sleeping Environment, and New Variables to Consider in Reducing Risk." *Pediatrics* 116(5) (2005): 1245–1255.

"Teen Birth Rate Continues Decline, Fewer Childhood Deaths, More Children Immunized Children More Likely to Live in Poverty, Be Involved in Violent Crime." Federal Interagency Forum on Child and Family Statistics (July 20, 2005), http://www.nichd.nih.gov/news/releases/americas_childreno5.cfm.

Terry, T.L. "Extreme Prematurity and Fibroblastic Overgrowth of Persistent Vascular Sheath Behind Each Crystalline Lens, Preliminary Report." *American Journal of Ophthalmology* 25 (1942): 203–204.

———. "Fibroblastic Overgrowth of Persistent Tunica Vasculosa Lentis in Premature Infants, Etiologic Factors." *Archives of Ophthalmology* 29 (1943): 54–65.

"Tetralogy of Fallot." *American Heart Association* (2006), http://www.americanheart.org.

Theilen, U., and L. Shederdemian. "The Intensive Care of Infants with Hypoplastic Left Heart Syndrome." *Archives of Disease in Childhood* 90 (2005): 97–102.

Thoreau, Henry D. *Walden, An Annotated Edition*, ed. Walter Harding. New York: Houghton Mifflin Company, 1995.

Tingling-Clemmons, Michele A. "Welfare Reform Two Years Later: Which Way Is Up?" *National NOW Times* (Fall 1998), http://www.now.org/nnt/fall-98/.

Torpy, Janet M., Tiffany J. Glass, and Richard M. Glass. "Blood Transfusion." *Journal of the American Medical Association* 292(13) (2004): 1646.

Totheram-Borus, Mary Jane, Patricia Lester, Pin-Wen Wang, and Qing Shen. "Custody Plans among Parents Living with Human Immunodeficiency Virus Infection." *Archives of Pediatric and Adolescent Medicine* 158 (2004): 327–332.

Tow, Abraham. "The Care and Feeding of the Premature Infant: With Special Reference to Simple Milk Mixtures." *Medical Clinics of North America* 20 (1936): 951–960.

Treasury Working Group on Child Care. *Investing in Child Care: Challenges Facing Working Parents and the Private Sector Response.* Washington, DC: United States Department of the Treasury, 1998.

Turner, Bobbie Green. *Federal/State Aid to Dependent Children Program and Its Benefits to Black Children in America, 1935–1985.* New York: Garland Publishing, Inc.

Tuttle, Jr., William M. *Daddy's Gone to War—The Second World War in the Lives of America's Children.* New York: Oxford University Press, 1993.

Tyson, Ralph M. "The Problem of the Premature Infant." *New York State Journal of Medicine* 34 (1934): 811–818.

Tyson, Ralph M., and Edward F. Burt. "Continuous Temperature Records of Premature Infants." *American Journal of Diseases of Children* 38 (1929): 944–952.

UNICEF. "UNICEF in Action: Eradicating Polio." *Immunizations Plus* (2006), http://www.unicef.org/immunization/index_polio.html.

U.S. Census Bureau. "Mothers Who Receive AFDC Payments: Fertility and Socioeconomic Characteristics." *Statistical Brief* (March 1995), http://www.census.gov/population/socdemo/statbriefs/sb2-95.html.

U.S. Census Bureau. *Immigration Legal History* (ILH). Legislation from 1790–1900: 3; and Legislation from 1901–1940: 3, Quota Law of May 19, 1921, Immigration Act of May 26, 1924 (n.d.): 3–6; Legislation from 1941–1960 (n.d.): 2–5; Legislation from 1961–1980 (n.d.): 1–6; and Legislation from 1981–1996 (n.d.): 1—7, http://www.uscis.gov/files/nativedocuments/legislation.

U.S. Department of Health and Human Services. *Temporary Assistance to Needy Families (TANF): Third Annual Report to Congress* (August 2000), http://www.acf.dhhs.gov/programs/opre/annual3.doc.

————. "Insure Kids Now!" *Health Resources and Services Administration* (n.d.), www.insurekidsnow.gov/.

U.S. Department of Justice. "Fair Housing Act," http://www.usdoj.gov/crt/housing/title8.htm.

Ventura, Stephanie J., T.J. Matthews, and Sally C. Curtin. "Declines in Teenage Birth Rates, 1991–98: Update of National and State Trends." *National Vital Statistics Reports* 47(26) (1999): 1–9.

von Kries, Rudiger, Berthold Koletzko, Thorsten Sauerwald, Erika von Mutius, Dietmar Barnert, Veit Gurnert, and Hubertus von Voss, "Breast Feeding and Obesity: Cross Sectional Study." *British Medical Journal* 319 (1999): 147–150.

Wagner, E.A. "One Year of Prematures at the Cincinnati General Hospital." *Journal of Medicine* 14 (March 1933): 13–16.

Wall, Stephen N., and John Colin Partridge. "Death in the Intensive Care Nursery: Physician Practice of Withdrawing and Withholding Life Support." *Pediatrics* 99(1) (January 1997): 70.

Wangner, Lola. "My First Baby." *Lady's Home Journal* (October 1904): 5–6.

Wapner, R.J., G.H. Davis, A. Johnson, V.J. Weinblatt, R.L. Fischer, L.G. Jackson, F.A. Chervenak, and L.B. McCullough. "Selective Reduction of Multifetal Pregnancies." *The Lancet* 335 (1990): 90–93.

Wasserstein, Wendy. "Annals of Motherhood—Complications." *The New Yorker* (February 21 and 28, 2000): 87.

Webb, C.H. "Concentrated Feedings in the Nutrition of Premature Infants." *Southern Medical Journal* 27 (1934): 608–613.

Weiss, Tara. "The New Mommy Track: Every Day Mom's Day for Savvy Employers." *Forbes* (January 23, 2007), http://www.forbes.com/2007/01/22/leadership-work-jobs-lead-careers-cx_tw_0123moms.html.

West, Mrs. Max. *Infant Care*, No. 8. Washington, DC: Government Printing Office, 1923.

"When Your Baby Is Premature—Advice for New Parents from Preemie-L Parents." *Preemie-L FAQ's and Advice Sheets* (n.d.), http://www.preemie-l.org.

Wilcox, Daniel A. "A Study of Three Hundred and Thirty Premature Infants." *American Journal of Diseases of Children* 52 (1934): 848–862.

Wilcox, L.S., J.L. Kiely, C.L. Melvin, and M.C. Martin. "Assisted Reproductive Technologies: Estimates of Their Contribution to Multiple Births and Newborn Hospital Days in the United States." *Fertility and Sterility* 65(2) (1996): 361–366.

Willinger, Marian, Howard J. Hoffman, Kuo-Tsung Wu, Jin-Rong Hou, Ronald C. Kessler, Sally L. Ward, Thomas G. Keens, and Michael J. Corwin. "Factors Associated with the Transition to Nonprone Sleep Positions of Infants in the United States." *Journal of the American Medical Association* 280(4) (1998): 329–335.

Willinger, Marian, Chia-Wen Ko, Howard J. Hoffman, Ronald C. Kessler, and Michael J. Corwin. "Factors Associated with Caregivers' Choice of Infant Sleep Position, 1994–1998." *Journal of the American Medical Association* 283(16) (2000): 2135–2142.

————. "Trends in Infant Bed Sharing in the United States, 1993–2000, The National Infant Sleep Position Study." *Archives of Pediatric and Adolescent Medicine* 157 (2003): 43–49.

Wilson, Kumanan, Ed Mills, Cory Ross, Jessie McGowan, and Alex Jadad. "Association of Autistic Spectrum Disorder and the Measles, Mumps, and Rubella Vaccine." *Archives of Pediatric and Adolescent Medicine* 157 (2003): 628–634.

Winicki, Joshua, Dean Jolliffe, and Craig Gundersen. "How Do Food Assistance Programs Improve the Well-Being of Low-Income Families?" *Food Assistance and Nutrition Research Report* 26-9 (October 2002): 1–3.

Winship, Scott, and Christopher Jencks, "Understanding Welfare Reform." *Harvard Magazine* (November–December 2004): 33–34.

Wolfe, Robert M., Lisa K. Sharp, and Martin S. Lipsky. "Content and Design Attributes of Antivaccination Web Sites." *Journal of the American Medical Association* 287(24) (2002): 3245–3248.

Woodward, Henry L., and Bernice Gardner. *Obstetric Management and Nursing.* Philadelphia, PA: F.A. Davis Company, 1942.

World Health Organization. "Global Polio Eradication Initiative." *Global Polio Eradication Initiative* (2006), http://www.polioeradication.org.

Wright, Anne L., and Richard J. Schanler. "The Resurgence of Breastfeeding at the End of the Second Millennium." *Journal of Nutrition* 131 (2001): 421S–425S.

Wuellner, Sister Mary Pulcheria. "Safe Nursing Care for Premature Babies." *American Journal of Nursing* 39 (November 1939): 1198–1202.

Youcha, Geraldine. *Minding the Children. Child Care in America from Colonial Times to the Present.* New York: Scribner, 1995.

Young, T. Kue, Patricia J. Martens, Shayne P. Taback, Elizabeth A.C. Sellers, Heather J. Dean, Mary Cheang, and Bertha Flett. "Type 2 Diabetes Mellitus in Children." *Archives of Pediatric and Adolescent Medicine* 156 (2002): 651–655.

Zahorsky, John. "The Baby Incubators on the 'Pike.' A Study of the Care of Premature Infants in Incubator Hospitals Erected for Show Purposes." *St. Louis Courier of Medicine* 31(6) (1904): 345–358; 32(1) (1905): 1–13; 32(2) (1905): 65–80; 32(3) (1905): 152–166; 32(4) (1905): 203–219; 32(5) (1905): 265–275; 32(6) (1905): 334–343; 33(1) (1905): 1–9; 33(2) (1905): 65–71; 33(3) (1905): 137–143; 33(4) (1905): 211–218.

Zelizer, Viviana A. *Pricing the Priceless Child. The Changing Social Value of Children.* Princeton, NJ: Princeton University Press, 1985.

Index

About the Author

ELIZABETH A. REEDY is a registered nurse with more than twenty-five years of experience in pediatric and neonatal nursing. She received her undergraduate degrees from Gwynedd-Mercy College in Gwynedd Valley, PA, and her master's and PhD degrees from the University of Pennsylvania in Philadelphia. She is currently an adjunct faculty member at Immaculata University.